THE PHENOMENOLOGICAL QUEST: BETWEEN AVICENNA AND HEIDEGGER

A Global Academic Publishing Book

THE PHENOMENOLOGICAL QUEST: BETWEEN AVICENNA AND HEIDEGGER

NADER EL-BIZRI
Associate Professor
American University of Beirut

SUNY
PRESS

Library of Congress Cataloging-in-Publication Data

El-Bizri, Nader
The Phenomenological Quest: Between Avicenna and Heidegger

1. Avicenna 2. Heidegger 3. Phenomenology

ISBN 1-586840-05-3

For information, contact
State University of New York Press, Albany, NY
www.sunypress.edu

DEDICATION

To Dina
for her intellectual inspiration
and emotional support;

To my family
for their patience and blessings.

TABLE OF CONTENTS

ACKNOWLEDGMENTS

It is a privilege to express my indebtedness to those scholars who have directly and indirectly contributed to this book. I am especially thankful to Professor Parviz Morewedge (State University of New York at Binghamton) for his valuable and inspiring scholarly support and intellectual guidance. I also want to show my gratitude to Professors Parviz Morewedge, and Rosemarie Morewedge Thee for their generosity. I also want to thank Professors Richard Bernstein (New School), Agnes Heller (New School), Dmitri Nikulin (New School), and Gail Soffer (New School) for their intellectual and scholarly rigor. I also have benefited from the valuable comments and suggestions of Professors Johannes Fritsche (New School), Majid Fakhry (Georgetown University), and Oliver Leaman (Liverpool J. M. University). I also consider myself fortunate to have had the opportunity to study with Professors Stanley Cavell (Harvard), Hilary Putnam (Harvard), and A. I. Sabra (Harvard). And this book owes much to the growing scholarly literature on Avicenna's philosophy. My thanks are also due to the members of the Hariri Foundation in Washington D.C. for their support. I also extend my thanks to Mr. C. Adamo and to Ms. C. Martin the secretary of the Graduate Faculty Philosophy Department (New School), and to Ms. Etin Anwar (SUNY, Binghamton) for her generous editorial assistance. I also acknowledge the assistance of the staff members of the New School, N.Y.U, Harvard University, and Cambridge University Libraries. I am definitely and deeply indebted to my parents and family (Mouhib, Souad, Fatmeh, CAbd al-Rahman, Nesrine, Samer, Zaher) for their love, patience, and encouragement. And more than anyone else, I am indebted to my wife Dina Kiwan, without whose intellectual inspiration and emotional support this book would have not been realized.

For the main ideas and thoughts expressed in this book and their shortcomings, I am alone responsible.

Nader El-Bizri --
New York City, 1999.

PREFACE

I- Problematics

Martin Heidegger claims that the history of metaphysics is a history of the oblivion of being while propounding that his "fundamental ontology" presents a "genuine" account of the question of being that attempts to overcome metaphysics and its oblivion of being. Yet, it is perhaps doubtful that, for more than two thousand years (from Aristotle to Edmund Husserl), no philosopher was able to come up with a "genuine" approach to the question of being, and that no philosopher attempted to overcome the metaphysical history of the oblivion of being. This issue becomes more polemical and problematic, given that it is unlikely the case that in the global intellectual history of Chinese, Jewish, or Islamic philosophy, no philosopher or philosophical tradition has successfully attempted to overcome the history of the oblivion of being. In the case of Islamic philosophy, it is well documented that the Near Eastern Muslim world of the Middle ages has had an impact on the intellectual history of Western science and metaphysics. However, it is not yet well documented that the same Near Eastern Islamic philosophical tradition does indeed testify to the development of a phenomenological philosophical tradition that took the question of being to be the most central question of philosophical investigations. Considering the particular case of the physician, philosopher, and poet: Avicenna ([Ibn Sīnā] 980-1037), it is known that his influential *al-Qānūn fī al-ṭib* (book on medicine) was translated into Latin (*Liber Canonis*) and many other languages, and was in currency since the late Middle ages and early Renaissance in Europe. It is also known that Avicenna's philosophical works have had a strong impact on Thomism and on the works of Maimonides among others. Moreover, Avicenna's philosophical contributions constituted the milestones of a phenomenological mode of investigation in ontology that impacted subsequent philosophical developments in the Near East, up to the recent modern times, and some investigators have already depicted some of the phenomenological dimensions that characterize his views. The celebrated scholar Henry Corbin pointed to these dimensions in his profound interpretation of the Avicennian visionary *Recital of Ḥayy Ibn Yaqẓān*. Joseph Owens briefly addresses this issue in *The Relevance of Avicennian Neoplatonism and Islamic Thought* (Owens, 1992, p. 47). And Parviz Morewedge points at the phenomenological character of Avicenna's consideration of the inner sense of prehension: *al-wahm* (which is addressed in Chapter 7 of this book). These scholars briefly point to the phenomenological character of Avicenna's philosophy without conducting further investigations on this issue. In this sense, this book presents one of the first elaborate investigations of Avicenna's phenomenological consideration of the question of being. The significance of this work lies in the possibilities it offers for the renewal of the philosophical re-constructive interpretation of the question of being in particular and of phenomenology and Islamic philosophy in general. The contemporary relevance of Avicenna's philosophical works is attested in the impact that Avicennism had on a philosophical tradition that could be characterized by its phenomenological approach to the question of being in a fashion that is akin to some of what Martin Heidegger innovatively attempted to show centuries later. Avicenna is one of the most influential of those phenomenologically inclined post-Avicennian metaphysicians like Shihāb al-dīn Yaḥya Suhrawardī (d. 1191), Naṣīr al-dīn al-Ṭūsī (d. 1274), and Mullā Ṣadrā (d. 1641). All gave shape to the course of development of a new strain in philosophy that we came recently to appreciate after the contemporary philosophical developments in phenomenology and ontology. The recent editions and translations, of post-Avicennian works, have revealed that with Avicennism a new tradition in philosophy has been established, and that tradition has been characterized by phenomenological inclinations in addressing the central question of being (*al-wūjūd*). Thus, Avicenna's works are now open to new interpretations that account for a rather undocumented phenomenological dimension that characterizes his philosophy and is further developed in the works of his successors. Given this intellectual history, one wonders whether Heidegger's account of the history of metaphysics has been incomplete, in the sense that his phenomenological approach to the question of being has not really had historical precedents throughout the history of metaphysics. It might be the case that, from the standpoint of considering Avicenna's and post-Avicennian philosophical works, there is a historical precedence that does indeed emphasize some of what Heidegger wanted to reveal. This issue becomes more contextualized given that the phenomenological salient features, that characterize Avicenna's philosophical consideration of being, do indeed affirm some isomorphic dimensions that one finds in Heidegger's "ontology." This eventually emphasizes the cross-cultural universal dimension that characterizes phenomenology across time.

II- Aims

This book investigates Avicenna's philosophical considerations of the question of being (*al-wūjūd*) in terms of addressing his ontological, epistemological, mystical, and linguistic views about being. This is conducted in the light of considering Martin Heidegger's critique of metaphysics and classical ontology. However, there is no enactment of a direct confrontation between Heidegger's thought and Avicenna's. And no assessment is undertaken in the sense of speculating whether Heidegger's critique of metaphysics applies to Avicenna's philosophical consideration of the question of being. Rather, the consideration of Heidegger's critique of metaphysics is mediated through an account of his theory of the subject/*Dasein*, and through a consideration of his views about modernity and technology. Some dimensions are addressed in such a way that a reevaluation of Heidegger's claims, about the historical significance of his fundamental ontology, becomes possible. This is the case given that Heidegger's account of the history of metaphysics does not reflect the historical precedence that Avicenna's philosophical consideration of the question of being presents. And, this becomes more of an issue given that Avicenna's philosophical consideration of the question of being initiates the beginnings of a whole living philosophical tradition that is phenomenological in character and that diverts from the Peripatetic categorical consideration of being in terms of οὐσία (*ousia*, i.e. substance)

Heidegger's views about *Dasein* reveal the existential, phenomenological, and temporal features that characterize his non-*ousiological* ontology. This departure from *ousiology* is also attested in Avicenna's philosophical accounts of being which give expression to a process/event ontology that departs from the Peripatetic ontological views. Moreover, the consideration of Avicenna's epistemological accounts reveals the phenomenological character of his theory of subjectivity. It also reveals that Avicenna's accounts divert from what later appears in Cartesian theories of the subject. And, this is the case given that Avicenna's views stress on the convergence between being and thinking, between being and *al-nafs* (soul-field/*Dasein*). The polemical Avicennian mystical insights pave the way for other modes of overcoming subjectivity by way of destining *al-nafs* to be oriented towards truth while being open to the perfection of its participation in being. Interpreting Avicenna's philosophical accounts of being, in the light of addressing contemporary concerns about the question of being, shows that the Avicennian accounts of being do overcome some aspects of classical ontology by overcoming ontological accounts that are substance or subject based. To sum up, Avicenna's consideration of the question of being does not reduce being into something that is other than itself.

In considering Heidegger's theory of modernity, the aim is to reveal the underlying features that characterize what Heidegger takes to be the threat of metaphysics as represented by the history of the oblivion of being. Yet, it is also the case that the site of this danger is the same place where the saving power emerges. It is in the light of considering the danger of the modern dispensation of being that Heidegger's critique of metaphysics acquires a broader cultural context while strenuously grappling with the possibilities of an attempted overcoming of metaphysics. The consideration of Heidegger's theory of modernity is undertaken in the light of addressing the history of the oblivion of being. This in itself points towards the Heideggerian criticized turn towards the poetic language which has been construed as being an attempt to overcome the language of metaphysics. With Avicenna, the overcoming of metaphysics is not declared as a task. Avicenna's accounts do overcome ontological accounts of being that are mediated through accounts of substance, essence, or metaphysical subjectivity. In this sense, and without being a philosopher of crisis, nostalgia, or utopia, Avicenna presents ontological, epistemological, mystical, and linguistic accounts, that offer rich possibilities to answer to some of Heidegger's concerns about being, *Dasein*, and the threat and salvation possibilities that issue from the standpoint of modernity.

III- A Remark About Avicenna

There is a historical as well as a scholarly tendency to consider Avicenna's philosophy as being incompatible with Islamic orthodoxy. This interpretation is itself advocated by the two philosophers: Abū Ḥāmid al-Ghazālī (1058-1111) and Aḥmad Ibn Taymīya (1262-1327) who side with traditionalist readings of Avicenna's philosophical accounts (mainly Avicenna's claim that God does not have knowledge of particulars). Some contemporary scholars, like J. J. Houben, and P. Morewedge, hold that Avicenna's philosophical system does not reflect an adherence to monotheism nor does it advance monotheism against other theological and religious systems. Other scholars such as Naṣr, do see that Avicenna's system is compatible with the monotheism of the Islamic orthodoxy. However, Houben holds that Avicenna upholds a non-religious "Monistic order of being" (which is akin to what is later echoed in Spinoza's ontology, without being based on accounts of substance [οὐσία]). Houben also holds that a "natural knowledge of God" is attributed to Avicenna's work according to which there is no distinction between the "natural" and "supernatural." On this account emanation becomes necessary and the relation of the human being with God is characterized by "naturalness" (Houben, 1956, pp. 207, 217, 220-221). Morewedge also advocates this position in his *Metaphysica of Avicenna.* So, in order to give a concise account of what Houben's and Morewedge's views entail, let us by way of illustration suppose that monotheism implies the following:

1- That it is logically possible that God exists and the world does not exist (Thus supporting an account of creation *ex nihilo*).
2- That salvation is conceivably affected by grace.
3- That prayer and intimacy between the worshipper and God are encouraged.

Based on these accounts, and in a manner that is akin to the Neoplatonic "One," Avicenna's conception of *wājib al-wūjūd bi-dhātihi* (the Necessary Existent due to Itself) entails the following:

1- The Necessary Existence of the Necessary Existent due to *Itself (wājib al-wūjūd bi-dhātihi*) necessarily implies the existence of the world in terms of emanation.
2- That salvation is not dependent on grace but is rather dependent on the subject as agent.
3- That the personal, spiritual, passionate, or even rational communication with the Necessary Existent represents a categorical philosophical error.

Given these accounts, Avicenna's Necessary Existent due to Itself (*wājib al-wūjūd bi-dhātihi*) is not the Ultimate Being or God of monotheism. Therefore, Avicenna's philosophy is not theosophic or religious. In this sense it is appropriate to refer to Avicenna's philosophy as being a medieval Near Eastern/Middle Eastern philosophy that has been mainly written in Arabic, in the Middle ages, in a civilization and culture (Arabic/Persian) whose dominant religion is Islam.

IV- Methodological Issues

Given that most of the relevant and important philosophical texts of Avicenna have not been translated into English. And given that what has been already translated into French or English is not sufficient, or is otherwise influenced by Thomistic, Orientalist, or Peripatetic interpretations. The investigations of this book have been conducted on primary Arabic philosophical texts of Avicenna that have not yet been fully translated nor were they sufficiently attended to in the Western scholarship. This includes main texts taken from *Kitāb al-Shifā', Kitāb-al-Najāt, Kitāb al-Ishārāt wal-Tanbīhāt, Kitāb al-Ḥudūd.* Other Arabic and French versions of the primary texts of the visionary recitals of *Ḥayy Ibn Yaqẓān*, *al-Ṭayr*, and *Salmān wa Absal* were also consulted. And the English translation of the *Dānish Nāma* from Persian gave deep insights about Avicenna's metaphysics. A Glossary of Arabic key terms has also been included in the end of the book to familiarize the reader with some of the used Arabic philosophical terms.

Regarding the format of the book, and for the purposes of clarity, conciseness, and analytic expository purposes, an *Analytic Synopsis* has been included to offer an abridged and outlined version of the main arguments and themes that are addressed in the chapters.

V- Shortcomings & Limitations

It would have been impossible to give a comprehensive account of Heidegger's philosophy while at the same time accounting for the complex and rich ontological, epistemological, mystic, and linguistic issues that figure in Avicenna's philosophical consideration of the question of being. It would have not also been possible to sufficiently contextualize Avicenna's phenomenological ontology in terms of accounting for the subsequent developments that one attests with the phenomenological tradition that characterizes the post-Avicennian philosophical heritage. In spite of the limitations in scope, one would hope that what has been presented in this book would offer a humble attempted contribution to bring together the research interests of phenomenologists from one side and Medievalists and Islamists from the other side. And to do so while pointing towards new possibilities of cross-cultural philosophical encounters.

PREFACE TO THE SECOND PRINTING

Fifteen years have passed since this present book was originally composed. Its theses have been reinforced through numerous journal articles and chapters that I published since 1999 on Avicenna and Heidegger. Ambiguities were reconsidered in depth through these publications. The main philosophical thrust has been maintained throughout my ensuing inquiries, albeit with nuanced elaborations that brought more clarity to this intellectual project and a deeper analytic understanding of its principal themes. The corpus is situated in-between two independent scholarship traditions, which necessitated novel methodological approaches that could not be restricted to those undertaken separately in "Avicennian" and "Heideggerian" studies. I aimed at finding conceptual and textual interconnections between them in view of exploring the potentials of their isomorphism. This work is not simply comparative in nature; it is rather philosophical in essence and surpasses the limits of exegetical commentary or documentation in historiography and philology. It is motivated by my reflections on the question of being, and by my endeavor to decode ancient texts and render their perennial questions relevant to contemporary philosophizing. I benefited over the years from exchanges with philosophers, historians, and philologists, especially through institutional research initiatives on "Arabic sciences and philsophy" and phenomenology, and by way of my close interactions with scholars such as Farhad Daftary (Institute of Ismaili Studies, London), Roshdi Rashed (Centre National de la Recherche Scientific, Paris), and Anna-Teresa Tymieniecka (World Phenomenology Institute, New Hampshire). It is my delightful duty to thank them all, and to express my gratitude to SUNY Press for the second printing of this book, which I will dedicate herein to my sons, Mouhib and Magdi.

Nader El-Bizri (Beirut 2014)

ANALYTIC SYNOPSIS

This analytic synopsis offers a concise and dense account of the main arguments and themes that constitute the abridged outline of each of the chapters of this book.

I- Preface

A- The aims of this book:

I. General

- i) To clarify the salient features and methods of the phenomenology of being in medieval and contemporary philosophy.

II. Particulars:

- i) To offer a new phenomenological reading of Avicenna's philosophy of being.
- ii) To critically reevaluate Heidegger's claims about the historical significance of his ontology:
  - a- Addressing the incompleteness in his account of the history of metaphysics. That his fundamental ontology does have features which have historical precedence in Avicenna's philosophical consideration of the question of being.
  - b- Addressing features of an alternative philosophical tradition that confirms the centrality of the question of being. That Avicenna's philosophical consideration of the question of being initiates the beginnings of a philosophical tradition that is phenomenological in character and that diverts from the peripatetic categorical consideration of being in terms of *ousia*.

c- Consulting primary Arabic philosophical texts of Avicenna that were not sufficiently attended to in the Western scholarship mainly the texts of:

1. *Kitāb al-Shifā', Kitāb-al-Najāt, Kitāb al-Ishārāt wal-Tanbīhāt, Kitāb al-Ḥudūd.*
2. Arabic and French versions of the primary texts of the visionary recitals of *Ḥayy Ibn Yaqẓān*, *al-Ṭayr*, and *Salmān wa Absal.*

B- Remark:

There is a historical as well as scholarly tendency to consider Avicenna's philosophy as being incompatible with Islamic orthodoxy. This interpretation is itself advocated by Abū Ḥāmid al-Ghazālī and Ibn Taymīya who side with traditionalist readings of Avicenna's philosophical accounts (mainly that God does not have knowledge of particulars). Some contemporary scholars like Houben and Morewedge hold that Avicenna's philosophical system does not reflect an adherence to monotheism nor does it advance monotheism against other theological and religious systems. Other scholars such as Naṣr, do see that Avicenna's system is compatible with the monotheistic of Islamic orthodoxy. In order to give a concise account of what these views entail. Let us by way of illustration suppose that monotheism implies the following:

1) That it is logically possible that God exists and the world does not exist (thus supporting an account of creation *ex nihilo*).
2) That salvation is conceivably affected by grace.
3) That prayer and intimacy between the worshipper and God are encouraged.

Based on these accounts, and in a manner that is akin to the Neoplatonic "One," Avicenna's conception of *wājib al-wūjūd bi-dhātihi* (the Necessary Existent due to Itself) entails the following:

1) The Necessary Existence of the Necessary Existent due to Itself (*wājib al-wūjūd bi-dhātihi*) necessarily implies the existence of the world in terms of emanation.
2) That salvation is not dependent on grace but is rather dependent on the subject as agent.
3) That the personal, spiritual, passionate, or even rational communication with the Necessary Existent represents a categorical philosophical error.

Given these accounts, Avicenna's Necessary Existent due to Itself is not the God of monotheism. Therefore, Avicenna's philosophy is not theosophic nor religious. One may refer to Avicenna's philosophy as being a medieval Near Eastern/Middle Eastern philosophy that has been mainly written in Arabic, in a culture (Arabic/Persian) where Islam is the dominant religion.

II- Introduction

I. Heidegger's acclaimed "genuine" consideration of the question of being, and his critique of metaphysics (as the history of the oblivion of being) are not considered in terms of:
   i) Enacting a direct confrontation between his thought and that of Avicenna.
   ii) Assessing whether Avicenna's philosophy is stamped by Heidegger's critique of metaphysics, thus not ceding to the thrust of the Heideggerian thought, rather taking that thought into consideration without fully adopting its ontological agenda.
   iii) Offering a direct account of the critique of the history of metaphysics in terms of accounting for:

a- The claim that the history of metaphysics is a history of the oblivion of being (i.e. that being is reduced into something other than itself).
b- The claim that the history of metaphysics leaves the ontological difference between being and beings unthought (and leaves the *differing* dimension of that difference unthought).

II. Heidegger's acclaimed "genuine" consideration of the question of being, and his critique of metaphysics (as the history of the oblivion of being) are rather considered in terms of:
i) Heidegger's theory of the subject which addresses:
a- The existential analytic of *Dasein* in terms of:
1. The worldliness of *Dasein* (mode of being-in-the-world).
2. The "care" structure of *Dasein.*
3. The "call of conscience" and the call for "thinking."
4. The authenticity of being of *Dasein* and death.
5. The temporality of *Dasein* and its finitude.
6. The solitude of *Dasein* and its relation to otherness.

ii) Heidegger's theory of modernity which addresses:
a- The critique of modern technology as the terminal phase of metaphysics.
b- The critique of the mode of revealing by way of the threatening *Ge-stell* (Enframing) of the essence of modern technology.

III. Avicenna's consideration of being (Arabic: *al-wūjūd*, Persian: *hasti*) is mediated through the following:
i) An ontology of being that:
a- Replaces the Peripatetic categorical ontology of οὐσία (*ousia*) by:

1. Accounting for the primordial being in the mind.
2. Analyzing being in terms of the modalities of impossibility (*imtināᶜ*, *istiḥāla*), contingency (*imkān*), and necessity (*wūjūb*).
3. Overcoming "essentialism" while drawing the distinction between essence and existence.

ii) An epistemology of being that:
a- Is integrated with Avicenna's ontology
1. By accounting for being in terms of the affirmation of the existence of *al-nafs* [non-substance based or metaphysically based account of the subject or soul-- (i.e. approached through an existential process based analytic)].
   a- This is attested in the process of the unfolding of *al-nafs* to a primordial ground of experience.
   b- This is attested in letting *al-nafs* be without offering claims about what that being is.
2. By accounting for intentional and phenomenological dimensions of knowledge as exemplified in Avicenna's consideration of the pragmatics of "the inner sense of prehension" (*al-wahm*).

iii) A philosophical mysticism that is characterized by:
a- Hermeneutic dimensions that are:
1. Related to the realization of truth (*ḥaq*/ἀλήθεια [*alētheia*], which is also the ultimate reality) as *taḥqīq* through *kashf al-maḥjūb* (i.e. unveiling of truth) – And this points to similar accounts

in Ibn ᶜArabī's *Futūḥāt,* and in Naṣīr Khūsraw's *Kashāyish.*

2. Related to *tanzīl* (revelation and descent) and to *ta'wīl* (as the return to the primordial self and ascent).

b- Self-realization and self-perfection as:

1. Being towards truth (*al-ḥaq*/ἀλήθεια which is also being towards the Necessary Existent due to Itself) and being towards the perfection and goodness of being.
2. An overcoming of subjectivity by tending towards the "union" which cannot be fully realized but with the rupturing event of a mystic death; and herein, union has three senses:

    a- It is union as *itiḥād*, as is the case with the religious ascribed rules of *al-sharīᶜa* (religious laws), when they are followed, the religious agent is thus in union with God's revelation (and this the state of affairs of the pious: *al-ᶜābid*).

    b- It is union as *itiṣāl*, represents a union by virtue of a common sharing between two realms where neither loses its individuality (like the mother and the father having *itiṣāl* in terms of the child, all intelligent beings share intelligence). This is the state of affairs of the ascetic (*al-zāhid*).

    c- It is union as *ḥulūl*, as a mystic union whereby individuation is lost and the mystic is in a union that describes the *baqā' al-fanā'* (i.e. existence in annihilation by union, existence by the rupturing death, as a return of no return). This is the state of affairs of the one endowed with gnostic knowledge, i.e. the gnostic (*al-^{C}ārif*).

III- The Metaphysical Tradition

Heidegger holds that the metaphysical tradition is characterized by the oblivion of being since that tradition reduces being into something other than itself. Based on this critique:

I. It is claimed that Aristotle has a reductive account of being due to the following:

- i) Holding that οὐσία (*ousia*, i.e. substance) is the sustaining and leading fundamental meaning of being to which all the categories are carried back. Thus adding that everything must have the saying of *ousia*; hence, despite the manifoldness in the ways being is addressed (categories, *actus* and *potentia* theory, true and untrue being) Parmenides' oneness of being is not compromised.
- ii) Considering being in terms of an analysis of *ousia* as that which is eternal, self-same, intelligible, and necessary.
  - a- Thus this *ousiology* is linked to what Heidegger takes to be the essence of technology whereby beings are construed as what is knowable, available, and ready for research.
  - b- Such *ousiology* is also linked to what Heidegger takes to be a correctness conception of truth as entailed by the mode of revealing of modern technology in terms of "Enframing" (*Ge-stell*).

iii) Considering the essence of a human being in terms of a *noetic ousiology* (i.e. positing the being of a human being in terms of accounts of substance and essence).

II. Yet it is the case that Aristotle does not reduce being into something other than itself, rather Aristotle divides being according to the following:

i) That metaphysics is a speculative inquiry that deals with the examination of being *qua* being, while also dividing the inquiry of being in terms of accounts of the categories: which are also divided into accounts of substance and accidents.

ii) That the manifold accounts of being are also expressed in terms of a theory of *actus* and *potentia*, and of true and untrue being.

iii) That the manifoldness in the senses of being does not contend or refute Parmenides' oneness of being, while accounting for the unity of multiplicity in terms of analogy.

III. Cartesianism and Subject-ism address being in terms of subjectivity:

i) Taking the *cogito ergo sum* to be the unshakable foundation (*fundamentum absolutum*) of all ontology.

ii) Considering the self in terms of a static conception of the self as substance. And doing so without accounting for its embodiment or its temporal determination (and both represent later Kantian objections to the *Cartesian* conception of the self that holds that: "I, as thinking being, am substance" or that "I am a simple substance" are empty sayings).

IV. Kant syntactically claims that being (obviously) is not a real predicate:

i) Claiming that being is not a real predicate. And that being acts as a *copula* between subject and predicate. And this is a consequence of the distinction between essence and existence that is undertaken in the context of considering abstract entities, whereby essence is taken to be prior to existents.

ii) Considering being to be a "positing" that is related to the "act of understanding." Being is thus determined from the side of thought and Kant's ontology is turned into a transcendental philosophy. According to Heidegger: the "being of beings" is taken (by Kant) to be the "objectness of objects."

iii) Considering being in terms of subjectivity and perception where:

a- Existence is bound up by the field (or horizon) of perception.

b- Existence is bound up by the subjective act of apperception (with its presupposed transcendental unity of apperception; given that being is determined from the side of thought).

c- Assimilating being to presence, whereby intentionality is determined or filled up by perception.

d- Stressing the interdependence between concepts and intuitions.

V. Hegel subordinates being to essence by:

i) Overcoming *ousiology* in terms of process ontology that focuses on subjectivity.

a- That the unfolding of being is a "dialectical process" that reflects a procession and reversion movement of identity, difference, and *Aufhebung* (A process that is

Neoplatonic in character while also being characterized by an essentialist [totality-based] tendency in metaphysics).

b- Mediating being through essence and subjectivity.

c- Showing that development/process supercedes the Absolute.

iv) Reducing being into essence, whereby being is the becoming of essence:

a- Taking essence, the notion, and ideas to be what is real, while taking being and the finite to be forms of conception (i.e. lacking true being).

b- Taking the truth of being to be essence, that the knowledge of being is mediated. And as an "indeterminate immediacy" and as a "pure concept," being is convergent with thinking.

c- Not being able to set εἶναι (*einai*: being in the Greek sense) from its relation to the subject. Being is thus "not set free" into its essence while unfolding as "presence."

IV- Heidegger's Theory of The Subject

Heidegger's "genuine" approach to the question of being (*Sein*) is mediated through the existential analytic of *Dasein* (as an ontological analytic of the subjectivity of the subject) which is undertaken according to the following salient features:

I. Being-in-the-World which shows that:

i) *Dasein* essentially belongs to the world.

ii) *Dasein*'s worldliness is not based on a containment picture of spatiality. *Dasein*'s "being-in" is neither a containment by envelopment (as is the case with Aristotle's account of space in the *Physics*), nor is it a containment by pervasion (as is the case with Plato's account of space in the *Timaeus*).

iii) *Dasein*'s worldliness is characterized by "being-in" which is also "being-toward" and "being-with-others."

v) *Dasein*'s worldliness is characterized by "care," and "knowing."

II. The Care Structure of *Dasein* entails that:

i) *Dasein* exists for the sake of itself.

ii) *Dasein* exists for the sake of others (Also for the sake of the neuter "they" or *das Man*).

II. The Call of Conscience calls for:

i) An authentic mode of being-in-the-world attested with *Dasein*'s bringing itself back from its everydayness to an "individuating" potentiality-of-being-itself in terms of:

a- *Dasein*'s "being-ahead-of-itself" as "running-ahead-of-itself," meaning that *Dasein*'s authentic mode of being is that of "being-towards-death."

b- *Dasein*'s "resoluteness" to be a potentiality-for-being itself within the limits of its own being.

c- *Dasein*'s estrangement from the everyday comforting and "tranquillization about death" (as an inauthentic mode of being in flight from death). Thus *Dasein* ought to estrange itself from the alienating everydayness world of *das Man*.

d- *Dasein*'s realization that its most extreme possibility is death.

ii) Thinking about what is most thought provoking:

a- To think about the question of being as the question of the meaning, place, and truth of being.

b- To think about death, as an "event" that allows *Dasein* to be in the world authentically.

c- Thinking about thinking in terms of re-collection, re-gathering, and thanking, i.e. to "commemoratively" think about the sending and granting of being.

III. *Dasein*'s authenticity of being is achieved in death given that:

i) *Dasein*'s wholeness is achieved in death. And "*Angst*" about death in the face of the "nothingness" of death discloses the certain and indeterminate most extreme possibility of *Dasein*'s potentiality-of-being (i.e. *Dasein*'s death).

ii) *Dasein* is finite and temporal, and its finitude is achieved in terms of its ownmost certain and indeterminate possibility to be itself, i.e. its death, given that *Dasein*'s being-in-the-world is a mode of being between birth and death.

IV. Temporality characterizes *Dasein* given that:

i) *Dasein*'s authenticity of being shows that:

a- Death pervades every aspect of *Dasein*, like it is the case with predication and Leibniz's monads, whereby every predicate pervades the wholeness of the monad.

b- *Dasein* is temporal and finite.

c- *Dasein*'s wholeness shows that *Dasein* "is not in time," "*Dasein* is time; and "temporality" constitutes the ontological meaning of *Dasein* while also being the transcendental horizon of the question of being.

d- Temporality reveals a stress on a process-ontology as characterized by *Ereignis* (as event of appropriation) already points towards a focus on process rather than focusing on substance. The use of a language that stresses on "events" is meant to be a move away from a consideration of being in terms of *ousia.*

V. The solitude of *Dasein* is critisized by Emmanuel Levinas in *Le temps et l'autre*, given that the solitude of *Dasein* is characterized by:

i) The Heideggerian impersonal existential analysis of *Dasein* that shows the insufficiency of claiming that being alone is a deficiency in being.

ii) Compromising the *otherness* of the *other (l'altérité de l'autre ou d'autrui)* despite what Heidegger holds viz. *Mitsein* (being-with) and *Miteinandersein* (being reciprocally with one another).

iii) Openness to a dissolution of the centrality of subjectivity in the face of death. Where it is claimed (by Levinas) that the subject is no more a subject in death. Death undermines subjectism.

V- Heidegger's Theory of Modernity

Heidegger's theory of modernity consists of critically addressing the terminal phase in the history of metaphysics as it is characterized by the following:

I. The *Vorhandenheit* (presence-at-hand) which entails:

i) The reduction of beings into present-at-hand entities
ii) The reduction of being into what falls under theoretical thematization
iii) The oblivion of the ontological difference between being and beings, and leaving the *differing* dimension of this difference unthought:
  a- That even a genus and species account of being and beings leaves the ontological difference between being and beings unthought.
iv) The stress on the metaphysics of production, *actualitas*, ἐνέργεια (*enērgeia*), and *ousia* (i.e. inscribing the question of being within the horizon of production).
v) Being coupled with the practical construing of beings in terms of the "circumspective" practicality of the *Zuhandenheit* (readiness-at-hand, handiness, or availability).

II. The metaphysical basis of science which reveals that:
  i) Metaphysics pervades all spheres of human existence.
  ii) Metaphysics underlies the scientific reduction of beings into present at-hand entities.
  iii) Scientific thematization serves the purposes of metaphysics and its oblivion of being, thus leaving the ontological difference between being and beings unthought.

III. The *Ge-stell* (Enframing) the mode of revealing that:
  i) Reduces objects and humans into an objectless "standing reserve" (*Bestand*) by means of setting-in-order and challenging forth to reveal the real as standing reserve.
  ii) Monopolizes all other modes of revealing of truth, thus:

- a- "Enframing" endangers the essence of truth by turning all modes of revealing into a securing of the "standing reserve."
- b- "Enframing" is the "danger of all dangers."
- c- Stresses on a monopolizing "correctness" conception of truth that dismisses the mystery of the sending and self-withdrawing of being (Enframing as *Ge-stell* thus blocks truth).

IV. The "saving power" which:

- i) Grows where the danger of "enframing" is (Based on the polemical Heideggerian poetic turn towards the language of being that is exemplified in Holderlin's verses).
- ii) Reveals other modes of revealing than the mode of revealing of the essence of technology and its "enframing."
- iii) Shelters the essence of the human being (that is threatened by "enframing" yet at the same time preserved by "enframing" in order to secure the ordering of beings as "standing reserve").
- iv) Makes a turn towards poetry as a mode of revealing (by ποίησις, *poiēsis*) that shelters truth and the meaning of being (turning in this towards a poetic dwelling on this earth, which is also characterized by the "gathering" of what Heidegger calls the "fourfold").
- v) Thinking about revealing in terms of granting, i.e. in terms of what calls for thanking.

VI- The Ontology of Being

Avicenna's ontology overcomes the Peripatetic realist *ousiology* in terms of two approaches to the question of being:

I. The primary analysis of being as what is primordial and familiar to the mind:
   - i) The consideration of being in terms of a primary encounter in the mind without being an available (handy) concept to ontology.

II. The analysis of being in terms of the modalities which depends on the following:
   - i) A consideration of the modalities in relation to:
     - a- Causation.
       1. Necessary existence (*wūjūb al-wūjūd*) in terms of external existential causes (*ᶜilal wūjūdīya*).
       2. The distinction between cause and agent in relation to existence and subsistence.
       3. That the activity of an agent is due to the agent's will and nature, or due to an accidental condition to it.
       4. That causes are either existential causes (*ᶜilal wūjūdīya*) or essential causes (*ᶜilal māhīya*), and that existential causes are what cause something to exist rather than the essence of that which exists.
     - b- Potentiality and actuality (*al-quwa wal-fiᶜl*)
       1. In relation to causality.
       2. In relation to existence.
       3. Logical analysis of the modalities (with a focus on the modality of *mumkin*).
       4. The *mumkin*/possible (of common sense [*al-ᶜāma*]) is not the same as the *mum-*

kin/contingent (of the elect learned [*al-khāṣṣa*] and philosophers).

ii) A consideration of the modalities in terms of:

a- An ontological consideration of impossibility

1. The impossible being (*mumtani*^{c} *al-wūjūd*) is that which cannot exist.

b- An ontological consideration of contingency

1. Contingent being is a necessary existent due to what is other than itself (*wājib al-wūjūd bi-ghaīrihi*) i.e. it is caused.
2. Contingent being (*mumkin al-wūjūd*) is that whose essence is other than its existence.

c- An ontological consideration of necessity that:

1. Reveals the Necessary Existent due to Itself (*wājib al-wūjūd bi-dhātihi*) as being irreducible to anything other than itself, that it is not *ousia* (*jawhar*), nor genus, nor species.
2. Reveals the epistemic priority of being over the Necessary Existent due to Itself.
3. Reveals the Necessary Existent due to Itself as being that who does have quiddity (*māhīya*) and whose essence (*dhāt*) is none other than Its existence (*wūjūd*). It is that which is not caused nor is it due to anything but Itself (in that sense it is pure perfection).
4. Reveals that the Necessary Existent due to Itself is One (*wāḥid, aḥad, awal*) and simple, and no *differentia* (*faṣl*) or composition (*tarkīb*) applies to it.

5. Reveals that no accidents apply to the Necessary Existent due to Itself, and Its only essence is existence.

d- Concluding that the Necessary Existent due to itself is not accounted for in terms of *ousia* based ontology. The consideration of the Necessary Existent due to Itself as being pure perfection points to an initiation into "*einaiology*," focusing on "to be" rather than on *ousia.*

VII- Being & Essence

Avicenna draws a distinction between essence and existence that entails:

I. Avicenna's distinction has an ontological basis that relies on the analysis of being in terms of the modalities.

II. Avicenna's distinction between essence and existence is undertaken in the context of:

i) A syntactic inquiry (*lafẓī*) in terms of which essence is taken to be prior to existents.

ii) A non-syntactic [actual] inquiry (*ghaīr lafẓī*) that consists of:

a- Non-conceptualist (*ghaīr ẓihnī*) empirical and perceptual consideration of entities and experiences in terms of which existents are taken to be prior to essence.

b- Conceptualist (*ẓihnī*) consideration of concepts and abstract non-existent entities in terms of which essence is taken to be prior to existence.

III. Avicenna's distinction between essence and existence does not solely entail essentialism given that:

i) The essentialism claim is based on incomplete readings of the primary sources:

- a- Reading Avicenna's work under the influence of the Thomistic scholarship, as is the case with É. Gilson and the reference to Gilson that John Caputo does.
- b- Referring to Thomas Aquinas' metaphysics as being a metaphysics of existence (*esse*) on the basis of accounts that could be traced back to Avicenna's philosophical consideration of the question of being. Yet still taking Avicenna to be an essentialist metaphysician (as is the case with Gilson's and Caputo's accounts).
- c- Reading Avicenna's work under the influence of early Orientalist translations and interpretations, and this influence is mainly due to the innovative works of A. M. Goichon and her influential consideration of the essence/existence distinction.
- d- The linguistic confusions in the rendering of the terms *māhīya*, *dhāt*, *huwīya*, *anīya*, and *wūjūd*. Some of these accounts are also elucidated in Jamīl Ṣalībā's Arabic encyclopedia of philosophy. And they are also analyzed in the body of this book in terms of grammatical and syntactical consideration of the Arabic language.

ii) Avicenna's distinction gives primacy to existence.

- a- With Avicenna existence is shown as being an advantage and a perfection and goodness (*khayrīyat al-wūjūd*).

b- Avicenna's analysis of being through the modalities of contingency and necessity supports his metaphysics of existence (i.e. his existentialism).

c- The account of the participation in being (*al-tashkīk*) which varies in intensity between an existent and another.

VIII- The Epistemology of Being

Avicenna's epistemological consideration of being is characterized by:

I. An ontological consideration of being in terms of:

i) The "Suspended Person Argument" (also known as: "The Floating Man Argument") which affirms self-existence in terms of:

a- Differing from the Cartesian *Cogito* conception of the self as substance (The *Meditations* of Descartes).

b- Reflecting isomorphic dimensions that are attested in Kant's transcendental unity of apperception (*Critique of Pure Reason*) and in Heidegger's existential analytic of *Dasein* (Being and Time). And in the de-alienating of *Dasein* from the world of everydayness and the comforting of the neuter "they" or *das Man.*

c- Offering a conception of the self in terms of a hermeneutic return process that does not account for the self in terms of static states but takes time to be a determinant horizon of the conception of the self.

d- A confirmation of being in terms of "I-ness," i.e. an encounter of being in terms of the "I" (*al-anā*).

1. Stressing on the convergence between being and thinking without the need

to continually affirm to myself that "I am" (in the Cartesian fashion). This account is closer to the Kantian unity of apperception that gathers the representations of the self.

2. Considering being in terms of the immediacy of knowledge and experience (*al-ᶜilm al-ḥuḍūrī*).

II. The intentional and phenomenological characterization of knowledge:

i) The inner sense of prehension (*al-wahm*):

a- *Al-wahm* as one of the higher inner senses (*al-ḥiss al-bāṭinī*).

b- The ascription of meaning and perception.

c- The pragmatics of successful concrete actions.

d- The hermeneutic and phenomenological dimensions that characterize the translation and interpretation of *al-wahm*.

1. The rejection of translations that take *al-wahm* to be, estimation, apprehension, instinct, imagination, or nervous response.
2. The consideration of *al-wahm* as a pragmatic and act-oriented process that accomplishes successful acts in the face of concrete circumstances (Morewedge interprets *al-wahm* as "the pragmatic process of prehension").

e- Confirming Avicenna's account of the self in terms of a hermeneutic process of return (which also figures in the philosophical mysticism of the Visionary Recitals, as addressed in chapter 7 below).

IX- The Authenticity of Being

The philosophical mysticism of Avicenna is attested in his Visionary Recitals (The trilogy cycle of the *Recital of Ḥayy Ibn Yaqẓān*, the *Recital of the Bird*, and the *Recital of Salmān wa Absal*). Henry Corbin is one of those scholars who emphasize that Avicenna's recitals display features of a philosophical mysticism that accounts for hermeneutic interpretations of rhetoric, allegory, and gnsotic features. While other scholars, like A. Amīn and A -M. Goichon, do emphasize that the recitals are allegorical reiterations of the metaphysical demonstrative views which are impacted by a focus on logical analysis and on tracing Aristotelian influences.

The philosophical mysticism of the recitals (in accepting H. Corbin's approach) does overcome the consideration of the question of being through a metaphysical or epistemological account of subjectivity; and this is due to:

I. Hermeneutic dimensions that are characterized by:
   i) Orientation that invites the mystic to journey towards the orient as the source and origin of being and awakens the self to its estrangement and alienation (as is the case with Corbin's reading of *The Recital of Ḥayy Ibn Yaqẓān*).
   ii) *Taḥqīq* as the realization of truth (*al-ḥaq*) in terms of an "orientation" that leads to the unveiling of truth (*kashf al-maḥjūb*, as a happening of ἀλήθεια [*alētheia*]). And the realization of truth is a mystic path that is represented by the temporal and dialectical process that is attested between the *maqāmāt* (stages) and *aḥwāl* (states) of the mystic. Whereby the self is in constant change on the path of self-realization in quest for truth.
   iii) The Islamic Neoplatonic consideration of *tanzīl* (as revelation and descent) which is followed by the interpretational move of *ta'wīl* (return to the primordial

self, or ascension [*mi*ʿ*rāj*]). And this itself is taken to be a re-enacting of the Prophetic *mi*ʿ*rāj* from Jerusalem, while also accounting in it for the mystic journey that is undertaken by the ʿ*ārif* (gnostic).

II. Accounts of the "other" in terms of an indirect consideration of φιλια (*philia*, i.e. friendship):

i) Linking friendship to a "brotherhood of truth" (*ikhwat al-ḥaq*) as being a community of mystics that seek truth (*al-ḥaq*) as the origin of their provenance and being. And this might be deduced from the preface of the recital of the bird, where the bird is a mystic icon that symbolizes the soul. And it might be addressed in allusion to the "Brethren of Purity" (*Ikhwān al-ṣafā*ʾ). Where purity represents a realm in which the mystic icon generates a transmutation of the world.

ii) Distinguishing between good and bad friendship in terms of ʿ*ilm al-firāsa* (By interpreting physiognomy bad companionship is revealed in a hermeneutic move of *ta'wīl* of a face to face encounter with the other – as it might be implied in *The Recital of Ḥayy Ibn Yaqẓān*).

iii) Breaking the solitude that characterizes the mystic's journey (*safar al-*ʿ*ārif*) which itself may be subjected to the same critique that Levinas advances viz. Heidegger's impersonal existential analytic of a solitary *Dasein*, which compromises the "otherness" of the other.

III. Self-perfection and self-realization:

i) In the de-alienating mystic quest of truth (as *taḥqīq*, which is also realization or more particularly realization of truth), and of being as perfection and goodness (*khayrīya*).

ii) In quest of the mystic union (*al-ḥulūl*) which is not realized but after the existential wholeness that the rupture of death brings about. Yet union in the sense of *itiḥād* and *itiṣāl* represents the mode of being towards truth that is not yet realized in its fullest sense.

IV. The polemical aspects of symbolism and the ascription of meaning in interpretation.

i) Interpretations that refute *ta'wīl* based on a logical and expository analysis of the Visionary Recital (as is the case with A. M. Goichon's consideration of *The Recital of Ḥayy Ibn Yaqẓān*).

ii) Interpretations that accentuate the role of *ta'wīl*, symbolism, and orientation in terms of accounts that address the recitals through the allegorical aspects of poetry and rhetoric (as is the case with Henry Corbin's analysis of the cycle of the trilogy of the visionary recitals of Avicenna).

a- The tension between the demonstrative/expository approach and the allegorical/hermeneutic approach (as exemplified in D. Gutas' emphasis on the Aristotelian impact on Avicenna's philosophy while reducing the importance of allegory, and *ta'wīl* in addressing the recitals). And this tension may also reflect the tension between the *ousiological* metaphysics and a hermeneutic openness to the movement of meaning interpretation and ascription.

X- Language & Being

The linguistic account of being is characterized by:

I. An onto-theological inclination not to confuse being with an entity or a being:

  i) This involves issues related to the use of the verbal "to be" and how this ties to the use of "is" and "to be" as a copula or to the use of existence as predicate.

  ii) The use of the verbal "to be" in Semitic languages (including the Arabic language) presents a linguistic context that meets the demands that the use of the verbal "to be" in English, French, or German might require, in order not to reduce being into a mere copula or to confuse being with beings:

    a- In Arabic, the use of the verbal "to be" is silent, in the sense that there is no "is" or "was" form that act as a copula (*wūjūd rābiṭ*). "Being" or "to be" become evoked when the question of being (*al-wūjūd*) is asked, or else, being is silently underlying the saying and the writing.

II. Hermeneutic dimensions:

  i) Regarding the univocity or equivocity of meaning ascription while preserving a basis for common understanding and fusion of horizons (the case of Hans Georg Gadamer).

  ii) Regarding the incommensurability line in interpretation and translation (the case of Jacques Derrida).

  iii) Regarding the relation between European hermeneutics and *ta'wīl* (the focus on language, intentionality, meaning, interpretation, and the relation of the self to what is other than itself).

III. Relationship between language and truth:

i) The case of *ta'wīl* and the unveiling of truth:
   - a- *Ta'wīl* is a return to the *al-awal*, as the primordial ground of the self or the primordial being "The One" (i.e. the Necessary Existent due to Itself).
   - b- *Ta'wīl* is a hermeneutic exegesis of the self, the world, and language:
     1. *Ta'wīl* is a hermeneutic ascent that affects the return of what has been brought down in descent by *tanzīl* (revelation).
     2. *Ta'wīl* is a self-exegesis that takes place in terms of interpreting the relation of the self to its origin and the source of its being.
     3. *Ta'wīl* reveals that the self cannot be accounted for in terms of substance.
   - c- *Ta'wīl* is *taḥqīq* in the sense of being a movement towards the realization of truth as is the case with the self that moves towards the source of its being and truth.
   - d- *Ta'wīl* is a *taḥqīq* (realization of truth) by way of *kashf al-maḥjūb* which transcends the construing of truth as correctness and takes truth to be a happening, an event, an occurrence as unconcealment and unveiling.
   - e- Risks of extremism in doctrinal accounts of *ta'wīl* that might lead to anthropomorphism (i.e. *tashbīh* that confuses being with beings) and *bāṭinnīya* (as an esoterism that compromises the literal exoteric meanings).

IV. Poetizing and mystery:

i) The relation between poetry and truth in Heidegger's consideration of modernity figures in relation to his account of the saving power that grows where the danger of all dangers is. That it grows at the same place where Enframing (*Ge-stell*) poses the threat to the essence of truth and to the sheltering of the question of being.

ii) The relation between truth and mystery, in the unveiling of truth, is meant to show that where the occurrence of the light takes place, that very lightning is also pervaded by darkness. That for every sending of truth there is also a self-withdrawing of what grants that truth (As an interplay of concealing and unconcealment). And this is advanced in objection to the correctness conception of truth that is entailed by the *Ge-stell* of modernity.

iii) The poetic dimensions of being in the world that resist "enframing" are attested in dwelling in the world poetically, i.e. in the gathering of the fourfold of a world that "worlds" in which the "thinging" things offer a spot for the gathering of the "fourfold":

a- A "thinging" thing may be represented by the consideration of the "bridge" in Heidegger's consideration of building, dwelling, and thinking.

b- A "thinging" thing, in a "worlding" world, is also exemplified in a work of art. As it is the case with the polemical consideration of the "peasant's shoes" in Van Gogh's painting – In Heidegger's "The Origin of the Work of Art" (which itself is debated by M. Heidegger, M. Schapiro, and J. Derrida – *Restitutions*, in *La Vérité en Peinture*).

iv) Avicenna wrote poetry and it was complementary to his scientific as well as his philosophical and mystical writings.

XI- Concluding Remarks

I. Avicenna overcomes classical ontology by:

i) Overcoming an *ousia*-based ontology in terms of a Neoplatonist account of processes and events (i.e. like is the case with Heidegger's conception of *Ereignis*).

ii) Showing the compatibility and complementary character of existentialism and essentialism depending on the sort of inquiry that is lead, either as syntactical or conceptual analysis, or as empirical investigation.

iii) Overcoming the ontology of metaphysical subjectivity that considers the self as substance.

II. Heidegger's consideration of the history of metaphysics is incomplete:

i) He did not give consideration to Avicenna's philosophy that takes the question of being to be central to it. He did not account for what is "other" within the history of Western Metaphysics (as if contributing to the obliteration of the "otherness" that characterizes that history).

ii) His claims about the historical significance of his ontology are to be re-valuated given that they emerge from his incomplete reading of the history of metaphysics. This is the case given that Heidegger did not account for Avicenna's consideration of the question of being and the centrality of that question within the subsequent developments of the Avicennian phenomenological ontology.

iii) The course of development of Avicennism diverts from the peripatetic categorical and *ousiological* ontology, while pointing towards the emergence of a process/event ontology that displays isomorphic features with what Heidegger claims to be his "genuine" fundamental ontology (i.e. phenomenology of being).

III. The need for future research work that addresses the subsequent ontological tradition that develops with the successors of Avicenna (like Ṭūsī, Suhrawardī, and Mullā Ṣadrā) which is beyond the scope of this book to address:

i) In order to investigate the course of development of that philosophical tradition apart from its links with medieval and ancient philosophy.

ii) In order to further investigate the salient phenomenological and hermeneutic features that characterize that tradition, and eventually offering a context that allows us to re-examine the Avicennian heritage.

iii) To show that Avicennism and its subsequent development offer alternative perspectives on the question of being.

iv) To show that Avicennism and its subsequent development offer alternative hermeneutic and phenomenological methods in ontology:

a- This is the case, given that this would offer a contribution to the contemporary concerns in renewing philosophy and metaphysics in an epoch that is considered by some to be the epoch of "the closure of metaphysics;" or more so the closure of a "particular" sort of metaphysics.

v) The subsequent developments of Avicenna's philosophy have lead to the emergence of a tradition that is characterized by the following:

a- Rejection of the Peripatetic tradition and the Aristotelian categories by accounting for "temporality/time" and "processes/motions" (Ṣadrā's "substantial motion" *al-ḥaraka al-jawharīya* is one example).

b- Giving prominence to the immediate knowledge and experience (*al-ʿilm al-ḥuḍūrī*); as is the case with Suhrawardī and Ṣadra.

c- Accounting for the world in terms of phenomena (as is the case in the conceptual inquiry [*ẓihnī*]), while also accounting for the world in a non-phenomenal manner (*ghaīr ẓihnī*) – This is attested with Ṭūsī and Ṣadrā.

d- Replacement of creation *ex nihilo* by various accounts of emanation and illumination.

e- Addressing the question of being in terms of a fourfold process that accounts for:

  1. The primary encounter with being,
  2. The showing of *al-anā* (the "I") as the revealing of this primary encounter with being.
  3. The search for the origin of the self as what grounds being.
  4. The integration of the above stages of the unfolding of being within a conception of the unity of being as *wiḥdat al-wūjūd.*

INTRODUCTION

I- Issues and Themes

The main focus of this book is directed to the consideration of the question of being in the philosophical works of the physician, *wazīr*, poet, and above all one of the great metaphysicians of history: Abū ᶜAlī al-Ḥusayn Ibn Sīnā (980-1037), who was known in the Latin world as Avicenna. The interpretation of his philosophical approach to the question of being will be reconstructed in the light of addressing some aspects of Martin Heidegger's critique of metaphysics. It is known that Avicenna and Heidegger are celebrated philosophers who dedicated most of the thrust of their works to think about being. Addressing the question of being through an examination of their works offers some grounds for the re-consideration of contemporary accounts of ontology through the examination of a rich and complex philosophical heritage that has not been sufficiently studied by the contemporary Western scholarship. Addressing the philosophy of a Middle Ages great metaphysician, who is not well understood by a majority of western philosophers, might open up new possibilities to reevaluate contemporary accounts *vis à vis* ontology. Such investigation may reveal some rather concealed and unthought ontological rich issues that one would find in the intricate work of a metaphysician like Avicenna. This, in its turn, allows for a consideration of the incompleteness of Heidegger's claims about the history of metaphysics, and the acclaimed historical and philosophical significance of his own ontology. Avicenna develops, adapts, and even overcomes the *ousiological* Aristotelian and Peripatetic categorical tradition in ontology. In this sense, Avicenna's philosophy offers a ground from which a possible reply to Heidegger's claims can be formulated. The consideration of Avicenna's philosophical accounts of the question of being raises some questions about the comprehensiveness and completeness of Heidegger's claim that, from the time of Aristotle till the time of Edmund Husserl, philosophy was entrapped in thinking about being in terms of οὐσία (*ousia*), *essentia*, *substantia*. What is at stake, is whether the Heideggerian "thought of being" has hastily declared, through a critique of metaphysics as first philosophy, that we have reached the epoch of overcoming metaphysics, the epoch of the end of philosophy at the beginning of thinking. It is tempting, yet problematic, if one tends to surrender to the thrust of the Heideggerian critique by hastily claiming that we are at the end of philosophy as metaphysics. . This becomes more of an issue if such claims are not sufficiently grounded through a comprehensive reconstructed examination and re-interpretation of the history of metaphysics itself. And this is especially the case if such re-interpretation is undertaken in the context of addressing some leading metaphysicians like Avicenna, who obviously have been left unconsidered by Heidegger's critique of the history of metaphysics. It might seem intellectually discomforting to think that Heidegger's consideration of metaphysics touches upon the works of Duns Scotus, Thomas Aquinas, and Meister Eckhart without any significant consideration of the influential Avicennian heritage.

One of the main features of Heidegger's critique of metaphysics is best expressed in the Heideggerian claim that being has fallen into oblivion almost throughout the history of Western Metaphysics. This claim reflects an interest in thinking about the unthought ontological difference between being and beings in terms of addressing what opens up the ontological difference in its very own *differing*. The critique of metaphysics expresses a Heideggerian concern with a particular side of the history of metaphysics that has been dominated by making and productivity. Such particular history is that of the metaphysics of *Vorhandenheit*, of ενέργεια (*enērgeia*), οὐσία (*ousia*), and τέχνη (*technē*), which all fall under the rubric of the metaphysics of making or of productivity. This sort of metaphysics is also coupled with a *Zuhandenheit* sense of circumspective practicality of readiness, and availability. Heidegger's critique of metaphysics is directed towards the essentialist line in thought, and it is also advanced in objection to an *ousia* ontology. Heidegger's ontological inclination hopes to effect a shift from *ousiology* to *einailogy* (εἶναι [*einai*]: to be, be-ing) by way of stressing the existential aspect of a metaphysics of *esse*. To think about being in terms of ἀλήθεια (*alētheia*), as unconcealment, is to think about being as truth and meaning by way of emphasizing the convergence of thinking and being. This requests thinking about language in terms of thinking about "the language of being." All of these issues underlie Heidegger's critique of metaphysics and onto-theology, and they offer a background against which the investigation of Avicenna's thought of being takes place.

II- Aims and Particulars

The aims and findings of the philosophical investigation, of Heidegger's phenomenological ontology and Avicenna's thought of being, clarify some aspects of the philosophical consideration of "being" in contemporary and medieval philosophy, while accounting for phenomenological methods of investigation in ontology. This involves an interpretive as well as a comparative philosophical investigation of a medieval philosophy in the light of considering a contemporary phenomenological approach to the question of "being." In this sense, the examination of some aspects of the universality of the phenomenological method in ontology becomes possible, given that isomorphic phenomenological dimensions are to be found in Contemporary European philosophy and in a Medieval, yet living, Islamic/Near Eastern philosophy. On this view, the universality of the phenomenological method is supposed to take into account the attempts to overcome the dichotomies of the world/self, of ontology/epistemology, and of other binary oppositions. Furthermore, the consideration of Avicenna's thought of being is accounted for in terms of presenting a clear formulation of some main phenomenological dimensions that characterize his thought. And, this is undertaken in terms of making use of primary Arabic texts that have not been adequately attended to prior to this investigation.

III- Contextual Issues

The philosophical development of the Avicennian heritage reflects a divergence from the Peripatetic categorical substance-ontology. This development attests the rise of process/event based ontologies which appear in the works of Avicenna's successors like Shihāb al-dīn Yaḥya Suhrawardī (d. 1191), Naṣīr al-dīn Muḥammad Ṭūsi (d. 1274), and Ṣadr al-dīn Muḥammad Shīrāzī [Mullā Ṣadrā] (d. 1641). Those philosophers testify to the rich developments in the intellectual history of the Muslim world. Their works attest to the rise of rich and complex philosophical accounts that depart from the Peripatetic and Aristotelian heritage. This state of affairs is also attested in the works of philosophers from the school of Isphahān, the school of Khurasān, and the school of Kirmān. The non-Aristotelian language that appears in the works of the successors of Avicenna points to a philosophical development that is not well recognized by the Western scholarship. After the Western/Latin philosophers lost their contacts with the Muslim intellectual life, the course of development of Islamic philosophy has been almost veiled. The divergence from the Peripatetic and Aristotelian tradition led some scholars to relegate Islamic thought to the realms of theosophy. This has been the case due to a failure to recognize the fact that the shift from the Aristotelian tradition was at the same time issuing innovative developments in Islamic philosophy that pointed towards process and event-based ontological accounts. The phenomenological, epistemological, and ontological tone that one encounters in the work of Muslim medieval philosophers leaves them standing open to a correlative contemporary reception of their philosophies. And this would be the case without strictly confining Islamic philosophy to a historical epoch that is usually taken as not being in direct touch with our own epoch and its ontological dispensations. The consideration of the successors of Avicenna, and the examination of primary Arabic texts, reflect a philosophical interest that does not merely mediate the interpretation of Islamic philosophy through a consideration of Aristotle, Alexander of Aphrodisias, the Neoplatonists, Augustine, or the Latin and Jewish scholastics. These sorts of comparative scholarly investigations usually do not carefully attend to the primary Arabic or Persian philosophic texts, nor do they study the philosophical works in terms of their own philosophical merits, away from doctrinal or ideologically inherited ways of receiving them. Interpreting Avicenna's philosophy in the light of Heidegger's critique of metaphysics might offer a context for a humble attempt to bring-together the works of Islamist philosophers, Medievalists, and Phenomenologists.

IV- Heidegger's *Dasein*

In addressing Martin Heidegger's thought of "being," the focus is turned towards the main features that characterize his notion of *Dasein*. This is undertaken in terms of attempting to resist ceding to the thrust of Heidegger's critique of the history of metaphysics by not directly confronting it. And more importantly not to apologetically cede the reading of Avicenna's philosophy to a tortuous attempt to save that philosophy from the grip of the Heideggerian critique of metaphysics. Therefore, the consideration of Heidegger's thought of being will not be endorsed in terms of focusing on a direct examination of the corrective requests that he advances in his critique of the metaphysical tradition (i.e. classical ontology). In this sense, the examination of Heidegger's consideration of the question of being will not directly address the Heideggerian innovative claims about the oblivion of being, the unthought ontological difference between being and beings, or the *differing* dimension of this difference in the "clearing," or "openness of the open." What is rather of interest is Heidegger's theories of subjectivity and of modernity as they reflect his accounts of the analytic of *Dasein* and the dispensation of being in the modern age. This is the case given that Heidegger's accounts of *Dasein* shed a light on his direct ontological account of being.

And, his accounts of modernity and technology express his own critique of the manifestations of metaphysics in the modern world by reflecting the endangering dispensation or sending of being in our epoch.

According to Heidegger, the availability of being in classical ontology does not entail the availability of being for thinking. Rather this availability marks some sort of oblivion of being, in the sense of taking being to be an "available concept" for classical ontology. On Heidegger's view, "all ontology,..., remains fundamentally blind and perverts its innermost intent if it has not previously clarified the meaning of being sufficiently and grasped this clarification as its fundamental task."[1] This ontological priority is coupled with an ontic priority that concerns itself with the question of beings. However, according to Heidegger, *Dasein* is unlike beings in the sense that the ontological *Dasein* is "ontically" distinct from other beings. After all, *Dasein* is the being that is "concerned *about* its very being." And, on Heidegger's view, "the understanding of being is itself the determination of the being of *Dasein*."[2] The investigation of Heidegger's conceptions of *Dasein* is mediated through a consideration of temporality that (according to Heidegger) constitutes the central problematic of all ontology by constituting the ontological meaning of *Dasein* and the transcendental horizon of the question of being. After all, the analysis of *Dasein* in *Being and Time* maintained that human understanding is situated in a temporal structure that involves particular projections. The existential interpretation of the being of *Dasein* as "care" reflects the salient dimensions that characterize *Dasein's* "being-in-the-world" that constitutes the fundamental a

---

[1] Martin Heidegger, *Being and Time*, trans. by Joan Stambaugh (Albany: State University of New York Press, 1996), p. 9.

[2] *Ibid*, p. 10.

priori worldliness structure of *Dasein*.[3] Another feature that characterizes Heidegger's account of *Dasein* is expressed in terms of what Heidegger takes to be the "call of conscience" and the authentic mode of being-in-the-world. The "call of conscience" summons *Dasein* to call itself from its own immersion in the everydayness of *das Man*. This call reveals *Dasein* as a futural being that reaches for its possibilities in projection. *Dasein* understands itself as being a being-towards-death which by virtue of its existential finitude understands its own potentiality-for-being. In "running-ahead," *Dasein* comes towards itself as a convergence of necessity and possibility. In attending to certain dimensions of *Dasein,* Heidegger attempts to overcome particular philosophical problems that emerge from the conception of the *Cogito* and the world/self dichotomy. The investigation of some main features of Heidegger's *Dasein* may help in clarifying some salient aspects of Avicenna's ontology which display features that develop in the direction of a process ontology that shifts from the οὐσία *(ousia)* and *substantia* ontology.

V- Avicenna's Philosophy

It is evident that Avicenna's work has not been granted the prominent philosophical status it deserves. This was, and perhaps is still the case, either due to cultural and linguistic reasons, or due to misconstruing interpretations. As the philosopher Lenn E. Goodman eloquently puts it:

> The name of Avicenna is well known in the west. His ideas less so. Many readers of philosophy know that philosophical inquiry and exploration were nourished and sustained in Arabic and Hebrew texts and discussions during the long period between the closure of Plato's Academy a thousand years after the birth of Socrates and the first light of the Renaissance, sparked

---

[3] On this reading, only *Dasein* is said to be in a mode of being that is that of *being-in-the-world*; beings [entities] in general are not said to be in the world in the sense of *Dasein*'s *being-in-the world*, they [entities] rather belong to the world.

> in part by translations of philosophical works from Arabic into Latin in late twelfth-century Toledo. But Few are aware of the exact nature of the philosophical contributions, if any, of the Arabs. Fewer still, even among specialists in philosophy and philosophical history, are aware of the abiding philosophical interest of the ideas and arguments of the great Muslim and Jewish philosophers who wrote in Arabic, of whom, at least in the area of metaphysics, Avicenna was the outstanding example.[4]

In the attempt to avoid similar pitfalls, the investigation of Avicenna's philosophy will be conducted in this book through an examination of original primary Arabic texts that reveal the question of being (*al-wūjūd*) as being one of the most fundamental questions of Islamic philosophy. The privileged role, that the question of being had, and still has, in Islamic philosophy, mainly emanates from profound philosophical concerns that are coupled with some theological interests. The Islamic philosophical concern with the question of being has been, in some instances, closely connected to the question of the divine.[5] However, the question of being was addressed by the *falāsifa* (philosophers) from the standpoint of the science of being (*ᶜilm al-wūjūd*), that is none other than ontology, which was methodically studied and rigorously formulated within Avicenna's philosophical works. However, Avicenna's science of being (*ᶜilm al-wūjūd*) was closely linked to his metaphysics (*al-ilāhīyāt*).[6] The influence that the *ᶜilm al-wūjūd* has on the theological aspects of metaphysics points to "*orthopraxis*" rather than orthodoxy. The Avicennian heritage has had its indirect impact on the *ashᶜarī kalām* schools. It influenced a variety of philosophical schools in Iran (mainly those of the illuminationist *ishrāqī* tradition). And, it

---

4 Lenn E. Goodman, *Avicenna* (London: Routledge, 1992), p. vii.

5 See also: Salem Mashran, *al-Jānib al-Ilāhī ᶜinda Ibn Sīnā* (Damascus: dār quṭayba, 1992), pp. 55-58, 72.

6 See also: Mahdi al-Yazdi, *Haram al-Wūjūd*, trans. by Muḥammad ᶜAbd al-Minᶜim al-Khāqānī (Beirut: dār al-rawḍa, 1990), pp. 7-9.

had its underlying influences within the Latin and Jewish schools of thought. Yet, having said that, Avicenna's philosophy was not spared criticism, and the most famous of his critics was the philosopher, *mutakalim*, *ṣūfī*, and reformist: Abū Ḥāmid al-Ghazālī (1058-1111). However, this critique did not compromise the central role that Avicennism plays in the course of development of *falsafa* or *ḥikma* (philosophical wisdom), especially in the Iranian later philosophic schools whose teachings might still be alive in contemporary religious seminaries. Avicenna has been one of the most systematic Muslim philosophers and metaphysicians who gave shape to the philosophical thoughts of his successors in Islamic Philosophy. Some hold that Avicenna's volumes of *Kitāb al-Shifā'* (The book of the Healing) constituted an encyclopedia of the Arabic Aristotelian canon. *Kitāb al-Shifā'* was known in Latin as the "*liber sufficientiae,*" and this major philosophy textbook of the middle ages was written in Arabic, the language of the *Qur'ān*, and the theological and philosophical *lingua franca* of the middle ages Muslim countries. *Kitāb al-Shifā'* comprises the main divisions of the sciences: Logic, Psychology (*De Anima*), Physics, Mathematics (the *quadrivium*: arithmetic, geometry, astronomy, and music), and Metaphysics.

As Bernard Carra de Vaux mentions, a Latin edition of *Kitāb al-Shifā'* was published in Venice in 1495, as a treatise that bear the title "*Metaphysica Avicennae sive ejus prima philosophia.*" This edition was divided into two volumes translated by François de Maccrata and Antoine Frachantianus Vicentinus (A reader in Philosophy at *Le Collège de Padoue*). De Vaux also mentions that the logic of *Kitāb al-Najāt* (The abridged version of *Kitāb al-Shifā'*) was translated into French by Pierre Vattier under the title "*La Logique du Fils de Sina*" wich was published in Paris in 1658.[7] *Kitāb al-Shifā'* and *Kitāb al-Najāt* (The Deliverance), were criticized by al-Ghazali

---

7 See: Bernard Carra de Vaux, *Avicenna (980-1037–Ibn Sina)* (Amsterdam: Philo Press, 1974), pp. 145-146.

(1058-1111) in his famous and influential critique of the philosophers in "*Tahāfut al-Falāsifa*" (*The Incoherence of The Philosophers,* 1095). A book that eighty five years later was in its turn attacked by Ibn Rushd (Averroes 1126-1198) in "*Tahāfut al-Tahāfut*" (*The Incoherence of The Incoherence* -- 1180). In all of this, Avicenna's philosophical works offer an eloquent testimony to his own creativity that surpasses the talent of a commentator. His philosophy rose by virtue of its own merits, and some also take him to be the formulator of a rigorous and comprehensive canon of an Oriental Aristotelianism.[8] Avicenna's philosophy might have been rigorously influenced by the works, of Plato, Aristotle, Alexander of Aphrodisias, the Neoplatonists, the Peripatetics, and the creative "dialectical theologians" *al-mutakallimūn* (the exponents of *kalām*), as well as being impacted by the works of al-Fārābī (870-950).[9] Yet, this does not mean that Avicenna's thought consists of footnotes to his philosophical predecessors. The innovative aspects of his work turn his philosophy into the site of cultural, intellectual, and philosophical convergence of Islamic, Latin/Christian, and Jewish philosophy (as well as having underlying Zoroastrian, Manichaen, and Buddhist influences). Avicenna's influence on Western philosophers is well illustrated by his influence on Thomas Aquinas, and his impact on Jewish philosophy is best illustrated in his influence on Mūssa bin Maïmūn (Maimonides). The later developments of Avicennism point in the direction of ontological and epistemological developments that are not solely classical or merely medieval. And it is in this spirit that his thought of being would be addressed in the context of this book.

The textual investigation of Avicenna's thought of being is addressed in terms of investigating some isomorphic dimensions that may be found in Heidegger's thought of "being." Avicenna's thought of being will be addressed in terms of the ontology of being,

---

[8] See also the introduction of F. E. Peters, *Aristotle and the Arabs* (New York: New York University Press, 1968).

[9] See: Lenn E. Goodman, *Avicenna* (London: Routledge, 1992), p. ix.

the epistemology of being, the ethics and authenticity of being, and the language of being.

As Soheil Afnan holds, if the central element of Platonic metaphysics is the theory of Ideas, and that of Aristotle is the theory of potentiality and actuality, Avicenna's metaphysics is the study of being qua being (Afnan, 1958, p. 108). Avicenna's ontology of being (*al-wūjūd*) reflects a shift from the Aristotelian categories of being while pointing towards some sort of a phenomenological encounter with the question of being. This is attested in investigating the semantics of Avicenna's ontology of being, and it is mainly illustrated by his ontological as well as logical consideration of being in relation to the modalities of necessity (*wūjūb*), contingency (*imkān*), and impossibility (*istiḥāla, imtināʿ*). Like all great philosophers, the groundwork of Avicenna's metaphysics is laid down in his logic.

The analysis of the modalities of being shows that, on Avicenna's view, being is either necessary or not necessary. Being is taken to be necessary in itself due to its own nature (*wājib al-wūjūd bi-dhātihi*). This is the case given that being that is not necessary due to itself is either impossible or contingent. Avicenna argues that: if the impossible-in-itself is that which cannot be, then being that is not necessary in itself is either contingent in itself (*mumkin bi-dhātihi*) or it is necessary by virtue of what is other than itself (*wājib al-wūjūd bi-ghaīrihi*). Being an existent (*mawjūd*) is a contingency. However, a contingency-in-itself is never realized. Rather, contingency is a potentiality to be that gets actualized by what is other than itself, i.e. by virtue of an external cause whose existence is prior to it. On Avicenna's view in the Logic, contingency is not possibility, in the sense that the non-existence of a contingent being does not entail impossibility. Avicenna argues that a non-contingent is not impossible while a non-possible is impossible, and this discussion of contingency is further explicated in the Logic of *Kitāb al-Shifā*ʻ and *Kitāb al-Najāt*. Avicenna's consideration of being in relation to the modalities of necessity, contingency, and impossibility, displays systematic, logical, and clear linguistic expositions of being, while reflecting a lucid and innovative dispensation of being that attempts to overcome some aspects of the Aristotelian *ousiology*. This development was extended and commented on by the successors of Avicenna; especially by those philosophers whose works had a central role in the later Islamic philosophical discourse.

Avicenna's distinction between essence and existence has been taken to be central to his metaphysics and to his ontology of being. Due to the influence that this distinction had on Thomism (and to a lesser extent on Maimonides' work) some Medievalists and Orientalists have been impacted by the centrality that this distinction occupies in St. Thomas' work. And this Thomistic influence lead some scholars to an exaggerated stress on the centrality of the essence/existence distinction in Avicenna's metaphysics. This state of affairs eventually overshadowed other important aspects of Avicenna's ontology of being and the metaphysical as well as logical analysis of being in terms of the modalities of necessity, contingency, and impossibility. The examination of Avicenna's metaphysics, under the spell of a Thomistic reading of the essence/existence distinction, might have led to a hasty and discomforting intellectual position that construes Avicenna's ontology as essentialism. John Caputo, a leading interpreter of Heidegger's thought, makes extensive references to the works of the Thomist scholar É. Gilson (In the context of his interpretation of St. Thomas' Avicennian heritage). Caputo's discussion of the essence/existence distinction adopts the standpoint that Gilson reflects in the reading of Avicenna's metaphysics as being the starting point of a long standing essentialist tradition that culminates in Hegel's Logic. This line of argumentation already supplies Caputo with sufficient secondary scholarly arguments that apparently enabled him to readily stamp Avicenna's metaphysics with Heidegger's critique of the tradition. The question that ought to be raised in this regard is whether the position of secondary scholarly sources is accurate, given that some of the scholars that propagate the claim that Avicenna is essentialist, are after all scholars that have not consulted or studied the primary sources. And these scholars primarily rely on secondary sources that mediate Avicenna's metaphysics through the Thomist scholarship that over-emphasizes the implications of the essence/existence distinction and neglects other important dimensions of Avicenna's philosophy. In some instances, even the reading of primary sources has been mediated through the accounts of earlier orientalist scholars, whose broader philosophical concerns in ancient, medieval Latin, and Jewish philosophy, influenced their reading of Islamic and Arabic philosophy. The Medievalists who consult primary sources, yet who are still under the spell of earlier Orientalist views, do not attempt to review some of their positions by going back to a closer examination of the texts and to a questioning reception of dominant translations and interpretations. There is a hermeneutic need to return to the primary texts and re-examine them in the light of new philosophical concerns. This is also needed in the light of questioning and adopting new methodological inclinations in translation and interpretation. This becomes a pressing issue given the seriousness of the philosophical consequences that might arise if we readily take Avicenna's metaphysics to be the metaphysics of essentialism.

Avicenna's intentional epistemology of being gives expression to another dimension that characterizes his consideration of the question of being (*al-wŭjŭd*). The prototypical *al-nafs/Dasein* dimension that lies in Avicenna's "Suspended Person Argument," finds an echo in Descartes' *Cogito* argument, and reflects a close affinity to "Brain in a vat" contemporary arguments of the Analytic tradition in Philosophy. Yet, the *al-nafs/Dasein* dimension is not based on an account of substance or metaphysical considerations of subjectivity. The "Suspended Person Argument" (or what has been known as the "Floating Man Argument") points towards an experiential field whereby the self or subject is not a substance or unity but is rather what generates itself. It is a *nafs* as a self/soul field of experiences that is self-generated from an experiential process (Almost similar to what one encounters in the notion of "prehension" of Alfred North Whitehead). The self-generated experiences are not therefore taken to be a state, they rather describe a vector. In this sense, the self is not a self-same substance. It is rather a potentiality-for-being-itself (Almost like what characterizes the authenticity of being in *Dasein's* being-in-the-world). The self is experiential, existential, and its being is stamped with the mark of becoming. And this account of the experiential *nafs/Dasein* dimension is to be considered in terms of reflecting on the hermeneutic notion of *al-ta'wīl* that represents a return back to the ground of the self as a return to *al-awal* (as primordial self). It also points to the non-alienating dimension in the conception of the unity of being (*wiḥdat al-wūjūd*), and the praxis of *tawḥīd* (unification) as it relates to *wūjūd* (existence or being), and to the conceptions of *anā* (I), and *dhāt* (essence, or essential self). Both, *al-ta'wīl* and *wiḥdat al-wūjūd*, are ways that accentuate self-realization and the retrieval of the self from its concernful absorption in the world. They also attend to a state of affairs that is similar to the thrownness of *Dasein* in existence and its unauthentic mode of being that is immersed in the everydayness of what Heidegger calls the "they-self" (*das Man*). Another dimension that marks Avicenna's epistemology of being is reflected in the pragmatics of Avicenna's account of the intentional inner sense of prehension *al-wahm*, and in the examination of prehensive perception (*al-idrāk bil-wahm*). This also points towards the immediate existential experience of knowledge (*al- ʿilm al-ḥuḍūrī*), which was later elaborated and developed in the works of the philosophers Suhrawardī and Mullā Ṣadrā.

The authenticity of being plays a major role in Avicenna's consideration of being. This is especially the case in relation to a discussion of ἀλήθεια (*alētheia*) in the *ṣūfī* ethics and praxis of *tawḥīd* (unification) and *taḥqīq* (going toward truth) as *kashf al-maḥjūb* (the unveiling of the veiled). This evidently presents some grounds for the consideration of the ethical dimensions that figure in *Dasein*'s authenticity of being, self-realization, and the call of conscience. It also manifests some links with Heidegger's later considerations of the truth of being in terms of unconcealment as a revealing of truth that brings beings from their hiddenness. And where *Dasein* is considered as the clearing in which the truth sent by being occurs. The unity of being, that figures in *wiḥdat-al-wūjūd* and in *tawḥīd*, finds echoes in the Heideggerian stress on the unity of being as recollection and gathering-together of every epoch of being which is rooted in the unity of being of *Dasein* that conjoins infinite possibilities with finite actuality.

In the analysis of the linguistic accounts of being, language is revealed as being a site of hermeneutic dimensions that express the encounters with the question of being. The examination of language offers venues for a possible overcoming of metaphysics. This is attested in terms of meta-mystic dimensions that polemically characterize some features of Avicenna's philosophy. And one might say that the attempt, to linguistically overcome metaphysics, finds some expression in the debatable and polemical poetic turn that one attests in Heidegger's thought.

VI- Modernity and the Obliteration of the Tradition

In the light of the extensive and profound preoccupation with the question of being (mainly as exemplified within the scope of this study by Avicenna's thought of being). And in the light of the centrality that the science of being (*ʿilm al-wūjūd*) has occupied in the history of Islamic philosophy and ontology, one would wonder whether Heidegger's critique of the history of metaphysics, and his claims about the oblivion of being, are complete? This question is meant to be advanced in support of an attempted reevaluation of Heidegger's position *vis à vis* metaphysics in general, and its medieval dispensations in particular. The consideration of this question ought to take into account the link that Heidegger attempts to make between metaphysics and the essence of technology. This also means that what is taken into consideration is the link between metaphysics and the radical form of availability and ordering manipulation that Heidegger calls *Ge-stell* (Enframing). And, it is this form that destines revealing to be an uncovering of beings and the world as *Bestand* ("Standing Reserve"). On Heidegger's view, the essence of technology, that is "nothing technological," yet concealed in technology, spreads throughout the history of metaphysics. Being a manner of "presencing beings in unconcealment," technology is tied to the "essence of truth." Yet, the truth in question is a particular kind of truth that is based on a correctness conception of truth that, in its very unconcealment, conceals other conceptions of truth. A correctness construal of truth endangers the relation to the essence of truth and the happening of ἀλήθεια (*alētheia*). And, this state of affairs gives expression to a Heideggerian Theory of Modernity that underlies his critique of the history of metaphysics as the history of the *Vorhandenheit* ("presence-at-hand") of productivity and making.

As it was mentioned above, the main aim of this book is to interpret Avicenna's thought of being in the light of Heidegger's critique of metaphysics. Yet, one wonders whether it would be the case that an examination of Avicenna's philosophy might offer ways by virtue of which a reevaluation of the completeness of Heidegger's critique of the tradition becomes possible. This issue might be addressed in terms of showing the incompleteness of the Heideggerian critique of metaphysics which itself represents a metaphysical philosophical tendency to occlude or assimilate the tradition of the other. This in itself is problematic given the historical and philosophical gap that Heidegger did not address in his avoidance of the Arabic and Islamic philosophical heritage that found its place within the folds of the history and destiny of Western Metaphysics. And it is also accentuated in terms of showing that the Avicennian and post-Avicennian heritage brings about a historical precedence that affirms what Heidegger wanted to address while being historically and philosophically antecedent to Heidegger's thought. What is also of relevance to this case is wondering whether Avicenna's thought of being and that of his successors open up realms of rich possibilities embedded within the profound course of development of a living Islamic philosophical inclination in thinking. The question that remains to be addressed is that of wondering whether such possibilities would help in raising contemporary claims that contribute to a renewal of philosophy by way of reconsidering the question of being in particular, and phenomenology and Islamic philosophy in general. This ought to be undertaken while stressing on the philosophical openness to universality in an epoch that some of our contemporaries take to be the epoch of the End of Philosophy, the Closure of Metaphysics. In thinking about Avicennism, thinking (*Denken*) is indeed turned into a remembering, thinking is thus commemorating and thanking.

CHAPTER 1
THE METAPHYSICAL TRADITION

Based on the thrust of the Heideggerian critique of classical ontology, one could claim that Aristotle may have questionably reduced being to οὐσία (*ousia*, i.e. substance), Kant syntactically held that being is not a real predicate, and Hegel turned essence into the last determination of being. The history of the reduction of being into something that is other than itself may be claimed to be the history of the metaphysical oblivion of being. At least this is the account that some Heideggerian scholars held in their interpretation of the history of philosophy in general, and the history of ontology and metaphysics in particular. In this chapter, I attempt to present a brief account of the ontological tradition as exemplified by Aristotle, Kant, and Hegel. This brief expository introduction will consist of addressing some basic aspects of classical ontology that might have incited Heidegger's critique of the history of Western Metaphysics. The accounts presented on Aristotle's reduction of being into οὐσία (*ousia*) will constitute a general background that will help in determining some dimensions of Heidegger's and Avicenna's contributions to the question of being. The section on Kant's discussion of being in relation to predication, along with the section treating Hegel's *essentialism*, both will have some bearings on the fifth chapter that deals with the Avicennian distinction between essence and existence. This introductory exposition of the tradition is meant to offer a quick reference to arguments that will help in clarifying the Heideggerian concern and corrective ontological request, and it will also provide a broad account of some of the main philosophical developments in addressing the question of being.

I- Aristotle's οὐσία (*ousia*)

In addressing Book Θ (IX) of Aristotle's *Metaphysics*, Heidegger offers a textual interpretation of the Aristotelian metaphysical theory of potentiality (*potentia*) and actuality (*actus*). Quoting Aristotle, Heidegger writes that dealing with "beings in the primary sense" has led our inquiry to that which "all other beings are referred back to," i.e. οὐσία (*ousia*).[10] On this reading, and quoting Aristotle, one could say that "everything that is (the other categories than *ousia*) must in and of itself have the saying of *ousia*." On Heidegger's interpretation of Aristotle, the categories are beings, they are "co-being with *ousia*." On this view, the discussion of *potentia* and *actus* is not a category question yet it is still a questioning about beings.[11] Regarding the manifold of the being of beings, beings are said and addressed sometimes in the mode of the categories and sometimes in terms of the theory of potentiality and actuality. Yet, this two fold way of addressing beings is reconsidered in chapter 10 of Book IX of the *Metaphysics* where Aristotle holds that the "most authoritative being [*das Seiende*] is true and untrue being." A fourth way of addressing beings is expressed in chapter 2 of Book VI (E) of the *Metaphysics* as "accidental being."[12] Based on this interpretation, beings are distinguished in four ways. And as Aristotle holds in chapter 7 of Book V (1017a7) of the *Metaphysics*, "for as the forms of the category are said in various ways, so being has various meanings." In the same chapter V7 (1017a35f) one reads that being means "the being," insofar as "the being is this and nothing other." In another part of Aristotle's *Metaphysics* (Z 1, 1028a13ff.) "first being" means *ousia*. Yet given the "manifoldness" of beings, would Aris-

---

10 Martin Heidegger, *Aristotle's Metaphysics, Θ 1-3: On the Essence and Actuality of Force*, trans. by Walter Brogan & Peter Warneck (Bloomington & Indianapolis: Indiana University Press, 1995), p. 2.

11 *Ibid*, pp. 5-7.

12 *Ibid*, pp. 9-10.

totle contend Parmenides' unity of being? As an indication of the manifoldness of beings, Aristotle refers to the manifold of the categories and the fourfold ways of addressing beings. However, accounting for the manifoldness of beings does not entail that Aristotle refutes or disavows Parmenides' proposition that "being is the One." Manifoldness and unity are thus recognized as belonging to one another. Reading Aristotle in terms of Heidegger's interpretation would lead us to say that "being is said with an eye to something that is somehow common to all the various ways, and which cultivates a community with these so that these many are all of the same root and origin."[13] On this view, oneness belongs to the essence of being, and both are said in multiple ways. And on Heidegger's reading, Aristotle's account of the oneness of being is taken by way of analogy not by way of accounting for it in terms of a talk about genus and species. If beings are addressed in many ways, this manifoldness in their meaning may still imply that a oneness pervades these significations. Yet, if Aristotle does not take being to be a genus, then being is not comprehended as a concept. However, Heidegger refers to Aristotelian accounts of some sort of "sustaining and guiding basic meaning" upon which the other meanings "can be said." Referring to the first sentences of Θ 1, one reads that "the sustaining and leading fundamental meaning of being, to which all the other categories are carried back, that is, *ousia*." Yet, on Heidegger's interpretation, beings are not kinds of *ousia* but ways of being related to *ousia* as the first category and as the sustaining and guiding fundamental meaning of being.[14] *Ousia* is always said along with the various meanings of being. Yet, Heidegger raises an objection to the Middle Ages scholastic conclusions that the fundamental meaning of being in general was *ousia*, and that the Artistotelian doctrine of being is a "substance

---

[13] *Ibid*, p. 24.

[14] *Ibid*, p. 35.

doctrine."[15] Nevertheless, this does not preclude the fact that being is related to *ousia* and that *ousia* is always said along with the meaning of being. Yet, to further elucidate some aspects of Aristotle's study of being away from Heidegger's focused textual reading of Θ 1-3 of the *Metaphysics* one may have to address additional aspects of Aristotle's account of being in relation to *ousia*.

In the *Metaphysics* V 7 (1017a7-30), Aristotle distinguishes between categorical being and accidental being. In view of Aristotle's position that non-substances are said to be in relation to substances, substances are taken to be "the ontologically basic beings." The primary being is substance (*ousia*), and "the science of being can be achieved through the study of substance." Yet this does not necessarily entail that the science of being ought to be restricted to ousiology nor does this readily entail that Aristotle's doctrine of being is a doctrine of substance (*ousia*). But given that non-substances inhere in substances, a study of non-substances leads back to the study of substance, thus ousiology would still act as the Aristotelian ground for the inquiry about being.[16]

In Book VII (Z) of the *Metaphysics*, the question of the being of a being is the question about the "what" that indicates the substance of a thing. Aristotle would also say "that which is primarily and is simply (not is something) is substance." The "what is" question is a question of essence that asks about the "whatness" of being. Yet, this question is turned into being a question about substance.[17] In both instances, whether with substance or essence, what is meant is nothing other than *ousia*. If being has many senses, all of these are

---

15 *Ibid*, p. 37.

16 Charlotte Witt, *Substance and Essence in Aristotle, An Interpretation of Metaphysics VII-IX* (Ithaca and London: Cornell University Press, 1989), pp. 58, 60, 61-62.

17 Aristotle, *Metaphysics*, ed. by W. D. Ross. (Oxford: Oxford University Press, 1924), Book VII, 1, 1028a; Aristotle, *A New Aristotle Reader*, ed. by A. J. Ackrill (Princeton: Princeton University Press, 1987), pp. 284-285.

articulated in such a way that they all relate back to that which is primarily the "what" which indicates the substance of a thing. All the ways in which being is articulated relate back to that which unifies them, and this is none other than substance, essence, or *ousia*. The Aristotelian tradition posits the question of being as a question about *ousia*. To inquire about being is primarily to inquire about *ousia*, be it essence or substance. In *What is Metaphysics?* Heidegger's claim that "the nothing belongs to being" is advanced by way of criticizing *the ousia* construing of being, where *ousia* is taken to be the substance or the subject that underlies the constitution of the beingness of an individual being. It is this sense of being (as *ousia*, essence, substance, or subject) that Heidegger attempts to criticize and overcome in his critique of the "metaphysical tradition."

If physics studies a particular genus of a thing-that-is; i.e. it studies particular beings, the discipline that studies a thing *qua* a thing-that-is, is a discipline that moves to the study of the beingness of the particular being. Yet, the question of the beingness of beings starts by wondering about "what" a particular being is. In chapter 5 of the *Categoriae* (2a),[18] Aristotle draws a distinction between a primary substance (*ousia*), that is neither said of a subject nor being in a subject, and secondary substance (*ousia*) as genus and species. On this reading, the secondary *ousia* becomes more of an *ousia* when it gets closer to the primary *ousia*. Secondary *ousia* is either a general or universal, as species or genus, or it is an individual. And, in this sense, *ousia* is constitutive of the being of an entity. Aristotle would also take species to be nearer to primary *ousia* than genus, and this is implied in asking what a primary *ousia* is. And the answer will be more "informative" by giving the species.[19] In the *Categories* (V,

---

[18] Aristotle, *Categories*, trans. by J. L. Ackrill (Oxford: Clarendon Aristotle Series, 1963); Gr. text: L. Minio-Paluello (Oxford: Oxford Classical Texts, 1956).

[19] *Ibid*, V, 2b.

2b) primary *ousia* gains priority since its nonexistence entails the impossibility for anything to exist. The primacy of primary *ousia* is also due to the fact that it is indisputable that every primary *ousia* underlies a "certain *this*," whereby the thing revealed is an "individual and numerically one." It is in the sense of this primary first *ousia* that *essentia* and *quidditas* are to be understood. This claim reflects the Heideggerian view that first *ousia* underlies our "modern" conception of essence.[20] Aristotle's account of being is based on an account of the categories that consist of substance (primary and secondary) and nine accidents. The primary first substance is a concrete individual that is the core and basis for the realization of entities. For example, one could say that on this account, "greenness" is realized by the mediation of the grass, as when we say: "the grass is green." The primary *ousia* is that which bears the attributes. It is that unit which is at the ground of all secondary substances, and without it there is no possible existence. The certain "this" of secondary *ousia* is unlike that of primary *ousia*, in the sense that the "this" of secondary *ousia* is "nothing but a qualification" while the primary *ousia* is without qualification. First *ousia* underlies therefore all accidents.[21] It is the primordial affirmation that is presupposed by any inquiry. First *ousia* is the essence of a thing and its form. It answers to the question *to ti ēn einai*, what is it to be? From the standpoint of this account in the *Metaphysics* (VII, 1032b) one could also formulate a response to Platonic realist inclinations that consider universals as being mind-independent.

---

20 Regarding this point, see: Werner Marx, *Heidegger and the Tradition* (Evanston: Northwestern University Press, 1971), pp. 18-19.

21 In reference to Aristotle's *Categories* (V, 3b) Werner Marx holds that, the first *ousia* that is resting in itself, lies at the ground of and is present for all determinations and accidents. See: Werner Marx, Heidegger and the Tradition (Evanston: Northwestern University Press, 1971), p. 22.

In Book V of the *Metaphysics* (1015a-b) Aristotle holds that necessity is "not open to persuasion" and is "contrary to change." Necessity implies that what is the case is that "which cannot be otherwise." This entails that what is necessary cannot be in more than one state. And therefore it is that which is simple. Aristotle then adds, that the things that are called one in the "primary way" are things whose "substance is one." Necessity is not only said of things, it also extends to an opinion (δόξα, *doxa*) that cannot be otherwise (Though *doxa* is open to change and thus is also open to error). As stated in Book IX of the *Metaphysics* (1051a30, 1051b30-1052a) these opinions are either true or false and cannot be sometimes true and at other times false. This is the case given that in the strictest sense truth and falsity are being and non-being. The necessity of opinions or propositions implies that what they depict is either true or false. And, this entails that if something exists in a particular way, then this thing cannot exist otherwise. It either exists in that way or it does not exist at all. This state of affairs reflects some sort of completeness in the "intelligibility" of *ousia*, which also entails that errors can be "corrected" and that the particular being is eventually knowable.[22] To say that what is true is as such necessarily and cannot be otherwise implies that what is true is necessarily true and cannot be sometimes true and at other times false. This also implies that what is true by necessity is a complete fact that is necessary, self-same, and knowable. Error blocks the way of accessibility to what is true by necessity. The only *ousiological* change that is admitted is that of generation and corruption (an issue that is problematized and overcomed by Avicenna, and is avoided by Spinoza in terms of accounting for modes that depict change in relation to the one substance). The path towards what is true by necessity is diverted due to errors that eventually will be corrected, or at least one hopes to be able to correct them by virtue of trials, observations, and experiments. The path of correctedness may then be the path of truth. I

[22] *Ibid*, p. 39.

say "correctedness" in reference to corrected errors, rather than in reference to correctness abstracted from error. Error is responsible for the loss of the path to truth that may be found again by virtue of corrective measures and attempts. On such a view, truth is accessible when errors are corrected by virtue of methods, trials, observations, and experiments. What is true by necessity is a fact that is awaiting discovery. This picture is almost the same as what Heidegger portrays in his theory of modernity as being a "standing reserve" (*Bestand*) that the *Ge-stell* (Enframing) of modernity entails. According to Heidegger, the essence of technology entails a "correctness conception" of truth and a destining to revealing of truth by way of "enframing" that turns all that is into a standing reserve. The correctness conception of truth, and the mode of revealing truth by way of "enframing," both pose a threat to the essence of truth and monopolize revealing by way of overshadowing and concealing all other modes of revealing. This state of affairs is already implicitly found in the essence of technology that we encounter from the standpoint of modernity. However, the essence of technology that is nothing technological is already to be found in the origins. The Aristotelian *ousiology* already displays the features and consequences of the essence of technology with its *Ge-stell* and correctness conception of truth. Construing all beings as standing reserve is also a construing of beings as being ultimately knowable, discoverable and ready for research and inquiry. This is the case given that such path would supposedly lead to a completeness of intelligibility when the correctness of all errors is in place. "Eternalness," "self-sameness," "necessity," and "intelligibility," all characterize *ousia* (as nature, essence, and substance). The labyrinth of trial and error, and of attempted corrections, is the labyrinth of possibilities that might lead by way of discovery to facts that are eternal, self-same, necessary, and intelligible. The realm of beings is therefore ordered in such a way as to be open to discovery and research. It is ordered by way of being turned into a standing reserve that is available and ready to be used in the very same destining to reveal by way of "enframing." Mystery is then turned into an anticipation of the discovery of what is standing ready and available for discovery. What is discovered is as such complete. Therefore, what is true is revealed as being correct, self-same eternal, and necessary. Discovery does not have a way back; what is discovered does not get concealed. Thus, the sending of truth is not self-withdrawing. The correctness conception of truth does not involve the dynamics of withdrawal and unconcealment, and no mystery of self-withdrawal is implied. Unconcealing as unveiling is distinct from discovery in the sense that what is disclosed is not taken to be available or ready for use or enframed as standing reserve. Rather, what is disclosed also withdraws. And, this is not the case with a correctness conception of truth. The necessity of something that exists in a particular way and not otherwise implies that this existent is universal. Yet, this does not entail that it is eternal. Since when that thing does not exist according to the necessity that is implied in its way of existence that thing ceases to exist. However, it might be argued that its necessity implies that it cannot be otherwise. And, when we say that it does not exist according to its necessity of existence, we are then presupposing that it could change and therefore be otherwise, even if this "being-otherwise" entails its nonexistence. That which is necessary is eternal given that it stays necessary. Yet that which is necessary is either necessary due to itself or necessary due to something other than itself. The former is eternal while the latter is not, since its necessity is due to what is extraneous to it. It is thus a caused and dependent necessity that ceases with the cessation of what brings it forth. And, that which brings it forth is external to it. The universality, self-sameness, intelligibility, and eternity of what is necessary differ between what is necessary due to itself and what is necessary due to what is other than itself. According to Werner Marx, the Aristotelian account of *ousia* is presented in terms of eternity, self-sameness, necessity, and intelligibility.[23] With Avicenna, the distinction, be-

[23] For an elaboration of Werner Marx's discussion of the form and meaning of the Aristotelian *ousia* under eternalness, necessity, self-sameness, and intelli-

tween what is necessary in itself and what is necessary due to something other than itself, leads to a difference in accounting for *ousia* which will turn *ousia* into being ontologically dependent on what is other than itself in order for it to be necessary. *Ousia* is necessary due to what is other than itself. Yet, only what is necessary due to itself is eternal, self-same, one, simple, and necessary. If this state of affairs is expressed in terms of causality, then, one would say that a being does not come into being unless its four causes exist, given that the teleological cause is the one that stands amidst the causes as the necessary one. *Ousia* is therefore thinkable due to its links to νοῦς (*noūs*) that brings it into the light. On this view, a human being ought to act according to his/her essence as rational animal; an essence that is as such (so to speak) dictated by a *noetic ousiology* (whereby νόησις [*noesis*] implies the availability of a complete accessibility, while *ousia* implies eternalness, self-sameness, necessity, and unchanging nature). One could thus assume that there could be completeness in the attributes of a self-evident *ousia*.

II- Subjectivity and the Overcoming of Metaphysics

The overcoming of metaphysics is meant to be a reception and encounter with being whose truth is not reduced to the order of the evidence of beings or of presence (And this is attested in Heidegger's following works: *Was ist Metaphysic ?, Zeit und Sein, Zur Sache des Denkens*). The articulation of the ontological difference between being and beings is expressed in terms of temporality which constitutes the horizon of thinking about the question of being which is the most fundamental and original of all the questions of metaphysics. Being, the true theme of philosophy is not of our making. The Aristotelian approach studies being as a being (*Seiende*), and philosophy studies what characterizes a being by considering that being in its being (*Sein*). If being is where the meaning of "all that is"

---

gibility, see: Werner Marx, *Heidegger and the Tradition* (Evanston: Northwestern University Press, 1971), pp. 17-43.

gets recollected, being is nevertheless still the most universal and vacuous concept. In Heideggerian terms, a philosophical meditation on beings presupposes a meditation on "the difference between being and beings."[24] The ontological difference between being and beings allows being to emerge as that which is different from beings. According to the Heideggerian thrust, the oblivion of being is also attested in (Metaphysical) theories of transcendental consciousness that attempt to fashion philosophy as a science. Heidegger argues that Descartes posits the *cogito sum* as the *fundamentum absolutum et inconcussum* (unshakable absolute foundation) of all ontology. On Heidegger's view, Descartes claims that, with the *cogito sum*, he is preparing a new and secure foundation for philosophy.[25] This entails subsuming the question of being under the rubric of the *cogito sum*. Moreover, this also entails that Descartes had to neglect the question of being given that the "absolute certainty" of the *cogito* does not require the consideration of the meaning of its being. Descartes' approach does not elucidate the manner of being that characterizes the *res cogitans* apart from its determination as *ens*, and particularly as *ens creatum*. This conception of "createdness" is taken by Heidegger to be a production conception that is structurally linked to the ancient concept of being. This ontological indeterminateness is not fully resolved even by Kant. What lacks is an "ontological analytic of the subjectivity of the subject."[26] The link between time and the *cogito sum* is not fully elucidated even in the Kantian doctrine of temporality. The understanding of being is still gained from a certain relation to temporality that is characterized by presence (*Anwesen-*

---

[24] See also: Robert Brisart, *La Phénomenologie de Marbourg, ou la Résurgence de la Métaphysique chez Heidegger a l'époque de Sein und Zeit* (Bruxelles: Publications des Facultés Universitaires Saint-Louis, 1991), p. 21.

[25] Martin Heidegger, *Being and Time*, trans. by Joan Stambaugh (Albany: State University of New York Press, 1996), p. 21.

[26] *Ibid*, p. 21.

heit). And, according to Heidegger, this is reflected in the determination of the meaning of being as παρουσία (*parousia*) or οὐσία (*ousia*), whereby being is understood in terms of presence.[27] Even if Husserl elucidates the *cogito sum* and gives weight to the explication of consciousness, yet, according to a Heideggerian reading, one still attests an ontological indeterminateness even with the stress on intentionality. However, consciousness is imposed as that which is originary and constitutive and most fundamental from the position of its presence. The horizon of consciousness theories from Descartes to Husserl is taken to be that of a definite mode of time that is that of presence. And, this in itself manifests what the Heideggerian critique takes to be the symptoms of a contemporary oblivion of being. In this sense, the critique of the history of metaphysics covers the works of philosophers from Aristotle to Husserl, and the ontological objection to ousiological accounts of being stretches to cover metaphysical accounts of subjectivity.

III- Kant and the Reality of Being

One of the traditional articulations of the difference between being and beings, that is also characterized by what Heidegger takes to be an oblivion of being, is the Kantian thesis that being is not a real predicate. This thesis figures in sections A598, B626 of the *Critique of Pure Reason*. There, Kant holds that "being is obviously not a real predicate; that is, it is not a concept of something which could be added to the concept of a thing. It is merely the positing of a thing, or of certain determinations in and of themselves. Logically, it is merely the copula of a judgment."[28] According to Heidegger, what strikes the reader at first is that this Kantian thesis about being is rather "abstract, meager, and pale." He then adds that this thesis seems to be offending for those who fail to consider "what Kant has

---

[27] *Ibid*, p. 22.

[28] Immanuel Kant, *Critique of Pure Reason*, trans. by Norman Kemp Smith (New York: St. Martin's Press, 1965), A598, B626.

said in elucidation of it."[29] In Kant's thesis, one can detect two main assertions. The first assertion holds that "being is obviously not a real predicate" while the second assertion holds that "being is merely the positing of a thing." Then Kant adds that "logically" being (which is not a real predicate and is a positing) is "merely a copula of a judgment." On this view, being acts as a copulative bond that connects a subject to a predicate. In a logical use, being acts as a link in the following form: A *is* B. The "is" herein serves as a copulative positing of the predicate in relation to the subject. Thus, the "is" has a logical function and not a substantive one. However, the "is" has also an "ontic" use when it figures in statements of the form: A is, or B is. In this sense, the "is" indicates that either A or B exists. In another section of the Transcendental Dialectic of *the Critique of Pure Reason*, one reads that "the small word 'is' adds no new predicate, but only serves to posit the predicate in its relation to the subject."[30] The verbal "to be" in its form "is" is then used as a bonding copula between a subject and a predicate. Therefore being is not a real predicate, and being rather acts as a copula. To say that being is not a real predicate is also to say that being, as empty as it is, is still different from beings. Yet, it also implies that being does not belong to the concept that determines what something is. This means that "being" (as predicate) does not add anything to the understanding of what makes a being what it is. Therefore, being and existence are distinct from the quiddity or essence of beings. This distinction reflects an interpretation of the old [Avicennian] distinction between existence and the reality and essence of a being. The Kantian thesis, that "being is (obviously) not a real predicate," is a consequence of the [Avicennian] distinction between existence and essence. Existence is distinct from the reality of a thing in the sense that this reality

[29] Martin Heidegger, "Kant's Thesis about Being," in *Pathmarks*, ed. by William McNeill (Cambridge: Cambridge University Press, 1998), p. 338.

[30] Immanuel Kant, *Critique of Pure Reason*, trans. by Norman Kemp Smith (New York: St. Martin's Press, 1965), B627.

represents the *thingness* of a thing, while existence is distinct from the essence of a being in the sense of being distinct from the *whatness* of that being. On the Kantian view, to say that "x" exists does not add a predication that determines the quiddity of "x." After all, Kant says that, "in the mere concept of a thing no mark of its existence is to be found."[31] And the use of the verbal "to be" in the form of "is" is a use that occurs within a predicative judgement. The use of "is" as copula turns being into that which posits a relation between a subject and a predicate. Herein, being acts as a copula between a being and several of its predicates. In terms of predicative judgements, being expresses an inherent relation in the reality of a subject, while in terms of judgements of existence, being takes a central position with regard to the existence of the subject as a thing. The categories of modality (possibility, existence, and necessity) do not add anything to the determination of a being in its reality, yet they do figure in relation to our faculty of knowledge.[32] To consider a being in terms of possibility, of necessity, or of existence, does express some aspects of the relation of that being to our faculty of knowledge. It also implies that our relation and experience of a being differs if this being is an existent being or is rather a mere possible being. The thing that accords with our formal conditions of experience is also in accordance with the material conditions of experience that are filled up with perception.[33] On this account, perception converges with existence. A thing that is in accordance with our formal conditions of experience is also a thing that is perceived as being a material existent. The existence of something implies that this thing is perceived. This also entails that perception characterizes

---

[31] *Ibid*, A225, B272.

[32] For further considerations of this point, see: Robert Brisart, *La Phénomenologie de Marbourg, ou la Résurgence de la Métaphysique chez Heidegger a l'époque de Sein und Zeit* (Bruxelles: Publications des Facultés Universitaires Saint-Louis, 1991), p. 33.

[33] *Ibid*, p. 33.

the existence and actuality of a thing. The concept of something precedes the perception that fills up that concept with its content. The existence of a thing is bound up with our perceptions. And the knowledge of the existence of things extends as far as perception.[34] Perception expresses some sort of an empirical relation between the perceiver and the perceived. In perception we have a subjective act of apprehension whereby the apprehended perceived being is as such perceived by a perceiving being. In this relation between subject and object, we do not attest a clarification of the ontological difference between being and beings. This is the case since a relation between perceiver and perceived occurs in the realm of beings. Given the convergence between perception and existence, can one then infer from this that existence is granted in perception? Or is it the case that from the fact that something exists, this thing would therefore be perceived as a being that is already present? Is it the case that existence is what is presupposed by perception or is it the other way round? If the existence of something is presupposed by its perception, then this thing is taken to be already that which has been produced. It is therefore that whose existence has been already brought into effect. And, this reflects a medieval conception of existents that construes them as *ens creatum*, i.e. as created entities that were produced.

In sections A598, B626 of the *Critique of Pure Reason*, Kant held that being is "merely the positing of a thing." According to Heidegger, such assertion implies that being as a "positing" is merely a "ground." In reference to the Latin *positio* and *perceptio*, Heidegger takes being to be a setting, a placing, or a lying at the ground. "Positing" is thus interpreted by Heidegger as being a "placing of something before us," as is the case with the act of the understanding that posits something as object.[35] Heidegger then adds that

---

[34] Immanuel Kant, *Critique of Pure Reason*, trans. by Norman Kemp Smith (New York: St. Martin's Press, 1965), A226, B273.

[35] Martin Heidegger, "Kant's Thesis about Being," in *Pathmarks*, ed. by

the understanding posits by way of synthesis. Thus, positing is a gathering or bringing together. Even in its logical and copulative function, being is a positing in the sense that it brings together a predicate and a subject in a judgment. Being and synthetic unity are thus brought together. According to Heidegger, being (as positing) is thus determined in relation to the "synthetic unity" of "transcendental apperception." Being and its modalities is thus determined in relation to the understanding.[36] On Heidegger's reading of Kant's thesis about being, the "being of beings" is understood to be the "objectivity of the object of experience." In "positing," being thus changes into "objectness," and Kant's ontology becomes a transcendental philosophy.[37] Yet, objectness (*Gegenstandigkeit*) is understood in terms of its relation to a human subject. Being that is obviously not an ontic predicate is as such a "transcendental/ontological" predicate. According to Heidegger, being as such is determined from the side of thought. And thought would provide the horizon for the determination of the being of beings as positing, whereby positing finds its essential provenance in presencing or presence. On Heidegger's view, Kant's thesis about being "points forward toward the speculative-dialectical interpretation of being as Absolute Concept."[38]

The distinction between *essentia* and *existentia* underlies the medieval conception of being. The question of *essentia* asks about what a thing is, *quid sit res*? The question of *existentia* asks whether a thing is, *an sit res*? To the question that asks what a thing is, the response is accounted for in terms of the *quidditas* or the *essentia realis*. And, this is also traced back to the *Zêta* book of Aristotle's *Metaphysics* and the influence of an *ousia* ontology. What Thomas Aquinas understands by *quidditas* is that in relation to its *quid*, a be-

---

William McNeill (Cambridge: Cambridge University Press, 1998), p. 341.

36 *Ibid*, pp. 348, 349

37 *Ibid*, p. 350.

38 *Ibid*, pp. 360, 361, 363.

ing has being before even being in actuality; i.e. that it has being before existing. The *quidditas* would then be designated as the *forma, natura, definitio*, or *essentia.*[39] A being by virtue of its quiddity is not a being that we could qualify as being an existent. Such being cannot exist but in actuality. It is by virtue of its *actualitas* that a being exists. And, as long as a being exists, it is as such in terms of being an effect of a cause that brings it into existence. The existent would be the product of a process of production. The effectivity of reality is then construed in terms of the *actualitas*. This might have been what one attests in Thomas Aquinas' account of *essentia* and *existentia* where the *esse* or *existere* are what happens externally to *essentia*, as if that which belongs to reality does so accidentally. The *essentia realis* cannot bring something into existence. It is not sufficient by itself, and some sort of an external agent is required to bring forth that existence. Such account takes beings to be of the order of the *ens creatum* (While with God, *essentia* and *existentia* are the same, where God is *actus purus*). Beings do not exist due to their essences rather they participate in existence. Beings pass from possibility to effective reality. On Heidegger's account, the ontological difference between essence and existence would then entail that being or existing is the effect of the phenomenon of making or productivity. On Heidegger's account, such a phenomenon of making or productivity, inscribes ontology within the horizon of production which is not dissociated from profound developments within theology and its accounts of creation. On Heidegger's point of view, the antique ontology of the ancient Greeks, and the ontology of Christianity, both display characteristics of a conception of being that permits to transcribe the Greek ontological account of being to a Chris-

---

[39] Regarding this point and the Heideggerian account with regard to the quiddity of an entity, also refer to: Robert Brisart, *La Phénomenologie de Marbourg, ou la Résurgence de la Métaphysique chez Heidegger a l'époque de Sein und Zeit* (Bruxelles: Publications des Facultés Universitaires Saint-Louis, 1991), p. 38.

tian consideration of creation and of beings as *ens creatum*. On Heidegger's view, both the Greek and Christian ontology are inscribed within the horizon of production that is centered on the notion of *actualitas*. And this notion of *actualitas* assimilates being to effectivity and presence, while also characterizing the Kantian *Wirklichkeit* (reality). And this is what Heidegger after all designates as *Vorhandenheit* (presence at hand, or objective presence).[40] Whether with *actualitas*, *Wirklichkeit*, or *Vorhandenheit*, being figures in the horizon of a definite mode of time that is that of the present.

If with Kant, perception is being, and perception is a simple and pure apprehension of an object by a subject, with Husserl perception is dynamic and is an intentional comportment that displays larger possibilities than that Kantian conception of perception. The introduction of intentionality gives more depth to the consideration of perception and its link to being. And, this is also attested in Avicenna's epistemological accounts of being which give expression to a phenomenological consideration of perception in terms of the pragmatics and intentional sense of prehension that is entailed by *al-wahm* (And this will be later addressed in the sixth chapter of this book). Regarding the Husserlian account, consciousness is taken to be intentional, and this reveals the correspondence between an *intentio* and an *intentum*. The intentional act is filled up with the perceptual act in such a way that intuition completes the givenness of an object. Perception fills up intentionality, since intentionality and the acts of consciousness do not guarantee by themselves the objective sense of what they target. It is perception and intuition (categorical or sensible) that complete the correspondence between *intentio* and *intentum*. Being is not the mark of the object standing up and against us, rather it is the mark of the experience of our own proper immanent consciousness. Yet, being has to be given to us externally in terms of objective correlatives. Without intuition concepts are

---

40 *Ibid*, pp. 41-42.

empty, and without concepts intuition is blind. This is a Kantian dictum that shows that "without sensibility no object would be given to us, without understanding no object would be thought. Thoughts without contents are empty, intuitions without concepts are blind."[41] This calls for making our concepts sensible and our intuitions intelligible. Husserl would illustrate the limits of this scheme, by showing that intuition is more extended and less limited than how it has been expressed in Kant's view. On Husserl's view, perception is not merely a pure and simple apprehension. Rather perception involves acts of intentionality that are more complex than apprehension. Therefore, these acts liberate perception from mere sensibility. The objectivity of something is not exhausted in a mere sensible reality, rather it involves a complex account of intentional acts of ideation. The phenomenological extension of perception takes place on the scene of intentionality that does not collapse an object to being a pure and simple object. Intentionality rather gives objectivity a more fundamental and originary constitutive sense. The shift away from the ontology of objects, as is the case with reducing being to perception, is a Husserlian shift towards the ontology of the subject. Yet, in both instances, the ontological cedes to the ontic. And, in a Heideggerian account, perception ought to testify to the difference between the "discovery" of beings and the "disclosure" of being.[42] Even with the Kantian convergence of being and perception, beings are not accessible but through perception. Therefore beings are not accessible but by virtue of a comprehension of being. Yet this does not emancipate the Heideggerian critique of the tradition. From what has been encountered so far, founding ontology is also a founding that focuses on subjectivity. However, according to Heidegger, the ques-

---

[41] Immanuel Kant, *Critique of Pure Reason*, trans. by Norman Kemp Smith (New York: St. Martin's Press, 1965), B75.

[42] Robert Brisart, *La Phénomenologie de Marbourg, ou la Résurgence de la Métaphysique chez Heidegger a l'époque de Sein und Zeit* (Bruxelles: Publications des Facultés Universitaires Saint-Louis, 1991), p. 61.

tion of being underlies the determination of the knowing subject, and the determination of subjectivity is of an ontological order of being.

IV- Hegel's Line of Essentialism in The Science of Logic[43]

According to Hegel, being-for-other and being-in-itself are the two moments of something. Being as self-relation is also the non-being of the otherness; where otherness represents the non-immediacy of the being of self-relation. Consequently, one would also say that being has the non-being of otherness in itself. Being-in-itself and being-for-other are therefore the determinations of one and the same thing that in its own nature relates itself to the other as one of its own determinations. Determinate being (that contains otherness as one of its moments) contains negation in itself and passes over into otherness.[44] The affirmative determinate being that passes over into otherness is by virtue of its determinateness a being that has a limit that is also the non-being of its other. On Hegel's view, something is what it is by virtue of its own limit. Yet, the limit of something implies that a thing and its other either one of them has being or one of them does not have being. Therefore, the limit is the "quality" of a thing.[45] However, according to Hegel, every limit as limitation also implies self-transcendence as an "ought" to rise above the limitation. Every limit is coupled with the "ought" to sublate that limit. Limit is coupled with its "self-sublation." Since every thing that is finite has the limit and the ought to transcend the limit as the moments of its determination, then every finite is self-contradictory and therefore "sublates itself" in the sense of ceasing to be what it is and becoming an other finite.[46] According to Hegel, the infinite is

---

[43] G. W. F. Hegel, *Hegel's Science of Logic*, trans. by A. V. Miller, ed. by H. D. Lewis (Atlantic Highlands, NJ: Humanities Press International Inc., 1996).

[44] *Ibid*, pp. 119-125.

[45] *Ibid*, pp. 126-129.

[46] *Ibid*, pp. 133-137.

the "true being" that is above its limitation. It is the "being which has restored itself out of limitedness;" marking itself as the affirmative determination of the finite.[47] However, this positing of the infinite reduces the infinite into a "category of being" that is "confronted" by the finite as its opposite. In this sense, the infinite is posited over against the finite. This bad binary positing of the infinite over and against the finite reduces the infinite into being merely the "limit" of the finite. It therefore leads to the inference that the infinite is itself limited and finite. This "bad infinity" is the "infinity of the understanding" whereby the "understanding" finds satisfaction in the unresolved contradiction between the finite and the infinite without being able to pass over into a positing of a "genuine" infinity.[48] However, when we say that the infinite of the understanding is the limit of the finite, we also imply that with the limit we do posit the "ought" to transgress the limit. And, this "ought" posits a new limit and a new "ought" and so on in an infinite regress. Yet, even with this progress into infinity, Hegel still holds that the infinity of "infinite progress" will always be burdened by the finite. And this entails that the "infinite progress" is itself finite. Hegel holds that, in its immediate determination, the infinite is only the "beyond of the finite" as a negation of the finite. Therefore, the infinite is the negation of itself in its own self, as a negation of the finite. The infinity of the finite consists of a self-sublation in terms of which the "infinite progress" describes a "closed system" of newly arising limits and a transcending of these limits. The infinite of the faculty of understanding is supposed to be unattainable. It is supposed to be "not there," while the genuine infinite is the "real" which is determined as "essence" and is described as a "circle" that is "bent back into itself," rather than being described as a "straight line" as is the case with the "infinite progress." This account would reflect that what is "real" is the Notion, the Idea, and Essence, while being, determinate being,

---

47 *Ibid*, p. 137.

48 *Ibid*, pp. 139-140.

and finitude are the more abstract and "the most familiar."[49] Saying that Essence, Idea, and Notion are the real, and being and the finite are the ideal, implies that being and the finite, are forms of conception in the Notion, and therefore they lack "true being."[50] Having said that, the question that arises is that which wonders what "true being" might be and what the "truth of being" might mean. Hegel would give the response in later sections of his Logic that are included in his Doctrine of Essence. Hegel plainly says that "the truth of being is essence."[51] Hegel holds that being is the immediate, "the most familiar." Yet, he also holds that the knowledge of being is mediated and that it starts from being then sublates it and passes over into essence and that such a movement is that of being itself. Essence is then taken to be "the absolute being-in-itself" that is "indifferent" to every determinateness of being. As an absolute, essence has no determinate being, it is "infinite being-for-self." Hegel then adds that essence is "absolute indifference to limit." This entails that in sublating itself, "essence converts itself into *ground* and passes over into *Existence* and *Appearance*." As a "sublated being," essence is "the negation of the sphere of being in general."[52] *Existence* is taken by Hegel to be the "undifferentiated unity of essence with its immediacy," while *Appearance* is that which "the thing is in itself, or its truth."[53] Hegel explicates his position by saying that:

> In the *sphere of being, determinate being* was the being in which negation was present, and being was the immediate base and element of this negation, which consequently was itself immediate. *In the sphere of essence, positedness* corresponds to determinate being. It is likewise a determinate being but its

---

49 *Ibid*, p. 142-149.

50 *Ibid*, pp. 154-155.

51 *Ibid*, p. 389.

52 *Ibid*, pp. 389-394.

53 *Ibid*, p. 479.

> base is being as essence or as pure negativity; it is a determinateness or negation, not as affirmatively present [*Seiend*] but immediately sublated.[54]

According to Hegel, "being is simply only the becoming of essence," while "the becoming of being" is further the "transition to essence."[55] On Hegel's view, and in a hint to the essence/existence distinction, a thing is distinguished from its existence as much as this thing is distinguished from its being. Existence is taken by him to be the unity of essence with its immediacy. Yet at the same time, existence is the "self-alienation" of essence in the sense that essence passes into existence which in its turn (as "essential existence") passes over into *Appearance*. Existence, as the totality of the world in and for itself, is the "determinate ground" of *Appearance*.[56] To sum it up, in essence, being emerges as existence, while actuality stands higher than existence and contains in itself possibility rather than being a mere immediate existence. According to Hegel, the unity of actuality and possibility is "contingency" which in its turn is contained in necessity whose absoluteness is the unity of being and essence.[57] The Absolute Necessary is the unity of being and essence. In other words, the Absolute Necessary is that whose being is essence and whose essence is being. And, this evidently reflects what figures in Avicenna's account of the Necessary Existent/Being due to Itself (*wājib al-wūjūd fī dhātihi*) whose essence is none other than existence. Yet, with Avicenna, the ontological account of being takes a different path than that taken by Hegel, since Avicenna's ontology of being does not readily entail essentialism. According to Hegel, essence is the "first negation of being" which thereby becomes "illusory being." The Notion is "the second negation" as the negation of

---

54 *Ibid*, p. 406.

55 *Ibid*, p.472, 475.

56 *Ibid*, pp. 483, 484, 499, 507, 509.

57 *Ibid*, pp. 551-552.

the first negation of being. Consequently, the Notion is restored as being the "infinite mediation and negativity of being within itself." On Hegel's reading of infinity, the Absolute is seen as a movement of infinity in finite beings. It is the movement of the same in the other whereby the finite is itself revealed as infinite. On Hegel's account: "something has truth insofar" it is an "Idea." The process of [an] Idea is the process of truth, and the occurrence of being is an occurrence of truth. This is also the case since being, as an indeterminate immediacy, and as a pure concept, is convergent with thinking. And the unfolding of being is a "dialectical process." Hegel's ontology is not *ousiological*. It is rather a "[dialectical] process" ontology by virtue of which being moves from being-in-itself (as substance) to being-for-itself (as subject). Yet, even if Hegel's process ontology escapes the confines of reducing being into *ousia*, it still gives a reductive account of being in terms of essence and the metaphysical subjectivity. In this sense, Hegel's account would still be stamped by the Heideggerian critique of metaphysics. As for Avicenna, his ontology of being is a process ontology that is not *ousiological*. And, his epistemology of being may rely on the metaphysical construal of subjectivity, yet such state of affairs is overcomed by his mystical accounts of the self which overcome the metaphysical dimensions in his epistemology. In other words, Avicenna overcomes the metaphysical substance and subject based ontologies.

In the context of examining Hegel's reception of Greek philosophy, Heidegger claims that Hegel was not able to set εἶναι (*einai*, i.e. "being" in the Greek sense) from the relation to the subject. On this reading, Hegel was not able to set being "free" into its own essence.[58] Heidegger then holds that Hegel's interpretation of the Greek doctrine of being shows that being unfolds as presence, given that ἀλήθεια (*alētheia*) holds sway without itself being thought of

58 Martin Heidegger, "Hegel and The Greeks," in Pathmarks, ed. by William McNeill (Cambridge: Cambridge University Press, 1998), p. 333.

in relation to its provenance.[59] On a Heideggerian account, the merits of Hegel's interpretation of the doctrine of being may be reduced to an indirect revealing to our thinking of the "not-yet" i.e. the "unthought" in philosophy.

59 *Ibid*, p. 335.

CHAPTER 2
HEIDEGGER'S THEORY OF THE SUBJECT

Heidegger's approach to the question of being is undertaken by the way of questioning which, in his own terms, "builds a way" that is that of a "thinking" that leads "through language."[60] On his account, "questioning" is the "piety of thought."[61] And one conducts a search about "beings" in their "thatness" and "whatness" by a way of questioning that answers to the question: "*what is that*?" Heidegger is concerned with the question of the meaning of being, as to ask "what is being?" Yet, in an attempt to answer the question concerning the meaning of being (*Sein*), one has to have some sort of guidance as to what is that which questioning is seeking. Faced with this requirement, "being" is available to understanding through its "indeterminateness" and "ambiguity."[62] On Heidegger's view, "everything" is "in being."[63] This staring point is itself a point of interest for our investigation of what Heidegger calls *Dasein*. Our inquiry

---

60 Martin Heidegger, "The Question Concerning Technology," in *Basic Writings*, ed. by David Farrell Krell (New York: Harper & Row, 1977), p 317. David Farrell Krell also indicates that this essay appeared in: Martin Heidegger, *The Question Concerning Technology and Other Essays*, trans. by William Lovitt (New York: Harper & Row). The German text appears in: Martin Heidegger, *Vortage und Aufsatze* (Pfullingen: Gunter Neske Verlag, 1954), pp. 13-44. It also appears in: Martin Heidegger, *Die Technik und die Kehre* (Pfullingen: Gunter Neske Verlag, 1962), pp. 5-36.

61 *Ibid*, p. 317.

62 For a detailed account of Martin Heidegger's exposition of the question of the meaning of being, refer to his introduction in: Martin Heidegger, *Being and Time*, trans. by Joan Stambaugh (Albany: State University of New York Press, 1996), pp. 1-5.

63 *Ibid*, p. 5.

about *Dasein*, and consequently about Heidegger's theory of the subject, is an inquiry that starts with the question of the meaning of being. However, this inquiry starts by asking "what is it for something to be in something else?" In other words, our question concerning the meaning of *Dasein* is also a question that concerns itself with the state of affairs of a mode of being that is that of "being-in." Questioning is constitutive due to its inquisitive grasp and the availability of being in ontology is not the availability of that which is being sought. Accordingly, being is "presupposed" in ontology in the form of being an "available concept."[64] Thus a concern with the meaning of the question of being is taken from the standpoint of the ontological priority of that question. On Heidegger's account, "all ontology, ..., remains fundamentally blind and perverts its innermost intent if it has not previously clarified the meaning of being sufficiently and grasped this clarification as its fundamental task."[65] Ontology has to turn the quest of the meaning of being (*Sein*) into being its "fundamental task." This ontological priority is coupled with an ontic priority that concerns itself with the question about beings. However, *Dasein* is unlike beings [entities] in the sense that *Dasein* is "distinctly different from other beings." The ontological *Dasein* is "ontically" distinct from other beings in the sense of being a being that is "concerned *about* its very being." And the understanding of being is itself the "determination of the being of *Dasein*."[66] On this account, *Dasein* concerns itself with "other beings that it need not itself be." *Dasein* essentially is in the world, and "being-in-the-world" essentially "belongs to *Dasein*."[67] On this reading, being-in-the-world constitutes *Dasein*'s fundamental structure. Accordingly, an inquiry about the meaning of *Dasein* is an inquiry that concerns itself with

---

64 *Ibid*, p. 6.

65 *Ibid*, p. 9.

66 *Ibid*, p. 10.

67 *Ibid*, p. 11.

the "*worldliness*" of *Dasein* and with the sense of "being-in" as such, and in the sense of "being-in-the-world" and of being-with (*Mitsein*) others. Thus the question concerning *Dasein*, as the question concerning Heidegger's theory of the subject, is also a question that concerns itself with the interpretation of "being-in" and of "being-with [*Mitdasein*]" as being the modes of being of *Dasein* in its *worldliness*. On Heidegger's view, "being-in-the-world," as the fundamental structure of *Dasein*, has an "*a prioristic*" status with respect to the questioning that concerns itself with the interpretation of *Dasein*. Given the essential priority of *Dasein*'s structure, as it is implied in *Dasein*'s *worldliness*, the analysis of what it is to "be-in" and to "be-with" would ground preparatory considerations of the interpretation of the "being of *Dasein*." As it was mentioned earlier, being-in-the-world is the fundamental constitutive structure of *Dasein*, and the demonstration of the being of *Dasein* is grounded on the fundamental preparatory interpretation of being-in-the-world. Being-in-the-world is to be taken as a whole, yet this does not prevent this "unified" structure from having some sort of "constitutive structural factors."[68] Being-in-the-world furnishes us with a "threefold perspective" that concerns itself with the question concerning the meaning of the "*in-the-world*," the question of "*being*" itself, and the ontological sense of "*being-in*."[69] The first question concerns itself with the analysis of the structure of "*worldliness*." The second question is concerned with the meaning of "*being*" as it is implied in the meaning of "*being-in-the-world*." The third question is concerned with the meaning of "*being-in*" as such in the sense of being a general question that acts as a fundamental starting point from which the interpretation of "*being*" and of "*in-the-world*" would be addressed.

---

[68] *Ibid*, p. 49.

[69] *Ibid*, p. 50.

I- Being-in-the-World and *Dasein*

In addressing the question concerning the meaning of "*being-in*" one is confronted with some sort of containment picture according to which something is said to be in something else in the sense of being contained by it. From the times of Plato, Aristotle, and of Simplicius after them, containment might have taken two main senses; one is that of envelopment and the other is that of pervasion. Some views on space might have taken containment to be envelopment (as it might have been implied by Aristotle's views in his *Physics* on "place as a boundary"). Other views give containment a sense of pervasion (as it might have been implied by Plato's views in his *Timaeus* on the "receptacle of becoming"). Heidegger's "being-in" does not from the onset imply containment. "Being-in" is not envelopment nor is it pervasion. And the analysis of "being-in" is not taken from an ontic position according to which something, as a being (an entity not *Sein*), is said to be in another being. Rather Heidegger's analysis of "being-in" is taken from the start to be a fundamental introductory analysis that is supposed to ground a preliminary demonstration of the being of *Dasein*. The Heideggerian analysis of "being-in" is taken to be some sort of a constitution[70] of *Dasein* that does not carry the spatial senses of being-in as they might be implied in a containment picture according to which, one thing is pictured as being contained by another. On this view, "being-in" designates the constitution of *Dasein* in the sense of being a "*formal existential expression of the being of Dasein* [but not of

---

70 Constitution does not take the sense of creation, however it still has the sense of being some sort of a "making" of what is constituted. The constitutive is that which makes what is constituted; as if it were the case that, that which is constituted does not (in a sense) exist prior to the constitution that *makes* it (constitutes it, produces it, brings it to what it is by associations, connections, etc...). Regarding the constitution of things and space one may refer to Edmund Husserl's views where the subject kinaesthetically constitutes space and things. As for the views of Maurice Merleau-Ponty, space itself is taken in its motivating sense to be constitutive of the engaged corporeal subject.

being in general] which has the essential constitution of being-in-the-world."[71] Being-in-the-world has rather the sense of being "absorbed" in this world. Being-in-the-world implies "being-together-with" the world and "being-with" others (*Mitsein,* and more so *Mitdasein*).[72] Again, as is the case with the interpretation of "being-in," "being with" does not carry the sense of having a spatial objective thing that is said to *be-with* another thing. "Being with" is an indication of *Dasein's* destiny as being "bound" with "the being of beings" that *Dasein* encounters in the world.[73] This view bases itself on an ontological consideration of *Dasein* that distinguishes between "being-in" as existential dimension and "being-in" as a spatial containment. *Dasein* has thus some sort of "facticity"[74] that designates an ontological factuality about how every *Dasein* is. Thus, the facticity of *Dasein* is also linked to the meaning of the being of *Dasein.* From what has been stated above, it might seem as if it were the case that Heidegger is denying the spatiality of *Dasein.* Yet, this is not the case since the fundamental structure of *Dasein* first points at the "existential spatiality" of *Dasein.*[75] However, this existential spatiality, and with it the "being-in" of *Dasein,* ought not to be analyzed nor understood ontically. Rather, this state of affairs ought to be interpreted from within the scope of an ontological inquiry. In this regard, Heidegger would take the ways of *Dasein*'s being-in as being ways of "taking care" that designate an ontological and *existential* state of *being-in*, of *being-toward,* and of *being-together-with* the

---

[71] Martin Heidegger, *Being and Time*, trans. by Joan Stambaugh (Albany: State University of New York Press, 1996), p. 51.

[72] *Ibid*, pp. 51-52.

[73] *Ibid*, pp. 51-52.

[74] *Ibid*, p. 52.

[75] *Ibid*, pp. 52-53.

world [of others].[76] "Being-in," in its priority and essential constitution of the being of *Dasein,* implies that "*Dasein* is never 'initially' a sort of being which is free from being-in."[77] Adding to that, the *a priori* primordial constitution of the being of *Dasein,* (as being-in) is "ontically as well as ontologically" a being-in-the-world as "taking care."[78] *Dasein* as the being that concerns itself with the being of other beings is also a being that concerns itself with knowing other beings. *Dasein* as "*care*" represents *Dasein*'s being-in-the-world in the form of "knowing the world."[79] In this sense, knowing the world is an "examplar" of *Dasein*'s being-in-the-world. Yet, knowledge as such is not to be understood in terms of a metaphysical subject/object distinction between *Dasein* as knower and the world as that which is to be known by *Dasein.* On Heidegger's view, knowing is a mode of *Dasein's* being-in the world. Thus knowing is grounded in being-in-the-world as that which constitutes the "being of *Dasein.*"[80] On this account, *Dasein* already exists in the world as a being-in-the-world that knows. Accordingly, *Dasein* is directed toward a world that is "discovered in *Dasein.*"[81] Given that "knowing" is *Dasein's* mode of being-in-the-world, one would be concerned with the "worldliness" of the world that *Dasein* knows. In order to have further insights about what it is to be-in the world, one has to examine the structure of the world; i.e. its "worldliness." Given this state of affairs, the worldliness of the world designates the structure of *Dasein*'s being-in-the world, which constitutes the onto-

---

76 *Ibid*, p. 53.

77 *Ibid*, pp. 53-54.

78 *Ibid*, p. 54.

79 *Ibid*, p. 55.

80 *Ibid*, p. 57.

81 *Ibid*, p. 58.

logical characteristic of *Dasein*.[82] On this reading, one could say that *Dasein* is already "wordly," and that *Dasein*'s *a priori* "wordliness" is not to be confused with the "objective presence" of beings (*Vorhandenheit*, presence-at-hand) that "belong" to the world rather than *being-in* it. This is the case given that *being-in* is a characteristic of *Dasein*'s "wordliness."[83] Yet, does *Dasein*'s *being-in* characterize *Dasein* with spatiality in the sense of taking *Dasein*'s worldliness to be a mode of being-in-space? *Dasein*'s spatiality attributes to the *being-in* of *Dasein* some sort of what he calls the character of "*de-distancing*" (a removal) and "*directionality*."[84] On Heidegger's account, "*de-distancing*" (roughly, as a removal of distance) constitutes a mode of being of *Dasein* according to which *Dasein* "circumspectively" *de-distances* something and brings it near in terms of *taking care* of that being or thing.[85] It is in its mode of essentially "dwelling in de-distancing" that *Dasein* is said to be spatial. And, it is in this manner that *Dasein* discovers space in terms of circumspective de-distancing. In circumspection (*Umsicht*), *Dasein* brings things into a nearness (*Nahe*) in the sense of having them *at hand* (*Zuhandene*, ready-to-hand). Given this state of affairs, *Dasein* is "directed" in de-distancing, since "every bringing near" has some sort of directionality.[86] *Dasein*'s spatiality is not *constituted* by the subject, rather space is taken to be *a priori* in the sense of being already

---

82 *Ibid*, pp. 59-60.

83 On this reading, only *Dasein* is said to be in a mode of being that is that of *being-in-the-world*; beings (existents) in general are not said to be in the world in the sense of *Dasein*'s *being-in-the world*, they (i.e. the existents) rather belong to the world.

84 Martin Heidegger, *Being and Time*, trans. by Joan Stambaugh (Albany: State University of New York Press, 1996), p. 97.

85 *Ibid*, pp. 97-100.

86 *Ibid*, pp. 100-101.

in the world, while the world itself is not taken to be in space. On this view, *Dasein* is taken to be spatial in a "primordial sense."[87]

II- *Dasein* and Care

From the analysis of being-in-the-world, it has been shown that, on Heidegger's account, the "subject" is primordially worldy. Heidegger's account is unlike those philosophical accounts that take the subject to be constitutive of space.[88] Given these conditions, the subject is already thrown into an intersubjective world. The mode of being of *Dasein* would thus be that of being-with-others. And this is implied in the *a priori* primordiality of *Mitdasein*. On this account, *Dasein*'s *being-in* the world is thus a *being-with* (others) in the world even if "existentially" no other is in fact perceived by *Dasein*. One could say that *Dasein* is "essentially being-with." This implies that an *existential* "being-alone" is in a sense a "deficient" mode of being-with.[89] *Dasein* does not take care of the other, rather *Dasein* takes care of beings that are objectively at hand (*Zuhandene*, or ready-to-hand). The other constitutes "a matter of concern (*Fur-sorge*)" for *Dasein* rather than being that which *Dasein* takes care of.[90] This concern reveals that *Dasein* is "essentially for-the-sake-of-others"[91] who, as others, are encountered by *Dasein* in "*their Dasein*." This entails that *Mitdasein* is already implied in the under-

---

87 *Ibid*, p. 103.

88 Edmund Husserl's accounts of the space constituting consciousness offer a complex, difficult, and detailed consideration of the constitution of space and things by and through the kinaesthetic systems of an intentional bodily subject.

89 Martin Heidegger, *Being and Time*, trans. by Joan Stambaugh (Albany: State University of New York Press, 1996), p. 113. But can one still claim that a self-burdened *Dasein* that is taken by itself and positing the *other* as a some sort of a threat for its own individuality is also a *Dasein* that is lonely in its solitude?

90 *Ibid*, p. 114.

91 *Ibid*, p. 116.

standing of *Dasein*'s mode of being in the world. And the mode of being of *Dasein* is that of being directed toward others.[92] Yet, *Dasein* discloses the other as being itself a *Dasein*. This state of affairs compromises *Dasein*'s own individuality and turns the other into a matter of concern instead of care. According to Heidegger, the primary factor of "care" is that of what he takes to be *Dasein*'s "being-ahead-of-itself," which means that *Dasein* exists "for-the-sake-of-itself" and for the sake of others. And in doing so, *Dasein* already exists for the sake of itself, and that *Dasein*'s existence for the sake of itself is also an existence for the sake of others. Having said that, one would still ask how would *Dasein* differentiate itself from, what Heidegger calls, the undifferentiated and indiscriminate *das Man* or the "*They*" of others? The "being-ahead-of-itself" is also a mode of being of *Dasein* in its existence for the sake of itself that indicates that *Dasein*'s "potentiality-of-being" has an "unfinished quality." [93] And "as long as *Dasein is*, it has never attained its wholeness."[94] Consequently this would mean that, "*Dasein* reaches its wholeness in death."[95] And this consideration of death will have bearings on our understanding of *Dasein*'s authenticity as well as understanding the authenticity and ethics of being as it figures in Avicenna's mystic Visionary Recitals.

---

92 *Ibid*, pp. 116-117.

93 *Being-ahead-of-itself* already implies that this state of affairs is temporal. Being-ahead-of-itself has the structure of an anticipatory projection from the present to the future; however this projection is towards a possibility that is indefinite yet certain. It is in his *Begriff der Zeit* (*The Concept of Time*) that Heidegger would give some insights as to how one could understand what he calls "the futural past" which accounts for the notion of time in terms of an interpretation of the certainty of death. And his analysis of time is reminiscent of St. Augustine's analysis of time and its measurement in the *Confessions*.

94 Martin Heidegger, *Being and Time*, trans. by Joan Stambaugh (Albany: State University of New York Press, 1996), p. 220.

95 *Ibid*, p. 221.

III- The Call of Conscience and Thinking

In his analysis of the self, Heidegger distinguishes between an authentic and inauthentic self. The inauthentic self shows the state of affairs of the "falling" and absorption in the world of everyday concern.[96] In the context of his examination of Heidegger and Wittgenstein, Stanley Cavell holds that, in Wittgenstein's *Philosophical Investigations*, everydayness is the "siting of skepticicsm." Yet, this implies that skepticism is not something that will be overcomed or refuted, rather skepticism is taken to be a "conclusion" of what Emerson calls the "human condition."[97] The sense of urgency with which the issue of the everyday is revealed, does not establish a philosophy of ethics that is separate from what Heidegger and Wittgenstein do as philosophy; both take philosophy to be "a way of life." According to Heidegger, to be its authentic self, *Dasein* has to bring itself out of its inauthentic mode of being. It must bring itself back to its "potentiality-for-being-itself." The "call of conscience" is what calls *Dasein* to its ownmost potentiality-for-being-itself. *Dasein* is ontologically under the threat of being alienated from its authentic mode of being-in-the-world. And alienation issues from *Dasein*'s "falling" which some commentators on Heidegger's work might attribute to an "initial alienation from God" that marks Heidegger's indebtedness to Christian theology.[98]

According to Heidegger, the call of conscience reaches only those who wish to hear it. The call that comes from "afar" reaches

---

96 *Ibid*, p. 164.

97 Stanley Cavell, *Conditions Handsome and Unhandsome: The Constitution of Emersonian Perfectionism* (Chicago: The University of Chicago Press, 1988), p. 61.

98 Allan Megill is one of those commentators who attribute the falling of *Dasein* to a primordial alienation from God. This account points to the contributions that St. Augustine offered in his account of the Neoplatonic fall of the soul. For further elucidation of Megill's view, see: Allan Megill, *Prophets of Extremity* (Berkeley: University of California Press, 1987), p. 118.

only those who want to be brought back.[99] The call "summons." It says "nothing" that is familiar to the discourse of *Dasein*'s inauthentic absorption in the world of everyday concern. The call calls for self-realization.[100] The caller is *Dasein* in its "uncanniness" as the being thrown into the world whose state of being in the world is that of being-not-at-home.[101] The call re-calls *Dasein* to the fact of its homelessness, to the fact that *Dasein* in its everyday concern has forgotten itself in an estranged world of *das Man*. The call of conscience recalls *Dasein* to its alienation by virtue of which this self tends to seek its return to itself. Thrown into existence, the essence of *Dasein* is to "project possibilities." *Dasein* has to reach for being. It has to recall itself as the "futural" being that exists "ahead of itself" while being aware of its finitude. In its absorption in the world of its everydayness, *Dasein* has in the company of others the feeling that "it is at home." However this feeling is deceptive, it veils *Dasein*'s human condition that comes to light due to "anxiety" by virtue of which *Dasein* experiences its unhomeliness. With anxiety, being-in-the-world emerges as being-not-at-home that has been veiled by *Dasein*'s everydayness. The falling from the authentic ownmost-potentiality-for-being into the world marks the emergence of anxiety at all times.[102] The call of conscience is a call that summons *Dasein* to return back to its potentiality for being. It is a call that summons *Dasein* to unveil its being-not-at-home as a way of bringing itself

---

[99] Martin Heidegger, *Being and Time*, trans. by Joan Stambaugh (Albany: State University of New York Press, 1996), pp. 249-250.

[100] Regarding this specific interpretation, see: Sonya Sikka, *Forms of Transcendence: Heidegger and Medieval Mystical Theology* (Albany: State University of New York Press, 1997), p. 203.

[101] Martin Heidegger, *Being and Time*, trans. by Joan Stambaugh (Albany: State University of New York Press, 1996), p. 255.

[102] As Allan Megill puts it: "there is no notion, here, of an 'age of anxiety'." See: Allan Megill, *Prophets of Extremity* (Berkeley: University of California Press, 1987), p. 119.

back to seek home. The call of conscience reaches those who want to "come back." And, this summoning to a return is also attested in the quest for a re-opening of the question of the meaning of being by bringing that question back from the history of its oblivion within the history of classical ontology. According to Heidegger, "resoluteness" (*Entschlossenheit*) constitutes *Dasein*'s authentic being-its-self that rests on *Dasein*'s being as a potentiality-for-being-itself within the limits of its own being. As Sonya Sikka puts it, "*Dasein* is, after all, thrown into its being-*Da* and can only resolve upon itself as having been thrown to be" (Sikka, 1997, p. 215). *Dasein* is ordered in its being and it is destined to be while being conditioned and limited by what it is. *Dasein* is also limited by the possibilities that are open for it in its potentiality-for-being. *Dasein* is in a mode of being that is that of "running-ahead-of-itself-in-anticipation," as "being-towards-death" according to which *Dasein* understands the "can" of its potentiality-for-being.[103] In its thrownness, and going ahead of itself in search for its potentiality for being, *Dasein* is after all in search for the paths that lead it back to itself. *Dasein* is in a search for the path of return.[104] As if it were the case that *Dasein*'s life is dominated by a compulsive regression towards death as a return to the site of quietude (Herein, one might find that Heidegger's views get so close to what one finds in Freud's consideration of the death-instinct and the trauma of birth). In "resoluteness" *Dasein* is retrieved from the being-alongside of its everydayness falling. However, resoluteness is bound up by the limits of what *Dasein* is. It is limited by "death,"

103 Martin Heidegger, *Being and Time*, trans. by Joan Stambaugh (Albany: State University of New York Press, 1996), p. 283.

104 Allan Megill would argue that "being-ahead-of-itself" has the implication that *Dasein* is perpetually trying to find its "way back to its ownmost potentiality-for-being." See: Allan Megill, *Prophets of Extremity* (Berkeley: University of California Press, 1987), p. 123; Martin Heidegger, *Being and Time*, trans. by Joan Stambaugh (Albany: State University of New York Press, 1996), pp. 191-192.

"guilt," "thrownness," and "facticity."[105] In its readiness to be called, *Dasein* is ready for the "happening" of the revelation of being. In the limits of what makes up the *Da* of *Dasein*, as Sonya Sikka puts it, *Dasein* "knows itself not to be merely *Da*, and not unlimited *Sein*, but *Dasein*" (Sikka, 1997, p. 219). This is granted in time, in the present moment that grants the visionary revelation of being. Presenting the past in recollection and remembrance is a handing over the inheritance. In repetition, *Dasein* discloses possibilities for itself. Yet, one does not attest a direct sense of a *Ṣūfī* union with *Dasein*, since *Dasein* is always there (*Da*), it is always in a strife in its being-in-the-world (*inamā khuliqa al-insān bi-kabad*, that the human being has been created with a strife). The notion of the voice, as being that of conscience, is to be interpreted in terms of *Dasein*'s own disclosure of itself as being a "potentiality-of-being-its-self." On this account, "the call of conscience" summons *Dasein* to its ownmost "potentiality-of-being-itself." The call of conscience individuates *Dasein*. However, the call entails speech and hearing. Accordingly, it has the structure of a discourse that "articulates intelligibility."[106] The call of conscience, and of its hearing, is also a *willful* call to have a "resolution," a decision, a "choice" of being an individual self. Yet, the call of conscience is supposedly made available to *Mitdasein* "by way of utterance in language."[107] However, Heidegger would say that calling lacks utterances, it is a form of speech of conscience that "*speaks solely and constantly in the mode of silence.*" And this "silent" call summons *Dasein* to free itself from its lostness in the they.[108] But

---

105 Sonya Sikka, *Forms of Transcendence: Heidegger and Medieval Mystical Theology* (Albany: State University of New York Press, 1997), p. 218.

106 Concerning the discursive aspect of "calling" and "hearing," see: Martin Heidegger, *Being and Time*, trans. by Joan Stambaugh (Albany: State University of New York Press, 1996), pp. 250-251.

107 *Ibid*, p. 251.

108 *Ibid*, pp. 252-253.

what is being said in a call that speaks in silence? The call says nothing, it does not even deliver an introspective speech. *Dasein* calls itself to its own potentiality-of-being. And, the call is "unfamiliar" to the everydayness lostness in the "they."[109] So is it then the case that the call of *Dasein*, which speaks to itself in the mode of silence, is the call of "subjectivity" that comes from the "*being* that *I* myself always *am*"? And is it the case that *understanding*, what the call calls for, is a *will* that "wants to have a conscience"? In "*What is Called Thinking*,"[110] Heidegger attempted to offer some sort of re-interpretation of his major work "*Being and Time"* in terms of opening it up to the "horizon of thinking." In this regard, and with respect to what one might make of Heidegger's "call of *Dasein*," one could read Heidegger's response to the question "What is *this* that *calls* on us *to think*?"[111] as being a horizon from which one could understand what summons *Dasein*. On Heidegger's account, that which calls on us to think brings us to face "thinking *qua* thinking" as being "essentially a *call*."[112] The call of conscience is the "ground" of itself.[113] And, as a transcending being, *Dasein* projects possibilities into the future while being situated toward itself in terms of "wanting to have a conscience." As Heidegger writes, "Understanding the summons means: wanting to have a conscience." The reception of the call implies that there is something that has been received, that it has been taken with a welcome, and as Stanley Cavell would say, "reception, or something received, if it is welcome, implies

---

109 *Ibid*, pp. 254-255.

110 Martin Heidegger, *What is called Thinking?*, trans. by J. Glenn Gray (New York: Harper & Row, 1968).

111 *Ibid*, p. 161.

112 *Ibid,* p. 161.

113 Regarding the analysis of these points in reference to Transcendence, see: Sonya Sikka, *Forms of Transcendence: Heidegger and Medieval Mystical Theology* (Albany: State University of New York Press, 1997), pp. 208-209.

thanks" (Cavell, 1988, p. 39). Such insight takes the readiness to receive, the readiness to hear the call, in the sense of welcoming it, to be a thanking for what is received, a thanking for what is received as a gift. To the question "what does thanks mean here?" The Heideggerian answer in "*What is Called Thinking?*" might be something like saying: "Perhaps thanks consist in thinking."[114] Thinking as recollection is giving thoughts to being, it is giving thanks for the gift of being. And, in "*What is Called Thinking?*" Heidegger asks whether thinking is a "giving of thanks."[115] On his view, thought is in need of "memory" it is in need of the "gathering of thought." And, "the gathering of thinking back into what must be thought is what we call the memory."[116] In an etymological and linguistic analysis, Heidegger links memory to thanks. On his view, we take the gift of thought with thanks, and the gift of thought is what is most-thought-provoking which is "recalled in thought" and to which we give thanks.[117] Thinking that recalls and gives thanks is thinking that "dwells within memory."[118] All of this implies that thinking that recalls, that thanks, and commemorates, is also thinking that shelters what gives fruit for thinking; i.e. it safe-guards what is most-thought-provoking. Recalling thought, thanking, and memory, all shelter what is most-thought-provoking. They also attest to the oblivion of what is thought provoking within the course of development of Western Logocentric thought that takes thinking to be "an assertion of something about something." The question "what is called thinking?" Opens up to the question of "what calls on us to think?" Heidegger

---

[114] Martin Heidegger, *What is Called Thinking?*, trans. by J. Glenn Gray (New York: Harper & Row, 1968). p. 139.

[115] *Ibid*, p. 139.

[116] *Ibid*, p. 145.

[117] *Ibid*, pp. 145-146.

[118] *Ibid*, p. 147.

would say that "thinking, *qua* thinking, is essentially a call."[119] Within the sphere of memory, thanking, recalling, and re-gathering, thinking is paying heed to the call within itself. Thinking that recalls, calls thinking to think according to its essential nature as thinking. It calls thinking to think about the difference between being and beings, where thinking and being converge. The gift of thinking, is that which gives fruit for thought. And what is the most-thought-provoking, is thinking about being.

IV- The Authenticity of Being and Death

It has been mentioned above that "*Dasein* reaches its wholeness in death,"[120] and that *Dasein*'s death is its "own." In taking its own death "upon itself," *Dasein*'s essential possibility of being is that of "coming-to-an-end."[121] However, the coming-to-an-end of *Dasein* could be an unauthentic ending in the sense of being a "demise" rather than being a "dying" or a "perishing." When *Dasein* dies inauthentically, it is in "demise." Only the (living) objectively present beings come to their end by perishing. The dying of *Dasein* is to be taken to be an authentic dying in the sense of being the mode of being in which "*Dasein* is toward [its own] death."[122] On this reading, "everyday, entangled evasion of death is an unauthentic being toward it."[123] The distinction between *demise*, *perishing*, and *dying*, is meant to be a distinction between death, as a physiological and biological ending, and a coming to an end in the mode of

---

[119] *Ibid*, p. 161.

[120] *Ibid*, p. 221.

[121] For further insights with respect to this point, see: Martin Heidegger, *Being and Time*, trans. by Joan Stambaugh (Albany: State University of New York Press, 1996), pp. 222-227.

[122] *Ibid*, p. 229.

[123] *Ibid*, p. 239. This point will be further discussed in the context of the analysis of being-toward-death and the everydayness of *Dasein*.

Dasein's being-toward-death. This distinction is to be undertaken from the standpoint of distinguishing between biological, ontic, ontological, and existential interpretations of *Dasein*'s being-toward-death.[124] On Heidegger's account, when *Dasein* exists it is already thrown into its *ownmost possibility* of being-toward-death. On this reading, *Dasein*'s "thrownness" into its being-toward-its-death is about *Dasein*'s being-in-the-world.[125] Yet, *Dasein*'s being-toward-death is concealed by the "estranging" and "comforting" of the "they" [*das Man*] and their *everydayness "constant tranquillization about death.*"[126] And, this tranquillization about death is undertaken in terms of the "estranging" and "veiling" of *Dasein*'s being-toward-death. In this regard, Heidegger would say that, "*they do not permit the courage to have Angst about death.*"[127] In its *Angst* about death, *Dasein* faces its ownmost possibility of being-toward-death. The lack of courage to have *Angst* about death implies that there is some sort of an *estrangement* of *Dasein* from facing its ownmost possibility as being-toward-death. The lack of courage to *have Angst* about death turns the constant tranquillization about death into being a constant flight from death. As Heidegger puts it, "as the end of *Dasein*, death is the ownmost nonrelational, certain, and, as such, indefinite and not to be bypassed possibility of *Dasein*."[128] Given this interpretation, how can *Dasein* maintain itself in an "authentic

---

[124] *Ibid*, pp. 229-231. Herein, Heidegger offers a rather detailed account of the existential analysis of death with respect to other interpretations of this phenomenon; whether those of fundamental ontology, or of the biology of life in its consideration of death as a "phenomenon of life."

[125] *Ibid*, pp. 231-233. Herein, Heidegger presents these points in the context of his discussion of the existential and ontological structures of death.

[126] *Ibid*, pp. 234-235. Herein, Heidegger offers an elaborate consideration of the analysis of being-toward-death with the everydayness of *Dasein*.

[127] *Ibid*, p. 235.

[128] *Ibid*, p. 239.

being-toward-death?" How would *Dasein* dis-entangle itself from the everydayness *flight from death*? On Heidegger's account, *Dasein*'s being-toward-death is a mode of *being-toward-a-possibility* which is to be *cultivated* and *understood* and *endured* as such in terms of being a possibility. *Dasein*'s being-toward-death shows a mode of being that is "anticipatory" of the possibility of death. *Dasein* reveals itself to itself as being a "potentiality-of-being" that is in anticipation of a *possibility*. In this sense, the anticipation of the ownmost possibility could be interpreted as being what Heidegger takes to be *Dasein*'s "authentic existence."[129] It is in terms of this authentic existence that the individualization of *Dasein* would supposedly take place. According to Heidegger, one could say that "death individualizes" in terms of being a "nonrelational," "certain," and "indefinite" possibility that is "not-to-be-bypassed." "They" (*das Man*) that do not have the courage to have *Angst* about death, do not permit *Dasein* to come to terms with its own death. The "they" distorts *Angst* by turning it into "fear." Consequently, the distortion of *Angst* does not allow *Dasein* to face its own death as the "possible impossibility of its existence." The non-distorted *Angst about death* is a non-cowardly overcoming of the fear of facing the ownmost potentiality-of-being of *Dasein* as being a being-toward-death. It is in this sense that a non-distorted fearless *Angst* "discloses" the most extreme possibility of *Dasein*'s potentiality-of-being. In this regard, *Angst* is a facing of the absolute threat of death in terms of a cultivation, enduring, and understanding of the extreme possibility of death which is to be found in the anticipation of that possibility. In this respect, Heidegger says that "*anticipation reveals to Dasein its lostness in the they-self, and brings it face to face with the possibility to be itself, primarily unsupported by concern taking care of things, but to be itself in passionate anxious freedom toward death which is free of the illusions of the they, factical, and*

[129] *Ibid*, pp. 241-242.

certain of itself."[130] The selfhood of *Dasein* is about both the "*they-self*" and that which could also be taken to be the "*I my-self.*" The they-self is about a selfhood that is "lost" in the everydayness of the indiscriminate "they." This lostness in the they-self is also a constant evasion from death that distorts *Angst* and turns it into a "cowardly" fear of facing death. The lostness in the they-self is some sort of a restraining prevention from dying authentically. Accordingly, the lostness in the they-self does not allow *Dasein* to find "itself" in its authentic being. Given its lostness in the "they," *Dasein* has then to find itself. In terms of the possibility of its potentiality-of-being, *Dasein* is already a "potentiality-toward-being-its-self." And, this is the "voice of conscience."[131]

V- Temporality and Death

In his book "*The Concept of Time*," Heidegger says that, "the question of what time is has pointed our inquiry in the direction of *Dasein*."[132] He then adds in the same context that *Dasein* is that entity which is characterized as being-in-the-world, and as being-with-others. *Dasein* is the entity which determines itself as "I am," which in its specificity as "I am," is constitutive of *Dasein*.[133] Heidegger then adds that *Dasein*'s *ownmost possibility of being* is that which constitutes its authenticicty; given that death as indeterminate certainty is the most extreme possibility of *Dasein* as being at an end. *Dasein*'s running ahead to its futural past is its ownmost possibility of being that stands before *Dasein* in certainty and utter indeterminacy. Under such state of affairs, *Dasein* is "not in time," rather *Dasein* "is time itself," given that the future is conceived as being the

---

130 *Ibid*, p. 245.

131 *Ibid*, p. 248.

132 Martin Heidegger, *The Concept of Time*, trans. by William McNeill (Oxford: Blackwell, 1996), p. 6E.

133 *Ibid*, pp. 6E-8E.

fundamental phenomenon of time.[134] Based on this view, one would say that the world of everydayness happens in the present that reflects the concern with the moment and the now. Therefore, in everydayness, *Dasein* is in time rather than being time. However *Dasein* is conceived as being [authentically] futural in running ahead to the certain yet indeterminate past.[135] On this account Heidegger says that "*Dasein* is time, and time is temporal." He then elaborates his account by saying: "*Dasein* is not time but temporality."[136] On Heidegger's view, thrownness is never a completed terminal act. It is rather a non-finished act that one is always open to. *Dasein* is thus not a "subject" or a "self" in everydayness. *Dasein* in thrownness is rather immersed in the everyday of the neuter "*das Man*," the They-self. And, in such state of affairs, *Dasein* is in a flight from its self-finitude. In experiencing the dread of the "nothing," *Dasein* is brought before being in the sense of being summoned to halt its immersion in an everydayness that is revealed as being a flight from its own self. *Dasein* is called into facing its own self rather than fleeing it by way of everyday preoccupations. The "nothing" is that which is unlike all beings, it is that which is ontologically different and Other. The "nothing" is *no determinate being*, and in being the negation of being, the "nothing" points to the ontological difference between being and beings. Anxiety, that arises in the experiencing of the "nothing," is an experiencing of the call of being as a "wonder of all wonders." What is experienced is that there is being rather than nothing. The wonder of wonders is that: "being is." Under such circumstances *Dasein* experiences the antique wonder that asks "why is there being rather than nothing?" The experiencing of the nothing reveals *Dasein*'s being as a mode of being-toward-death. Therefore, *Dasein*'s ownmost possibility of being is revealed as being a "possi-

134 *Ibid*, pp. 10E-12E, 14E.

135 *Ibid*, pp. 16E-17E, 20E.

136 *Ibid*, p. 20E.

bility of impossibility."[137] The existential movement of *Dasein* is revealed as being a movement between birth and death. And *Dasein*'s mode of being-in-between [birth and death], is what constitutes an authentic self-unfolding of *Dasein*'s existential mode of being-in-the-world. Wholeness implies that *Dasein* [necessarily] dies. The wholeness of *Dasein* implies that *Dasein* is a finite temporal being whose temporality (as the primordial ontological time) unifies the *ekstases* of future, past, and present. *Dasein* is temporal, since *Dasein*'s ownmost possibility is death. And, temporality does ground *Dasein*'s being-in-the-world. *Dasein*'s existentiality is futural and it describes the realm of *Dasein*'s possibilities. *Dasein*'s facticity as what is past describes *Dasein*'s actuality; and fall-ness is the present mode of selfhood. Each *ekstasis* of temporality, as existentiality, facticity, or fallness, grounds *Dasein*'s existential constitution as a whole finite being. On this account, possibilities imply that *Dasein* will have a future, while thrownness recollects *Dasein*'s past, and fallness reflects *Dasein*'s present. If possibilities are opened up by virtue of *Dasein*'s future, then death is the ownmost possibility of what the future will always hold. Therefore, the future brings "angst," since it reveals *Dasein* as being-towards-death. Yet, to have possibilities is to be alive while still revealing death as being the owmost possibility. On this account the self's personal identity is revealed as a wholeness that existentially moves between birth and death. If Hegel also thought of being and nothingness as being co-determined by one another, Heidegger pushes this thought to

---

[137] As Emmanuel Levinas says: "*La mort chez Heidegger n'est pas, comme le dit M. Wahl, 'l'impossibilité de la possibilité', mais 'la possibilité de l'impossibilité'. Cette distinction, d'apparence byzantine, a une importance fondamentale.*" ("Death according to Heidegger is not, like Wahl says, 'the impossibility of possibility', rather 'the possibility of impossibility.' This distinction, of Byzantine appearance, has a fundamental importance"). See: Emmanuel Levinas, *Le temps et l'autre* (Paris: Quadrige/Presses Universitaires de France, 1979), no. 5, p. 92.

broader realms whereby the realm of light is always pervaded by the realm of darkness, and where that which is revealed is pervaded by mystery. According to Emmanuel Levinas, "death [*la mort*] announces an event in which the subject is no more a master, an event with respect to which the subject is no more a subject."[138] On Levinas' interpretation of Heidegger's views, death is that which makes all other possibilities possible. Death is an event of liberty that acts as the limit of idealism.[139] This interpretation is similar to what one encounters in relation to the mystic death [of Absal] as depicted in Avicenna's Recital of Salmān and Absal. There Avicenna shows that the gnostic's death may constitute a liberating rupture (We will later discuss this account in relation to the authenticity of being as it figures in Avicenna's Visionary Recitals). The "death," that Levinas is addressing in Heidegger's thought, is "never a present"(*la mort n'est jamais un présent*).[140] Death as the limit of idealism marks the end of the mastery, "virility," and "heroism" of the subject. Death delivers a blow to the Cartesian account of subjectivity by delimiting the spheres of subject-ism. Being never a present, death is what determines the "future" in so far that this future is never a present. Levinas gets so close to an Avicennian mystic mood when he says that defeating death is not the problem of an eternal life, rather defeating death is "undertaking with the alterity of the event [i.e. death] a relation that is still personal."[141] Death as such is a relation with Otherness. It is an openness to a relation with what is mysteriously other. This means that the soul ought to retain a personal relation with the alterity of death. This mysteriously radical otherness of death defines the future rather than being defined by the future. And the future of

---

[138] *Ibid*, p. 57.

[139] *Ibid*, pp. 57-58.

[140] *Ibid*, p. 59.

[141] *Ibid*, p. 73.

death is characterized by utter otherness.[142] With an Avicennian mystic mood, the soul (*al-nafs*) is also in a primordial relation with the otherness towards which it is oriented. Death as the utter otherness constitutes a liberating rupture-event that grounds all other possibilities. The soul is destined to journey, and it is destined to retain a personal relation with Otherness. This orientation, this journey, and this mystic conception of death, all constitute icons, symbols, or signs that will be addressed in the consideration of the authenticity of being in Avicenna's Visionary Recitals. The face-to face encounter with Otherness is what the longing soul tends to in its serious orientation and journey. And death is the in-liberating event on the mystic path of the gnostic seekers of "union" *(itiḥād, itiṣāl, ḥūlūl).*

Heidegger's conception of *Ereignis* itself points to the conception of an ontology whose fundamental horizon is based on temporality and on processes and events. Heidegger gives the name *Ereignis* to the "belonging together" or "being for one another" of the human being and being. *Ereignis* is not an "event as such" rather it is used to designate a "happening of lighting" as "the happening of the disclosing of beings according to their proper manifestation." *Ereignis* would then be thought of as being the language of "the unfolding of being in language." In this sense *Ereignis* implies that the "word" is "granted."[143] *Ereignis* is an "appropriating-event" that grants the essence and *Wesung* of what is. *Ereignis* is the "event of appropriation" that ceaselessly grants the *essencing* or *presencing* of what is. Standing within *Ereignis*, is standing within the truth of how being presences, it is standing in the openness of the open. Standing in *Ereignis*, is standing in the truth of the "turning" where the centrality of the subject gives way to the centrality of being. *Er-*

---

142 *Ibid*, pp. 73-74.

143 Françoise Dastur, "Language and *Ereignis*," in *Reading Heidegger, Commemorations*, ed. by John Sallis (Bloomington & Indianapolis: Indiana University Press, 1993), pp. 364-365.

eignis is the site where truth is granted by being and not by a "constitutive" transcendental subject/ego that acts as the center of everything. *Dasein* is dependent on the gift of *Ereignis* that is beyond its own control.[144] After all, like lighting is coupled with mystery and darkness, so is *Ereignis* as "ap-propriative event" coupled with *Enteignis* as "ex-propriative event." However, the granting, the hearing, and the visionary revelation, all do not exact consent rather they require readiness and openness to the call. As Sonya Sikka cites from Heidegger, the shift from the centrality of the constitutive subject to that of being is also a shift from the subject to *Dasein* as a "perspective" of being itself, where *Dasein* is "the clearing of the unconcealment of being" as a way of "being-in-the-truth."[145] In this, *Dasein* is in a state of devotion and dedication to "be-in-the-truth" for the sake of the whole of being which reflects *Dasein* as "care" (*Sorge*). Resoluteness among possibilities would also be understood in terms of being a dedication to being, a way of being for-the-sake-of-being, the whole of being, as it is implied in *Dasein* as care. Being as not being the beingness of beings is unlike beings. Being is the ultimate other. Being is thus mis-represented and mis-understood in being taken to be the beingness of what is. The essence of being is concealed due to the lighting of beings, which hints to the self-withdrawing character of being. And Heidegger's consideration of "enframing" (*Ge-stell*) in the "*Question Concerning Technology*," cautions from the danger that "enframing" *(Ge-stell*) places on the essence of human beings by exposing humanity to the denial of other modes of revealing. In this sense, "enframing" (*Ge-stell*) posits a denial of truth (ἀλήθεια [*alētheia*], *veritas*), where modernity is revealed as being

---

[144] For a more elaborate account of the interpretation of Heidegger's views on *Ereignis* in his *Contributions to Philosophy* and in the *Basic Concepts*, see: Sonya Sikka, *Forms of Transcendence: Heidegger and Medieval Mystical Theology* (Albany: State University of New York Press, 1997), pp. 246-247.

[145] *Ibid*, p. 251.

the culmination of the history of the oblivion of being and of the crisis of nihilism.

VI- The Solitude of *Dasein*

It is claimed that Heidegger's *Dasein*, which is the being that concerns itself with the meaning of being, is depicted in *Being and Time* as being the "impersonal" and "solitary" being. In "*Le temps et l'autre,*" Levinas observes that: "*Toutes les analyses de Sein und Zeit se poursuivent soit pour l'impersonalité de la vie* quotidienne, *soit pour le Dasein esseulé*."[146] On Levinas' view, the "solitude" of *Dasein* burdens the self by its very own self. In this sense, solitude absorbs what is "other."[147] Even *Dasein*'s reciprocal relation to the other does not amount to being a "face-to-face" encounter with the other.[148] On Levinas' account, *Dasein*'s relation *with* the other is around something, around some sort of a "common term," primarily around a "truth." Hence, *Dasein*'s relation to the other is not an original personal "face-to-face" relation.[149] Levinas would then assert that the relation with the other as being-with-one-another (*Miteinandersein*) leads to some sort of a disappearance of the other (*la disparition de l'autre*).[150] In this regard, Levinas would like to show that, unlike what appears in Heidegger's view, the relation of the *self* to the *other* would not rise from the *Mit* of *Miteinandersein* (being-reciprocally-with-one-another). Levinas holds that the original relation of the self with the other is a personal "face-to-face" relation

---

146 Emmanuel Levinas, *Le temps et l'autre* (Paris: Quadrige/Presses Universitaires de France, 1979), p. 18. Holding that the analysis of *Being and Time* has been undertaken in terms of addressing the impersonality of everyday life or through an account of a *Dasein* that has been turned lonely.

147 *Ibid*, p. 13.

148 *Ibid*, pp. 18-19.

149 *Ibid*, pp. 18-19.

150 *Ibid*, p. 19.

that objects to the loneliness in *Dasein's* solitude and to the lack of *Dasein*'s personal existential character. On Levinas' view, the *Mit* of being-with does not describe the relation *with* the other.[151] In this context, it might be insightful, yet disruptive, to bring Jacques Derrida's voice to Levinas' picture. In his description of the manner *Dasein* relates to the other as "*friend*" [*ami(e)*], not in the mode of Levinas' face-to-face, Derrida would say that for Heidegger's *Dasein*: "The friend does not speak, but is also invisible. The friend does not appear [*parait*, *apparait*] any more than it comes to speak or to a decision [*il ne prononce, ou ne se prononce*]. The friend has no face, no figure [*figure*]. No sex. No name. The friend is not a man, nor a woman; it is not I, nor a "self," not a subject, nor a person."[152] One could read both Levinas' and Derrida's views as representing objections to the lonely solitude and impersonality that are somehow forced on *Dasein* in its everydayness and in its relation with the other. Levinas' translation of *being* and *beings* (*Sein, Seiendes*) takes them to be respectively "*exister*" and "*existant*" (existing and existent) instead of taking them to be "*être*" and "*étant*."[153] For Levinas, the *exister* is always seized by the *existant*; thus *being* is al-

---

151 *Ibid*, pp. 18-19. Herein, Levinas writes: "*Enfin l'autre, chez Heidegger, apparaît dans la situation essentielle du Miteinandersein--être réciproquement l'un avec l'autre ... La préposition 'mit' (avec) décrit içi la relation. C'est, ainsi, une association de côte a côte, autour de quelque chose, autour d'un terme, commun, et, plus précisément pour Heidegger, autour de la vérité. Ce n'est pas la relation du face-a-face. Chacun y apporte tout, sauf le fait privé de son existence. Nous ésperons montrer, pour notre part, que ce n'est pas la préposition 'mit' qui doit décrire la relation originelle avec l'autre.*"

152 Jacques Derrida, "Philopolemology: Heidegger's Ear (*Geshlecht IV*)," in "*Reading Heidegger*," *Commemorations*, ed. by John Sallis (Bloomington and Indianapolis: Indiana University Press, 1993), p. 165.

153 Emmanuel Levinas, *Le temps et l'autre* (Paris: Quadrige/Presses Universitaires de France, 1979), p. 24.

ways taken hold of by *beings*. According to Levinas, this state of affairs is attested in Heidegger's notion of *Dasein*'s thrownness (*Geworfenheit*) in existence.[154] Given the seizing of the *exister* by the *existant*, Levinas goes on saying that the *exister* does not exist, and that it is the *existant* that exists.[155] On this account, one might say that unlike Heidegger, who takes being/existing (Levinas' *exister*) to be the place of disclosure, Levinas inverses Heidegger's position by taking the existent (*existant*) to be the place of disclosure. Levinas' notion of "*il y a*" (there is) points towards some sort of absence. This "*il y a*" is anonymous since it does not have an object and it still points to some sort of being or existing that is other. As for the *exister* (existing), it is affirmed in terms of imposing itself as being that which cannot be refuted.[156] The "*il y a,*" as the anonymous and impersonal existence, is an *exister* without *existant*, i.e. existing without existent.[157] On this reading, the "*il y a*" pervades the *exister*; *it* thus allows for some sort of a dissolution of its distinction from the *existant.*[158] The "*il y a*" implies necessary existence (what may be called in Avicenna's parlance: *wūjūb al-wūjūd*, i.e. the necessity of existing). And this is expressed in terms of saying: *hunālika*, i.e. there is, *il y a*. The "*il y a*" supposedly dissolves the *exister/existant* dis-

---

154 *Ibid*, pp. 24-25.

155 *Ibid*, p. 25. Herein, Levinas says: "*Je dirais aussi volontiers que l'exister n'existe pas. C'est l'existant qui existe.*"

156 *Ibid*, pp. 26-27. Herein, Levinas elucidates some aspects of the link between the "*il y a*" and the "*exister.*"

157 *Ibid*, p. 28.

158 This might imply that there is some sort of dissolution of the subject/object distinction. In this regard one might also claim that in "*The Question Concerning Technology*," Heidegger shows a manner by which the subject/object distinction gets dissolved in the modes by which subjects and objects are turned in "Enframing" (*Ge-stell*), as the name for the essence of technology, into "standing-reserve" (*Bestand*).

tinction, and *Angst*, if not distorted, makes *Dasein* anticipate its own elimination. It is about taking its position *here* (Levinas' *ici*) that *consciousness* comes to itself rather than by taking an anticipatory position in a futural *there* (Heidegger's *da*) that consciousness comes to itself. In this respect, Levinas says,"*La mort chez Heidegger n'est pas, comme le dit M. Wahl, "l'impossibilité de la possibilité", mais "la possibilité de l'impossibilité*."[159] According to Levinas, death "announces" an event with respect to which the "subject is no more subject."[160] On Levinas' account, the "passive" subject reaches the limits of "possibility" with death. And, in its "mystery," death renders impossible any assumption of possibilities. This position does not take death as being that which is "assumed" and anticipated, rather a "heroic" subject always searches for a "last chance" to survive. Yet, it is the case that "death *comes*," and "it does indeed come" (*la mort vient, elle vient*).[161] Levinas makes use of his concept of time in order to show that *Dasein*'s "anticipation of its futural death" is a "present" that is projected into the future rather than being an "authentic future."[162] Levinas wants to reveal the "otherness" of the future. He wants to show that a relation with this future is not a relation with one's own self. Levinas wants to account for otherness which he takes as not being the case with Heidegger's conception of *Dasein*'s individualization that takes place in terms of facing death. Levinas wants to disclose the relation with the future as

---

159 Emmanuel Levinas, *Le temps et l'autre* (Paris: Quadrige/Presses Universitaires de France, 1979), p. 92. Levinas holds that death according to Heidegger is not like what Wahl says: the impossibility of possibility, rather death is the possibility of impossibility.

160 *Ibid*, p. 57. Herein, Levinas openly says: "*La mort annonce un événement dont le sujet n'est pas le maître, un événement par rapport auquel le sujet n'est plus sujet.*"

161 *Ibid*, pp. 58-61.

162 *Ibid*, p. 64.

being a relation with the other (*autrui, et altérité*). This relation with the future and death, is a relation that is accomplished in a flesh and blood personal "face-to-face" intersubjective relation with another person (*autrui*). It is a relation without "mediation" that supposedly breaks the solitude of "*un Dasein esseulé*."[163]

[163] *Ibid*, pp. 68-69, p. 89.

CHAPTER 3
HEIDEGGER'S THEORY OF MODERNITY

I- The *Vorhandenheit*

Classical ontology mediates the question of being through logical investigations. The encounter with being thus passes through the light shed on it by the λόγος (*logos*). And, pure perception and being are revealed as being the same νοεῖν (*noein*) and εἶναι (*einai*). Heidegger held that, "the Greeks had an appropriate term for 'things': *pragmata*, that is, that with which one has to do in taking care of things in association (*praxis*)."[164] In this interpretation, things are taken to be useful. This also entails that the determination of beings as useful things implies that these things are available and ready to be manipulated. In other terms, the πραγματα (*pragamata*) are present at hand (*Vorhandene*), and they are determined in terms of their essential μορφή (*morphè*) and εἶδος (*eidos*). *Morphè* reflects the figure of something and gives it its *eidos* as aspect. And both are the determinations of a being. The *morphè* acts as a determined configuration or production model, while the *eidos* acts as the prototype of the product. This eventually inscribes Greek ontology within the horizon of production that requires the *morphè* and *eidos* of what is to be produced.[165] With Kant, it might be argued that ontology is not inscribed in the horizon of production, and that being is not identical with production, rather that being is identical with per-

---

164 Martin Heidegger, *Being and Time*, trans. by Joan Stambaugh (Albany: State University of New York Press, 1996), p. 64.

165 Robert Brisart, *La Phénoménologie de Marbourg, ou la résurgence de la métaphysique chez Heidegger à l'époque de Sein und Zeit* (Paris: Grasset, 1993), pp. 91-93.

ception. Yet, this does not entail that being is irreducible. It is perhaps the case that with Kant we are not anymore within the realm of the metaphysics of production. However, if perception is a trait of pure and simple apprehension, then this would entail that the determination of beings is taken from the standpoint of apprehension rather than from the standpoint of being. The question of being is then addressed from the standpoint of an apprehending subject. Such state of affairs describes some sort of relation between a producer and its product. In a subject-based approach to the question of being one might still be inscribed within the ontological horizon of production. This account implies that beings are ready at hand (*Zuhandene*). And the significance of the Greek *ousia* inscribes ontology within the horizon of productivity. On this account, being is taken to be that which is available and present at hand. The originary sense of *ousia* underlies the *essentia* conception of the quiddity and essence of things. Beings that are inscribed within the ontological horizon of productivity are finite and handy beings. The basis of *ousia, esse, existere*, is what Heidegger calls *Vorhandenheit* (presence at hand).[166] On this reading, *Vorhandenheit* and *ousia* both imply the *Anwesen* (the present) which characterizes the circumspective and practical everyday praxis of *Dasein*. *Ousia*, *Wirklichkeit*, and *Vorhandenheit* all mark what may be called in Heideggerian terms: "the metaphysics of presence." Presence at hand and presence to the eye, both imply that what is present as such is also that which is part of the everydayness of *Dasein* and its *Umsicht* (circumspection) which reflects the inauthentic mode of being of *Dasein*. The being that supposedly shelters the meaning of being is the being whose understanding of its own existence is mediated through the oblivion of being. This is the state of affairs of an inauthentic mode of being in the world. In the natural attitude of the everyday circumspective concerns, the being that shelters the meaning of being ontologically

166 *Ibid*, pp. 96-97.

adheres to the present reality. And, in its inauthentic and alienated mode of being in the world, *Dasein* confuses its being with the being of beings it encounters in reality. Inhabiting the natural world in the form of alliance with beings is a path that leads to the forgetfulness of the essence of dwelling. Faced with these Heideggerian views, one wonders whether Heidegger deflates and depreciates the value of the *Lebenswelt* (Life-world) in his critique of metaphysics. And, this is perhaps the case given that Heidegger's disenchantment with the scientific reduction of reality into an objective factuality is turned into a nostalgic critique.

II- Metaphysics and Science

On Heidegger's view, metaphysics pervades most of the spheres of human existence, and this broad sense of metaphysics is the one that is intended in his call for an "overcoming of metaphysics." This account of metaphysics is presupposed in Heidegger's consideration of the relationship between metaphysics and the essence of modern technology. It is due to metaphysics that the question of the meaning of being has been occluded and eventually has fallen into oblivion. In the age of nihilism, in the age of the homelessness of humanity, in the age where nature is objectified, metaphysics dominates as the essence of technology. And, modern technology is the terminal phase of metaphysics that brings about a new beginning (that of a "Turn"). Faced with the peril of all perils, deliverance comes as the rising of the saving power from the same place where the danger arises. Wherein, the promise to overcome nihilism and metaphysics (as an essencing of technology) emerges. Heidegger pictures the essence of technology as being an uttermost danger that arises due to an uncreative gathering of all beings as standing reserve (*Bestand*). This uncreative gathering is that of the *Ge-stell* (Enframing). However, the human being that is gathered as standing reserve, or stock, is also revealed as being a partner in revealing and unconcealing, and herein lies the responsibility of bringing about deliverance through the sheltering of unconcealment that guards the essence of truth. This state of affairs reveals the depth of the relationship that ties the essence of a human being to the essence of truth and of being. Yet, this relationship has withdrawn from thought as it might be implied by Heidegger's claims about the oblivion of being. Being a partner in un-concealing and in revealing, is also being a partner in preserving revealing and attending to truth and to the mystery that pervades unconcealment. This also entails that unconcealment, that lets beings be, is pervaded by the mystery of a self-withdrawing revealing, as a self-concealing revealing.

Metaphysical presuppositions underlie science and its objectifying thematization of being. And metaphysics misconstrues being as being the beingness of beings. This state of affairs arises as a consequence of being directed toward mundane beings which are taken to be present-at-hand and therefore to be real. On this account, reality is construed in terms of the *Vorhandenheit* that overshadows other ontological possibilities of attending to the question of being. Intentionality implies that *Dasein*'s being-in-the-world is a mode of being-towards-the world, this also means that *Dasein* is oriented towards the world. Projection and resoluteness between possibilities takes place in being-towards-the-world, while thrownness and absorption in everyday concern (*Sorge*) represents a mode of being-in-the-world as being-alongside-the-world. And, being-alongside-the-world is expressed in terms of practical and non-theoretical interests in the world. The theoretical inclination emerges with the circumspective practical concern. In praxis and everyday concern things are taken as being ready-to-hand (*Zuhandene*). Yet, circumspection, in its "if-then" deliberations, allows for a way of looking at things as being present-at-hand (*Vorhandene*). In this sense, circumspection turns beings into the subject matter of theoretical investigations.[167] What

[167] Regarding the elaboration of this point and the shift from praxis to theoretical investigations, refer to: Martin Heidegger, *Being and Time*, trans. by Joan Stambaugh (Albany: State University of New York Press, 1996), pp. 327-331; Joseph J. Kockelmans, "Heidegger on the Essential Difference and Necessary

this reflects is that the theoretical way of looking at the world has been linked to the practical way of being absorbed in the world. The theoretical investigations do consist of an ontological inclination towards the world that reflects a new way of being-in-the-world while not being engaged in its practical everyday concern. The theoretical approach to the world delimits the realm of the objective present-at-hand entities. This theoretical understanding of beings is an objectifying thematization of beings that presupposes *Dasein*'s mode of being-in-the-world. And thematizing frees beings from the confines of practical use and throws on them a new light by virtue of which they become objects. Theoretical investigations do not approach things through their "equipmentality." Theoretical investigations focus on the observation of an objectified world. In this regard, the stress on intentionality reflects an attempt to overcome the theoretical construing of reality as being that which is merely objective. In drawing the contrast between philosophy and science, Kockelmans holds that unlike science, philosophy does not disregard intentionality and seeks to describe the "modalities of encounter and coexistence in their *noematic* and *noetic* aspects."[168] In thematization, formalization, and quantification, meaning is reduced to what is either objectively "countable" or "measurable."[169] The intentional orientation towards beings does inscribe the theoretical thematization within the horizon of the intentionality of meaning. This entails that the scientific and theoretical thematization rests on certain metaphysical presuppositions. The essence of science, as that which reflects what sci-

---

Connection between Philosophy and Science," in *Phenomenology and the Natural Sciences*, ed. by Theodore J. Kisiel & Joseph J. Kockelmans (Evanston: Northwestern University Press, 1970), pp. 153-155.

[168] Joseph J. Kockelmans, "Heidegger on the Essential Difference and Necessary Connection between Philosophy and Science," in *Phenomenology and the Natural Sciences*, ed. by Theodore J. Kisiel & Joseph J. Kockelmans (Evanston: Northwestern University Press, 1970), p. 160.

[169] *Ibid*, pp. 160-162.

ence rests on, is intertwined with metaphysics and the essence of technology. This state of affairs is revealed to us as such from the standpoint of our own historical epoch that is that of modernity. According to Heidegger, the essence of modern science belongs to the essence of modern technology that is not anything human nor is it anything technological.[170] If the sciences are not thinking, then what calls for thinking is what is unthought by the sciences.[171] Yet, thinking is not methodological nor is it situated in subjectivity in the sense that one encounters in Hegel's Science of Logic or in Husserl's focus on "the principle of all principles." On Kisiel's interpretation of Heidegger's account of thinking, thinking does not aim at having "ultimate evidence" nor does it reveal "absolute knowledge" as being situated in the "self-knowing subject." Thinking is a letting-be that is more like a revelation rather than being a "methodical" subjective manipulation. Thinking is "hermeneutical" while science is "mathematical."[172] The affinity between science and production is reflected in the scientific interest in what is actual and real, given that the actual is taken to be that which is complete and produced. What is "actual" is an object that loses its status as object (*Gegenstand*) due to the *Ge-stell* (enframing) of modernity that posits that object as some sort of standing-reserve or stock (*Bestand*). Under the *Ge-stell* of modern technology, what is true is merely what is correct, and beings are reduced into a stock or standing-reserve. This state of affairs shows that the modes of revealing of modern science and technology overshadow other possibilities of revealing. This is seen by Heidegger as being a threat to the essence of revealing and truth. What calls for

---

170 Martin Heidegger, *What is Called Thinking?*, trans. by J. Glenn Gray (New York: Harper & Row, 1968), p. 22.

171 *Ibid*, p. 33.

172 Theodore J. Kisiel, "Science, Phenomenology, and the Thinking of Being," in *Phenomenology and the Natural Sciences*, ed. by Theodore J. Kisiel & Joseph J. Kockelmans (Evanston: Northwestern University Press, 1970), pp. 174-176.

thinking is that which also calls for thinking about the possibilities of revealing that are excluded by the dominant scientific revealing as research (*Forschung*) which holds sway in the *Ge-stell* of modernity.

III- Technology and Enframing

In his essay "The Question Concerning Technology,"[173] Heidegger's main concern is to find a manner by which he could have access to the essence of technology. In this regard, he would claim that the essence of technology is "nothing technological." Yet, this essence is concealed in technology and is even prior to the scientific revolution. On this reading, Heidegger would take technology to be a pervading encompassing of all beings under a radical form of availability and ordering manipulation that he calls *Ge-stell* or "enframing." This state of affairs reveals the dominance of modernity in terms of its ways of thinking and imagination that are not separable from technological and scientific successes. Under such circumstances, thinking and imagination would not be independent from technology either by affirming or by refuting what it offers. In this regard, the modern age has dominant, technologically bound, totalizing ways of thinking, imagining, and questioning that are legitimated by scientific and technological successes. In this sense, the question concerning the essence of technology becomes a question concerning modernity. It is under the overarching modern enclosure of "enframing," that Heidegger takes beings and humans to be reduced into a "standing reserve" that serves an expanding technology that appropriates, manipulates, and turns all what it encloses into available

---

[173] Martin Heidegger, "The Question Concerning Technology," in *Basic Writings*, ed. by David Farrell Krell (New York: Harper & Row, 1977), pp. 287-317. David Farrell Krell also indicates that this essay appeared in: Martin Heidegger, *The Question Concerning Technology and Other Essays*, trans. by William Lovitt (New York: Harper & Row, 1977). The German text appears in: Martin Heidegger, *Vortage und Aufsatze* (Pfullingen: Gunter Neske Verlag, 1954), pp. 13-44; Martin Heiddeger, *Die Technik und die Kehre* (Pfullingen: Gunter Neske Verlag, 1962), pp. 5-36.

"stockpiles" that meet its purposes. This state of affairs shows technology, in its essence and enframing, as being a reductive mode of the revealing of truth. Technology and enframing reflect a mode of revealing that is that of "presencing beings in unconcealment." Technology is thus tied to the "essence of truth," while propagating a correctness conception of truth. Even if the essence of technology is nothing technological, this does not entail that a correctness conception of truth could sufficiently gain dominance due to the successes of technological and scientific inventions. And, according to Heidegger, herein lies the threat of technology and "enframing." Yet, in response to this threat, and on Heidegger's account, the same danger acts as some sort of a ground from which salvation would possibly rise. It is through its relation to the essence of truth, that technology would be related to a mode of revealing beings that is tied to art. On Heidegger's account, the work of art is a mode of revealing by virtue of which the safeguarding of truth becomes possible. This would be the case given that salvation concerns itself with the question of technology, the question of dwelling, and primarily with the sheltering of the meaning of being. Questioning about technology would initiate a "free relationship" to it that opens our human existence to its essence. On Heidegger's view, to take technology to be "neutral" is to be "utterly blind" to its "essence." According to him, "we ask the question concerning technology when we ask what it is."[174] Based on this account, Heidegger would then proceed by enumerating what in a first approach we might take technology to be. He would say that some take technology to be a "human activity;" while others either take it to be a "means to an end," or to be an *"instrumentum."* And such definitions of technology are "instrumental and anthropological." In a first approach to the definition of technology, Heidegger would not object to the instrumental "means to an end" construal of technology. On his account, the "means to an end" construal presupposes some sort of a "will to mastery" that "be-

[174] *Ibid*, p. 288.

comes all the more urgent the more technology threatens to slip from human control."[175] The "means to an end" picture might be "uncannily correct." Yet, this does not mean that what is correct is also what is true. On Heidegger's view, for something to be correct, it has to "uncover the thing in question in its essence." The correct would not become true unless the uncovering "of the thing in question in its essence" has already taken place. Even if a correctness conception of truth is based on instrumental accounts, it still does not sufficiently answer the question concerning the essence of technology and its "whatness." On Heidegger's view, "only the true brings us into a free relationship with that which concerns us from its essence." On this account, the instrumental construal of technology does not yet show us the essence of technology. In this regard, Heidegger would investigate instrumentality in such a manner as to seek the true by way of the correct.[176] If the instrumental construal of technology is based on a "means to an end" picture, then one has to investigate this picture in terms of causal links. In this respect, Heidegger enumerates and comments on various types of causes while asking whether causality itself is "veiled" with respect to the question of "whatness."[177] According to Heidegger, the four Aristotelian types of causes (*causa materialis, causa formalis, causa finalis, causa efficiens*) are ways by which something is "being responsible for something else."[178] These causal ways that come into "play of production" are "different" while still "belonging to one another" in terms of their common characteristic, that is that of "bringing something into appearance" by letting it "come forth into presencing."[179] Heidegger would say that, these four ways are "unifiedly governed by

---

[175] *Ibid*, p. 289.

[176] *Ibid*, p. 289.

[177] *Ibid*, pp. 289-90.

[178] *Ibid*, p. 290.

[179] *Ibid*, p. 291.

a bringing that brings what presences into appearance."[180] Based on Plato's account, of that which "passes beyond the non-present and goes forward into presencing," Heidegger would examine the notion of "bringing-forth" in terms of its ποίησις (*poiēsis*) and φύσις (*physis*) senses. In his usual etymological tracking of the Greeks, Heidegger takes *physis* to be a way of bringing-forth in terms of a "bursting of a blossom into bloom, in itself;" while for him, *poiēsis* is a bringing-forth "not in itself, but in another."[181] This bringing-forth, in its *physis* or *poiēsis* sense, "brings out of concealment into unconcealment," a state of affairs that passes insofar as "something concealed comes into unconcealment." And, all of this "moves" within what Heidegger would call "revealing" as "*alētheia*," "*veritas*," and "truth."[182] By his ways of questioning, Heidegger examines the notion of "revealing" which, on his terms, grounds every bringing-forth that gathers the modes of causality along with the instrumental characteristic of technology. On this account, technology would be "a way of revealing."[183] However, technology as a way of revealing, brings forth truth as correctness. Truth itself is correctness when it is taken in the sense of its technological unlocking and unconcealment. The correctness conception of truth is a presencing of a certain kind of truth by way of its technological and scientific construal. Truth as correctness describes what is brought forth and revealed by technology. Yet, this correctness sense of truth does not exhaust all the senses of what truth is. Again, it is the case that questioning builds the way of thinking, and leads through language. In this regard, Heidegger examines the Greek roots of technology as

---

180 *Ibid*, p. 292.

181 *Ibid*, p. 293.

182 *Ibid*, pp. 293-94

183 *Ibid*, p. 294.

"*technikon*" that belongs to "*technē*" which, in its turn, belongs to "*poiēsis*."[184]

On Heidegger's reading, τέχνη (*technē*) is a "bringing-forth" where "*alētheia*" (truth) happens.[185] On this reading, technology, from its roots as *technē*, is a mode of revealing that "does not unfold into a bringing-forth in the sense of *poiēsis*." Technology is rather a "setting-in-order" of the energy of nature "in the sense of challenging it."[186] According to him, "the revealing that rules throughout modern technology has the character of a setting-upon, in the sense of challenging-forth."[187] This state of affairs takes place in terms of "unlocking, transforming, storing, distributing, and switching about" the energies of nature. And these are "ways of revealing" that order beings in terms of taking them to be a "standing-reserve" (*Bestand*).[188] According to Heidegger, this "standing-reserve" is the way in which "everything presences" in terms of a "revealing that challenges." And, "whatever stands by in the sense of standing-reserve no longer stands over against us as object." On Heidegger's view, human beings accomplish this "challenging setting-upon" by virtue of which the real becomes "objectless." However, by doing so, humans are no less "challenged and ordered to do this."[189] The technological unconcealment challenges nature and orders it about in terms of revealing it as a standing-reserve that awaits presencing. Given that humans are more originally challenged than the energies of nature, they are not "transformed into mere standing-reserve."[190] Hu-

---

[184] *Ibid*, p. 294.

[185] *Ibid*, pp. 294-95.

[186] *Ibid*, p. 296.

[187] *Ibid*, p. 297.

[188] *Ibid*, p. 298.

[189] *Ibid*, p. 299

[190] *Ibid*, pp. 299-300.

mans take part of the ordering "as a way of revealing" without taking unconcealment to be their mere human "handiwork." On this account, humans respond to the call of revealing that challenges them to approach the objects of nature as "objects of research" until these objects "disappear into the objectlessness of standing-reserve."[191] In this sense, modern technology is revealed as being "no mere human doing." And that the challenging, that sets humans into "ordering" the real as standing-reserve, gathers humans in such a way as "to order the self-revealing as standing-reserve." Heidegger would call this challenging claim "enframing" (*Ge-stell*) which is also a "name for the essence of modern technology."[192] Under such state of affairs, humans do not have control over unconcealment, rather they are ordered about to challenge nature while themselves being turned into a technological standing-reserve of human resources and arsenals.

According to Heidegger, "enframing" is a gathering of the setting-upon that challenges humans to "reveal the real as standing-reserve." It is a way of revealing that pervades the essence of technology without itself being technological.[193] However, *Ge-stell* has also a sense of producing and bringing-forth, which relates it by essence to *poiēsis* as both being "ways of revealing, of *alētheia*."[194] *Ge-stell* (Enframing), thematizes nature in terms of a regulated and orderable system of information that gets reported through forms of causality.[195] Enframing is not technological, it is rather a way of revealing the real as standing-reserve. And, it does so in terms of challenging humans to reveal the real as standing-reserve while standing within enframing as standing reserve. In this sense metaphysics is problematized and the classical subject/object distinction is blurred,

---

191 *Ibid*, p. 300.

192 *Ibid*, pp. 300-301.

193 *Ibid*, p. 302.

194 *Ibid*, p. 302.

195 *Ibid*, p. 304.

since modern technology destines humans to reveal what is real as standing-reserve.[196] In this regard, Heidegger would say that, "Enframing, as a challenging-forth into ordering, sends into a way of revealing. Enframing is an ordaining of destining, as is every way of revealing. Bringing-forth, *poiēsis*, is also a destining in this sense." On this view, *poiēsis* as bringing-forth is also a destining which is tied to the essence of history, and the destiny of humanity is that of unconcealment. On this account, humans are free as long as they are destined to reveal truth. Humans let "the veil" that veils "the essential occurrence of all truth" appears as "what veils."[197] Heidegger holds that "the essence of technology lies in enframing" that "belongs to the destining of revealing."[198] Given that, humans would already be within the realm of enframing as destining. In this sense, humans are endangered by a destining that pushes what is revealed in ordering as being the destiny of revealing. Unconcealment, that brings-forth everything that shows itself, reveals the destining of revealing as being an ultimate danger. It is precisely in the successes of modern technology and its correct determinations that the danger holds sway in terms of taking enframing as being the destiny of revealing. In this respect, a correctness conception of truth itself reveals the manner by which science and technology pursue nature in terms of mathematizing it and turning its objects into calculable entities of research by way of revealing them in terms of the objectlessness of standing-reserve. One might say that technological and scientific revealing is not concerned with the essence of nature. Rather the main concern is directed to the manners by virtue of which nature is set up in such a way as to "play certain roles" that are made available and stored in order to serve use purposes. The danger is

---

[196] *Ibid*, pp. 304-306.

[197] *Ibid*, p. 306.

[198] *Ibid*, p. 307.

that "amidst of all that is correct the true will withdraw."[199] Modern science and technology advance a correctness conception of truth that, in its very unconcealment, conceals other conceptions of truth. In this regard, Heidegger says that, "the destining of revealing is in itself not just any danger, but the *danger*;" and that "when destining reigns in the mode of enframing, it is the supreme danger."[200] On this account, as soon as what is unconcealed concerns humans as standing-reserve, humans, as those who order the standing-reserve, "will have to be taken as standing-reserve." It is in this sense that humans would not be able to grasp the "enframing as claim" since humans stand "in attendance on the challenging-forth of enframing." The danger is in turning human destiny into a destining revealing, "that is an ordering" that conceals revealing as *poiēsis*. The danger of enframing lies in not merely being what conceals *poiēsis*; rather the danger is that turning revealing into a mere "securing the standing-reserve." On this view, enframing blocks truth. Hence, it is "destining and danger."[201]

IV- Salvation

Reaching the tragic and dramatic conclusion about the danger of enframing and that of the essence of technology, Heidegger shifts his attention to poetry. Citing Holderlin, "But where danger is, grows the saving power also."[202] Heidegger then says that, "to save" is to fetch something home into its essence, in order to bring the essence for the first time into its genuine appearing." On this account,

---

199 *Ibid*, pp. 307-308

200 *Ibid*, p. 308.

201 *Ibid*, p. 309.

202 Taken from F. Holderlin's *Patmos*. Cf. *Friedrich Holderlin Poems and Fragments*, trans. by Michael Hamburger (Ann Arbor: The University of Michigan Press, 1966), pp. 462-63; Martin Heidegger, "The Question Concerning Technology," in *Basic Writings*, ed. by David Farrell Krell (New York: Harper & Row, 1977), p. 310.

the essence of technology, has to bring about its own "saving power." It is in this sense that one might say that modern natural sciences historically prepare the way for "enframing" by way of positing nature in such a manner as to be revealed as standing-reserve. Enframing takes place in such a way as to be neither beyond human control nor entirely taking place through that human control. In this sense, one might claim that enframing is a horizon or a destining that encloses without being a "fate." Enframing is a destining that is of the greatest danger yet it is not a final inescapable fate. Heidegger repeats Holderlin's verse, "where danger is, grows the saving power also." On his view, the essence of technology "must harbor in itself the growth of the saving power."[203] In order to "behold the saving power in the essence of technology," one has to consider in what sense "enframing is (taken to be) actually the essence of technology."[204] This consideration has to examine what do we take "essence" to be. In Heidegger's etymological investigations, "essence" answers to the question concerning the whatness of a thing.[205] As it was mentioned, both enframing and *poiēsis* are taken to be ways of revealing that are characterized by destining. However, enframing as a destining way of revealing that challenges, "blocks" the *poiēsis* way of destining in bringing-forth. Enframing is the name of the essence of technology that is never understood in the sense of "*genus* or *essentia*." On Heidegger's account, technology "demands on us" to think in another way than that of thinking in terms of "essence." Returning to Greek thought, he would investigate the meaning of essence in terms of that which "endures" and "persists." On his account, that which endures or persists, is that which "is granted."[206] Yet, if what endures is also what grants; then, is it the case that en-

---

203 *Ibid*, p. 310.

204 *Ibid*, pp. 310-11.

205 *Ibid*, p. 311.

206 *Ibid*, pp. 311-12.

framing is a form of granting? And, if enframing is a destining of revealing that challenges, how would it then be a granting? In response to these questions, Heidegger would say that "challenging is anything but granting." He would then wonder whether enframing, in the sense of being the supreme danger, would still be called a granting. In response to this issue, Heidegger's position would be to accept to call enframing "granting." Yet this is the case given that the saving power grows from within the rise of the danger of enframing.[207] Every destining of revealing is as such a granting. Consequently enframing would be a granting; granted that it harbors the growth of "the saving power" which is a granting that "sends into revealing." In this sense, the saving power keeps "watch over unconcealment," and the essence of technology harbors the "upsurgence of the saving power."[208] Such state of affairs reveals the essence of technology as being "ambiguous." And this ambiguity points to a bringing-forth of the unconcealment of "truth." It is in this regard that enframing "endangers the relation to the essence of truth." It is the human that is needed in order to "save" the essence of truth. And enframing, that challenges the human into ordering objects as standing-reserve, is itself a mode of granting what "endures" the human. It is in this endurance that the saving power finds its place of growth in terms of what it offers as "restraint" that passes alongside ordering.[209] It is in this closeness, between ordering and restraint, between enframing and saving power, that the destining of revealing and ambiguous concealing interplay. And, it is in this sort of interplay that the safekeeping of the essence of truth takes place. In this respect, Heidegger says that, "we look into the danger and see the growth of the saving power." It is by recognizing the danger as a "danger" that the saving power starts to come into presence. It is in the concealing of the danger that what is concealed is coming into

---

207 *Ibid*, p. 313.

208 *Ibid*, p. 314.

209 *Ibid*, pp. 314-315.

unconcealment. It is in seeing enframing as a threat that the saving power is brought forth. Turning his gaze towards the Greeks, Heidegger would again ponder on the senses of *technē* and *poiēsis,* as being "the bringing forth of the true into the beautiful."[210] *Poiēsis*, as a way of revealing, contrasts technology as a way of bringing-forth. *Poiēsis* brings-forth of the true into the beautiful, and this reveals a way of revealing that is not that of challenging and ordering. Revealing the true into the beautiful reveals another kind of truth than that of correctness. *Poiēsis* contrasts in its truth the dominance of truth by enframing. As Heidegger writes, "the coming to presence of technology threatens revealing, threatens it with the possibility that all revealing to be consumed in ordering and that everything will present itself only in the unconcealedness of standing-reserve."[211] Returning to Holderlin's verse, Heidegger would take the poetical to be that which pervades "every revealing of coming to presence into the beautiful." In this sense *technē* belongs to *poiēsis* as a poetic revealing. In all of this, Heidegger's hope is that the essence of technology would one day "come to presence in the coming to pass of truth."[212] In this respect, he would say that since the essence of technology "is nothing technological," then human reflection on that essence "must happen in a realm that is,..., akin to the essence of technology and,..., fundamentally different from it."[213] And such realm is that of art; granted that a reflection upon art concerns itself with the question concerning technology. In this regard, the question concerning technology traces a way of thinking that opens up human existence to the essence of technology. This would mean that, "the closer we come to the danger, the more brightly do the ways into the saving power begin to shine and the more questioning we become. For question-

[210] *Ibid*, pp. 315-316.

[211] *Ibid*, p. 315.

[212] *Ibid*, pp. 316-17.

[213] *Ibid*, p. 317.

ing is the piety of thought."[214] By way of questioning Heidegger repeats after Holderlin: "...poetically dwells man upon this earth." This implies that it is not only the case that the poetical brings forth the true into the beautiful, rather it shows that the poetical dimension pervades our being-in-the-world. This links the question concerning technology to that of being-in-the-world, and to the question of dwelling-in-the-world. And, this reflects a concern with the place where truth happens. In this sense, Heidegger's concern shifts from what is technological to the place where revealing takes place. His essay "*Building, Dwelling, Thinking*" seeks further revelation of where the saving power grows. Arguing from the standpoint of our human "homelessness," Heidegger would set upon himself to show that building and thinking belong to dwelling and that "dwelling is brought to the fullness of its essence" when humans "build out of dwelling, and think for the sake of dwelling."[215] Dwelling is itself one way in which we as humans are on the earth. And dwelling in the fullnesss of its essence is care and a guarding against all that dominates, manipulates, and exploits with thoughtlessness. Given this view, is it then the case that the saving power grows out of preserving the question of the meaning of being? And is it then the case that, technology, science, and modernity in their enframing do endanger the manner we "mortals" are destined on the earth? And would it be the case that Heidegger's theory of modernity is also a theory about how our modern homelessness does not bring dwelling to the fullness of its essence; that as moderns we do not build out of dwelling, and think for the sake of dwelling? This question of dwelling discloses again what appears in the earlier writings of Heidegger concerning the homelessness of *Dasein*. Dwelling points in the direction of alienation and anxiety that are not characteristic of one age or another. With Heidegger's theory of modernity, homelessness is not solely the ontological condition of *Dasein*'s being-in-the-world,

---

214 *Ibid*, p. 317.

215 *Ibid*, p. 339.

rather it also extends to touch a whole community of *Dasein*(s). Homelessness is social and historical, yet this crisis is philosophically attested from the standpoint of modernity.

CHAPTER 4
THE ONTOLOGY OF BEING

I- The Primary Analysis of the Nature of Being

Avicenna mentions that being (in Persian: *hasti*)[216] is encountered immediately and definition (*ḥad*) or description (*rasm*) do not apply to it. Being-qua-being (*hasti*) reflects the most general (*ᶜāmm*) encounter in the mind (*al-ᶜaql*), and being is recognized by the mind as being necessary, contingent, or impossible. This familiarity with being does not entail that the Heideggerian sense of "the availability of being" to classical ontology applies to Avicenna's consideration of being. Avicenna does not take being (*hasti, wūjūd*) to be an "available" ontological concept. Immediate familiarity in the sense of *badāha* does not entail the handiness or self-evidence that do not necessitate the consideration of the question of being. According to Avicenna, if being has no definition nor description, and is recognized as such by reason, then being is also that which is neither genus

---

216 The Persian term *hasti* does not have an equivalent in Arabic, and the verbal "to be" is not used as an obvious *copula* in Arabic. Unlike Persian, Arabic is a Semitic language that does not have Indo-European roots. The Arabic term *wūjūd* designates existence and being. Yet, with the Persian text, the distinction between being and existence is determined in terms of the use of *hasti* and *wūjūd*, where *hasti* refers to being and *wūjūd* refers to existence. Some contemporary Arab scholars or thinkers attempt to use *kaynūna* to refer to being while they make use of *wūjūd* in reference to existence. The use of *kaynūna* seems to be accurate in terms of referring it back to its roots in the command: *kun*! (Be) and *kawn* (generation, or universe). In some instances one encounters the term *anīya* which also designates being or the "thatness" of that which is or exists. Some might have taken the lack of a *copula*, or the lack of a distinction between existence and being, to be a shortcoming in the Arabic language and in its use in metaphysical discussions. Chapter eight of this book, on the language of being, addresses issues related to the Arabic language and its copulative functions while attending to contemporary philosophical accounts about the question of being in Heidegger's thought.

(*jins*) nor *differentia* (*faṣl*), since nothing is more general than being.[217] This account has important philosophical implications, since it does not account for being and beings in terms of being two different species under one overarching genus. The analysis of species (*nawᶜ*, *anwāᶜ*), differentia (*faṣl*), and genus (*jins*), masks the "unthought" ontological difference between being and beings. On Heidegger's view, the ontological difference between being and beings, cannot be sufficiently accounted for in terms of species under one genus. On his account, a talk of species and genus defeats the purposes of drawing the ontological difference and keeps it unthought. Heidegger's requirements go further by claiming that the *differing* dimension of that ontological difference remains unthought.

Avicenna argues that everything derives from being. According to him, being is first divided into substance (*jawhar*) and accident (*aᶜrāḍ*). Yet, Avicenna then argues that the being (*hasti*) of substance "is not in a subject (*mawḍūᶜ*)" as it would have been the case with the being of accidents. On his view, the being of substance is a reality or a truth (*ḥaqīqa*). Unlike accidents, being is neither a receptacle nor in a receptacle, and form (*ṣūra*) is taken by Avicenna to be a substance and not an accident. This is the case given that form is the posterior principle to substance and cannot thus be an accident. On Avicenna's view, a receptacle completes its being and is "active" (*fāᶜil*) when it receives something in itself. And by doing so, the receptacle becomes matter (*hayūla*, or *mādda*).[218] On this view, substance is divided into, simple matter (*hayūla*), form (*ṣūra*), a composite (*murakab*), and a body-independent entity like the soul or the intelligence (*al-ᶜaql*). On this account, substance (*al-jawhar*)

---

217 Avicenna, *Dānish Nāma (Metaphysica of Avicenna)*, ed. and trans. by Parviz Morwedge (New York: Columbia University Press, 1973), p. 15.

218 This view reflects some of the accounts of the receptacle as they figure in Plato's *Timaeus* in reference to *Khora*, the receptacle of becoming and its relation to the eternal indestructible forms.

could be a body by being a composite (*murakab*) of matter (*mādda/hayūla*) and form (*ṣūra*).[219] And, in *Kitāb al-Ḥudūd* (Book of Definitions), Avicenna indicates that substance (*al-jawhar*) designates the "essential self" (*dhāt*) of a thing. He also holds that there exists a sort of substance that "subsists due to itself" (*jawhar qā'im bi-dhātihi*) as a primary οὐσία (*ousia*) that is neither in a subject (*mawḍūʿ*) nor in a receptacle (*maḥal*).[220]

II- On Cause (*ʿilla, sabab*) and Effect (*maʿlūl, musabab*)

According to Avicenna "for anything (x) having being (*hasti*) not from something known (y), where the being of the former (x) is known from the latter (y), the latter is called the cause of the former, and the former (x) is called the effect of the latter (y)."[221] This readily tells that the being of the effect is known from the cause, and that the being of the effect results from the being of the cause. According to Avicenna, causes are at first divided into two kinds. The first kind (x) of causes is that which resides in the essence of the effect and is part of it, the second kind (y) of causes is that which does not reside in the essence of the effect nor is part of it. The cause (x), that resides in the essence of the effect and is part of it, is itself divided into two kinds. The first type (x) of causes is attested in the *inner sense of prehension* (*al-wahm*) where the being of the cause is related to the being of the effect potentially and not actually. The second type (x) of causes is that which is necessary for the imagination to relate the being of the effect to the being of the cause. The first type of (x)

---

219 Avicenna, *Dānish Nāma (Metaphysica of Avicenna)*, ed. and trans. by Parviz Morwedge (New York: Columbia University Press, 1973), p. 16.

220 Avicenna, *Avicenne Livre des Définition*, trans. by A. M. Goichon (Cairo: *Publications de l'Institut Français de l'Archéologie Orientale du Caire*, 1963), pp. 23-24 Arabic Text, pp. 34-36 French Translation.

221 Avicenna, *Dānish Nāma (Metaphysica of Avicenna)*, ed. and trans. by Parviz Morwedge (New York: Columbia University Press, 1973), p. 41.

causes, that reside in the essence of an effect and are part of it, is a material type of causes (*causa materialis*). The second type of a cause (x), that resides in the essence of an effect and is part of it, is a formal cause (*causa formalis*). As for the final cause (*causa finalis*), or the cause of completion (*tamām*), Avicenna holds that it is a cause that is external to its effect. It is a cause that brings an effect, yet such cause does not yet exist. It is a cause that derives an effect, yet that does not yet exist. Another type of causes is reflected in the role that a maker/agent plays. This cause is the *causa efficiens* (efficient cause), and like the other causes it also follows from Aristotle's account.[222]

Avicenna holds that the final cause gains primacy over the other causes in terms of a teleological account that focuses on final purposes. When there is a final purpose behind the performance of an act, the final cause assumes a primacy over the other causes by turning into the "cause" of these causes. The teleological consideration of a final purpose reflects an account that takes the existence of something to be better than its nonexistence. It is in this sense that existence is a perfection, and that the existent is advantaged. Given that a final purpose is sought, the final cause is then the cause of all causes, and agents will perform acts in such a way as to realize that final purpose. What lies in the background of the attempted teleological path of realization, is a value that is assigned to the existence of what is sought whose existence is superior to its nonexistence. On this view, the existence of a final purpose, and of causes that lie behind the teleological pursuit of this purpose, all reflect Avicenna's account that assigns value to the cause that leads to the bringing forth of an effect. Consequently, a cause, by virtue of being a cause, is that which brings forth an effect. It brings a result that is realized on the path of seeking a final purpose that lurks behind the acts. This account reflects a consideration of the relationship between the essence of a thing and what is external to that thing as that which realizes it.

[222] *Ibid*, pp. 41-42.

On such a consideration, the existence of a cause, that is external to the essence of something, is given an important role in the realization of that thing. The essence of something might not be sufficient to its own proper realization. And this implies that a thing requires something else that is external to it. A cause that is external to a thing and does not reside in its essence is the existential cause of that thing. On Avicenna's view, a thing exists by virtue of something other than itself. And, an existent thing is due to what is external to it, and its essence is not enough to bring it into existence. The primacy of the existential cause (*al-ᶜilla al-wūjūdīya*) over the essence of a thing is reflected in terms of the role this cause plays in bringing that thing into existence. As Avicenna says, the thing "is not yet complete by its essence alone." However, the primacy of a cause over essence is constrained to things whose existence is not sufficiently warranted by their essence alone. There are cases where a cause is not entirely in the service of its final purpose. Under such cases, the cause produces an effect out of its own essence, and it does so not in response to a final purpose. On Avicenna's consideration of causes, one also notices that he distinguishes between two general types of causes. The first type is that which is due to reality (*ḥaqīqa,* or truth), the other is that which is due to appearance. On this account, apparent causes do not produce an effect by themselves rather they lead to an action that contributes to the action of other causes.[223] On Avicenna's view, the activity of an agent is due to its nature, to a will, or to an accidental condition to it. In the case of an activity that arises due to the nature of the agent, Avicenna uses the example of "fire [that] burns according to its own nature." Regarding the role of will, this is attested in a situation like that of "a man who moves something." As for an occurring accident, it is exemplified by the case of [heated] "water [that] burns something due to an accidental condition in it." After all, water would not burn due to its own nature, unless it is as-

---

[223] *Ibid*, p. 43.

sociated with the accident of heat.[224] On this account, when the alteration of certain circumstances occurs, it is then the effect or the result of an activity that is due to a new nature, a new will, or a new arising accident. The agent, that acts at certain times and does not act at other times, is an agent that has a capability to act whenever it is not restrained from acting by an external constraint. When a capable agent does not act according to its capability, then this agent is constrained by something external to it. On this account, to consider that the existence of a thing has more value than the nonexistence of a thing indicates that what exists accordingly has more advantage and is as such due to the conditions of its essence that admits change. And it is the case due to the surrounding circumstances of the external world that acts on its change, rather than constraining that change.[225] In the second volume of the metaphysics of *Kitāb al-Shifā'*,[226] Avicenna holds that there cannot be a cause of a cause *ad infinitum* since on that account, the cause of a cause is a first primary cause for the ensuing effects. On this view, if one considers A to be the cause of B, and B is the cause of C, while C is the cause of D, then by virtue of a chain of causation, one would say that A is the cause of B, C, and D. Avicenna then asserts that all causes are finite from whatever side we opt to account for them, and that the primary first principle of all causes is none but the One Necessary Being (*wājib al-wūjūd*). He then mentions that causes are finite since the disclosure of a final cause would turn that cause into a finite cause.

III- On Potentiality (*quwa*) and Actuality (*fiᶜl*)

On Avicenna's view, potentiality is either an active potentiality, or it is a passive potentiality. Active potentiality is that which is

---

[224] *Ibid*, p. 43.

[225] *Ibid*, p. 43.

[226] Avicenna, *Kitāb al-Shifā', Metaphysics II*, ed. by G. C. Anawati, Ibrahim Madkour, Saᶜid Zayed (Cairo: al-hay'a al-ᶜāmma lil-kitāb, 1975), pp. 327-328, 340.

"inherent in the agent's act," while passive potentiality designates a condition (*ḥāl*) of receptivity.[227] On this account, actuality describes the condition of that which has been realized. And, the contingency of being implies that a contingent entity "x" has being, in the sense that "it is," while itself not necessarily "existing." The contingency of being (at this stage of the analysis) is called the "potentiality of being." On Avicenna's view, being is either that of actuality or that of potentiality. That which is contingent has being, yet it does not yet exist in the sense of being actualized. Therefore, that which has being in potentiality is not yet that which has being in actuality. However, on Avicenna's view, that which has potential being, yet that does not yet actually exist, is that which is not yet something real. And what is not yet something real, is a contingent being "that has no advantage" (since the advantage derives from existing).[228] This is the case, given that what is not yet something real is a contingent being that would or would not exist. The being that is contingent, yet that is not yet realized, is a mere contingency that is not yet in union with a cause by virtue of which it will be brought from potentiality to actuality. Contingency, as a state of being, is no longer a contingency once the contingent being has been realized and brought from potentiality into actuality. Avicenna explicitly states that "the being of a substance is due to its own essence (nature, *dhāt*) while the being of being possible [contingent] is due not to its own essence but to that thing which is its possibility [contingency] of being. Thus, being possible [contingent] is not a distinct substance (*jawhar mufrad*). Being possible [contingent] is then either a condition of a substance, or a substance to which a condition is connected."[229] Avicenna holds that active potentiality is also of two kinds. The first is said to be "necessarily active at all times," and cannot "refrain" from action

---

227 Avicenna, *Dānish Nāma (Metaphysica of Avicenna)*, ed. and trans. by Parviz Morwedge (New York: Columbia University Press, 1973), p. 45.

228 *Ibid*, p. 46.

229 *Ibid*, p. 46.

(like fire cannot refrain from burning).[230] Regarding the second type of potentiality, it is active, yet it can refrain from action. This sort of active potentiality involves an action that has been constrained by an external agent that is responsible for the non-realization of the act. This is the case, given that this constraint is coupled with an ability (or capability) to act. Avicenna wants to illustrate how something comes into existence due to a cause by necessity, and that it is not possible for the necessity of a thing not to be realized.[231] On Avicenna's view, the act that is realized due to a cause is the effect of that cause by necessity. This state of affairs reflects how Avicenna links his views on causation to his consideration of actuality and potentiality (And this consequently will also appear in the consideration of the modalities of being). A cause is brought from the state of potentiality to the state of actuality when an act comes from it and is realized. In the case when it is possible for an act to either come from a cause, or not to come from it, then that cause is only "potentially" a cause.[232] Such remarks also feed into Avicenna's consideration of how the effect of a cause is linked to its essence or essential self. On his view, if the essential nature of a cause (*dhātihā*) determines the effect, then the essence of the effect is not yet realized. But what does one infer from such a statement, and how would it later affect our understanding of essence and its relation to the realized existence?

IV- The Analysis of Being in Terms of Its Modalities

Avicenna's ontology of being (*al-wūjūd*) reflects a shift from the Aristotelian categories to some sort of a phenomenological consideration of the question of being. This is attested in investigating the semantics of Avicenna's ontology of being that is mainly illus-

---

230 *Ibid*, p. 46.

231 *Ibid*, p. 47.

232 *Ibid*, p. 47.

trated by a logical and ontological analysis of being in relation to the modalities of necessity (*wūjūb*), contingency (*imkān*), and impossibility (*imtinā*ʿ). Like all great philosophers, the groundwork of Avicenna's metaphysics is laid down in his logic. Based on the analysis of the modalities of being, being is either necessary or not. Being is taken to be necessary in itself due to its own nature (*wājib al-wūjūd bi-dhātihi*), while what is not necessary in itself is either impossible or contingent. Avicenna argues that, if the impossible-in-itself is that which cannot exist, then being that is not necessary in itself is either contingent in itself (*mumkin bi-dhātihi*) or it is necessary by virtue of what is other than itself (*wājib al-wūjūd bi-ghaīrihi*). Being an existent (*mawjūd*) is being a contingent. However, a contingency-in-itself is never realized, rather contingency is a potentiality to be that gets actualized by what is other than itself, i.e. by virtue of an external cause whose existence is prior to it. On Avicenna's view in the Logic, contingency is not the same as possibility. This is the case given that the non-contingent is not impossible while the non-possible is impossible. This is the case in the Logic of *Kitāb al-Shifā*ʿ and that of *Kitāb al-Najāt*. Given this brief account of Avicenna's consideration of being in relation to the modalities, one might argue that we already attest some ontological dimensions that overcome some aspects of the Aristotelian *ousiology*. This development was extended and commented on by the successors of Avicenna; especially by those philosophers whose works had a central role in the later Islamic philosophical discourse. In the *Avicenna Latinus*, one reads that the quiddities of entities do not deserve being if abstracted from the Necessary Being due to Itself. A quiddity of what is abstracted in its relation from Necessary Being is a quiddity that deserves "non-being."[233] Contingent beings do have an inde-

---

[233] The French rendering of the Latin translation reads as follows: "*Quant aux autres choses [that is those things that are other than wajib al-wujud], leurs quiddités, comme tu le sais, ne méritent pas l'être, mais en elles-mêmes et en faisant abstraction de leur relation à l'être nécessaire, elles méritent le non-*

terminate relation to existence or nonexistence. And a nonexistent does not come back to existence, and if it does, it is not self-same. On Avicenna's account, there is no "return" into existence of that which is nonexistent and no self-sameness may be implied, since even in returning to another time, that which does not exist anymore does not return as the same. At least there is a temporal differentiating rupture that breaks the self-connectedness and self-sameness of self-identity. Existence is external to the substantial structure of beings. It is that which happens to them. Existence is a happening, it is what comes to happen to beings like *Ereignis* (i.e. event of appropriation). The metaphysical structures of necessary being and that of contingent being are different. Necessary being due to itself is true in itself. It is the source of its own being without borrowed existence; it always exists. Necessary being due to itself is the highest level of truth and intelligibility. Necessary being due to itself is truth while the contingent being is "false" in itself and "true" due to something else other than itself. After all, the contingent being does not find the reasons for its existence in its essence or in itself or its proper structure.[234] Contingent being cannot by itself actualize its very own existential potentiality. Beings vary in the intensity of their participation in being. However, the participation in being does not entail an equivocity in the meaning of being. And being is indeed applied to the (Aristotelian) categories in different degrees of applicability while still holding the univocity and sameness of its meaning. Without battling Parmenides' view, being is one, and it applies to the substance, then in a posterior order, it applies to the accidents by transcendental as well as predicative analogy (And this is close to the notion of *al-*

être." See: *Avicenna Latinus, Liber De Philosophia prima sive Scientia divina I-IV.* Édition Critique de la Traduction Latine Médiévale par S. Van Riet, introduction Doctrinale par G. Verbeke, patronage de l'Union Académique Internationale (Leiden: E. J. Brill, 1977), pp. 73*-74*. See also: Avicenna, *La Métaphysique du Shifa', Livre VIII, 6,* trans. by Anawati (Montréal: Texte dactylographie, 1952), p. 20.

[234] *Ibid*, p. 72*.

tashkīk that will be briefly addressed later).[235] Avicenna holds that "the being of that entity which has being is either necessary in itself due to its own nature or is not necessary."[236] He then states that the being which is not necessary due to itself is either an impossibility or a contingency. He then asserts that what is not necessary in itself and is impossible "can never be realized (*ḥāṣil*)." Therefore whatever is impossible is that which cannot actually exist. However, this does not entail that what is impossible cannot be, that it cannot have some sort of being. The being that is not necessary in itself, nor impossible, is contingent. And whatever is contingent is either contingent due to itself or is necessary due to the condition that its cause exists, while it is impossible if its cause does not exist. Contingent being is sub-divided into three determinations. The contingent being (*mumkin al-wūjūd*) is either as such due to itself, or it is necessary due to a cause that is external to it. As for the contingent being, that is not as such due to itself, nor is necessary due to its own cause, it is a being that is impossible. A contingent being is a potentiality to be or not to be. While contingent being, that is necessary due to its own cause, is being that has been brought into actuality by virtue of its own cause, and such being is the effect by necessity of a cause that exists. Contingent being, that is neither due to itself, nor is necessary due to its own cause, is not necessary due itself, nor is it contingent in itself, therefore it is an impossible being. In all cases, the impossible, is that which cannot exist, yet it is also that which is not entirely denied being. After all, an impossible being like the "round square," which is not a contingent being is impossible and never exists. Nevertheless, it is called an impossible being. A "round square" may be addressed in terms of accounts of squareness or roundness, and certain linguis-

235 *Ibid*, p. 66*.

236 Notice here that what is used is the term "nature" and not essence in reference to *dhāt*, or *dhātihi*. For the quotation, see: Avicenna, *Dānish Nāma (Metaphysica of Avicenna)*, ed. and trans. by Parviz Morwedge (New York: Columbia University Press, 1973), p. 47.

tic expressions may be used in reference to it. Such impossible being has certain predicates that qualify it, yet it never exists. It is an impossible being that cannot be realized in a logical sense. A "Unicorn" has certain qualities of horses. It is pictured as a horse, yet it also has wings. A unicorn is an impossible being that does not exist, yet it is nevertheless imaginable and can be represented. It can be imagined, while knowing that it is an impossible being that cannot be an existent in an existential sense. Such being is addressed or analyzed in terms of the modality of impossibility. As for a contingent being, it may be necessary due to its own existential cause. When the existential cause of this contingent being does not exist, this contingent being remains a potentiality. When its own cause exists, and a necessary existent arises due to it, this contingent being is realized. Regarding an entity that cannot exist nor can it be realized, impossibility would be a relevant modality that characterizes it. Avicenna summarizes this case by concluding that "any existing entity, for which existence is not intrinsically necessary, is contingent in itself. Therefore, this entity is a contingent being in itself and a non-contingent being with regard to something else (*ghaīr*)."[237] Contingency does not come out into existence unless there is a cause due to which this contingency is realized. Contingency in itself is "never" realized since it has not come out from an existing cause. Once a contingent being becomes an existent, it is as such by virtue of coming out into existence as the necessary effect of an existent cause. This is the case, given that the cause of an existent entity is that which is other than itself. By becoming an existent, the existing entity is "united" (*mutaḥida*) with its cause (*ᶜilla*).[238] This reflects that a cause is something else than an entity. And, a cause *qua* cause cannot be as such unless an effect emerges from it by necessity due to a union of that cause with what results from it as an existent.

---

[237] *Ibid*, p. 48.

[238] *Ibid*, p. 48.

V- Necessary Being (*wājib al-wūjūd*)

In Islamic philosophical texts, some refer to God as the Necessary Existent due to Itself (*wājib al-wūjūd bi-dhātihi*). And in this sense, *wājib al-wūjūd bi-dhātihi* can exist independently of the world that could be created *ex nihilo*. However, Avicenna's consideration of *wājib al-wūjūd bi-dhātihi*, as the Necessary Existent due to Itself, differs from what those philosophical texts propound. And Avicenna also differs from what the orthodox doctors of Islam would hold (And this has been indicated early on in the *Preface* and the *Analytic Synopsis* of this book). Avicenna's Necessary Existent due to Itself does not exist without entailing the existence of the world of contingency. Avicenna's Necessary Existent due to Itself is not epistemicly prior to being nor is it beyond being. The Necessary Existent due to Itself has epistemic posteriority viz. being (*wūjūd*) that is addressed from the standpoint of necessity (*wūjūb*). This is the case given that being is primarily encountered in the mind in immediacy. This preserves to being its logical, ontological, and epistemic priority. The study of being is prior to the study of the Necessary Existent due to Itself. The Necessary Existent is not self-evident and is thus derived from Necessary Being.[239] On this account, the science of metaphysics does not begin with the concept of the Necessary Existent due to Itself as a primitive term, but this concept is developed in the course of the inquiry.[240] Yet, this does not entail that the inquiry would lead to the claim that there is a demonstration (*burhān*) of the Necessary Existent due to Itself.[241] The consideration of the Necessary Existent due to Itself differs from the consid-

---

239 See M. Marmura's contribution to the *Avicenna Metaphysics* section in: *Encyclopaedia Iranica*, Vol. III, ed. by Ehsan Yarshater (London: Routledge & Kegan Paul, 1989), p. 75.

240 This point is addressed in: Parviz Morewedge, *Islamic Philosophical Theology* (Albany: State University of New York Press, 1979), pp. 191-192.

241 Avicenna, *Kitāb al-Shifā', Metaphysics II*, ed. by G. C. Anawati, Ibrahim Madkour, Sa^cid Zayed (Cairo: al-hay'a al-^cāmma lil-kitāb, 1975), p. 354.

eration of the Ultimate Being of monotheistic orthodoxy and it is also distinct from what figures in Descartes' ontological argument. This is so, given that in Descartes' case, the Necessary Existent is transcendent and does not have epistemic priority viz. the *Cogito*. And the awareness of the contingency of the *Cogito* leads to a search for what grounds the *Cogito* as that which is Necessary due to Itself. Avicenna's Necessary Existent due to Itself is akin to Plotinus' One in the sense that Its existence entails, by emanation, the existence of the world. The concept of the world is essentially contained in the concept of the Necessary Existent.[242]

The Arabic expression "*wājib al-wūjūd*," is at certain instances rendered as [The] Necessary Existent, and at other instances it is rendered as Necessary Being, or Necessary Existence. "*Wājib al-wūjūd*" could literally mean: that whose existence or being is necessary. It could also be [The] Necessary Existent or Being, where Being or Existent specify some sort of a *being* that is unlike beings or entities. The rendering of "*wājib al-wūjūd*" could also refer to necessary being as such without specifically designating a particular being or entity. Yet, *wājib al-wūjūd* designates what is ontologically different from beings and is not merely the "beingness" of beings. Unlike the contingent existent, the Necessary Existent cannot be united with any cause, nor is Its *wūjūd* (being or existence) in any way due to a cause. The being of the Necessary Existent is not associated with any condition that is external to It nor is It due to any other being. As it was indicated above, the cause for the existence of a contingent existent is prior to that contingent existent in essence. This is not the case with the Necessary Existent that exists due to Itself. Yet, *wājib al-wūjūd* is also divided into *wājib al-wūjūd bi-dhātihi* and *wājib al-wūjūd bi-ghaīrihi*. The *wājib al-wūjūd bi-dhātihi* is the Necessary Existent due to Itself, while the *wājib al-wūjūd bi-*

242 Parviz Morewedge, *Islamic Philosophical Theology* (Albany: State University of New York Press, 1979), pp. 210-211.

ghaīrihi is the necessary existent due to something other than itself. The Necessary Existent due to Itself exists due to Its own intrinsic nature (*dhāt*), and nothing that is not of Its intrinsic nature is needed in order for It to exist.

On Avicenna's view, the Necessary Existent due to Itself has no cause, while the necessary being due to something other than itself is a contingent being that has been realized by a cause that is external to it. The contingent is that which is not necessary due to itself but can be necessary due to what is other than itself. Unlike all contingents, the Necessary Existent due to Itself (*wājib al-wūjūd bi-dhātihi*) is not equivalent to any other being. Its truth and reality (*ḥaqīqa*) cannot be shared with anything else. It is ontologically distinct from all that is, in the sense that It is ontologically distinct from all beings.[243] The Necessary Existent due to Itself is that whose truth or reality is not shared with anything else, It is that which is ontologically other. As for the contingent being which may become a necessary existent due to something other than itself, the quiddity (*māhīya*) of that being is not sufficient for bringing it into existence. The *māhīya* (quiddity) of a being is not enough to bring about the existence of that being. The *māhīya* of a being necessitates something other than that being in order for that being to exist. Its existence requires an external "existential cause" (*ᶜilla wūjūdīya*) by virtue of which that being becomes a necessary existent due to something other than itself.[244]

On Avicenna's view, the Necessary Existent due to Itself is one (*wāḥid*) and only. It is that which is one essential self and nature (*dhātan wāḥida*).[245] Avicenna argues that there cannot be more

---

243 Avicenna, *Kitāb al-Shifā', Metaphysics II*, ed. by G. C. Anawati, Ibrahim Madkour, Saᶜid Zayed (Cairo: al-hay'a al-ᶜāmma lil-kitāb, 1975), pp. 37-38.

244 *Ibid*, p. 39.

245 *Ibid*, p. 43.

than one Necessary Existent due to Itself. And, this is the case given that there cannot be more than one Necessary Existent without having *differentia* (*faṣl*) that allows one Existent to be distinguished from the other. In case there is no *differentia* by virtue of which one Existent is distinguished from the other, then there is no sense in which these Existents could be distinct and not be one and the same. In case there is more than one Necessary Existent that is Necessary due to Itself, then these must be separated by what is external to them and other than themselves. This eventually entails that each of the Necessary Existents in question is Necessary due to Itself and due to what is other than Itself, and this does not hold. This problem may be addressed through a dialectical approach that accounts for what is determined in itself and what is determined by what is other than itself. Yet, even such dialectical account does not allow for the simultaneous occurrence of the determination of something due to itself and a determination of that thing due to what is other than itself. What Avicenna attempts to show is that there cannot be more than one Necessary Existent due to Itself. The Necessary Existent due to Itself cannot be accounted for in terms of a talk of genus (*jins*), species (*anwāʿ*), *differentia* (*faṣl*), substance (*jawhar*), accidents (*aʿrāḍ*), or definition (*ḥad*).[246] The ontological truth of the Necessary Existent is that It is what necessarily exists due to Itself and is not united with anything other than Itself. Avicenna says that "the necessity of being/existing [due to itself] cannot be but for one."[247] The Necessary Existent is One, and unlike beings, It cannot be analyzed or addressed in terms of species under one over-arching genus. On Avicenna's view the ontological difference, between being and beings, is not a difference in terms of species (*al-anwāʿ*) under one genus (*jins*). The Necessary Existent is not one as a number; It is rather beyond number, and It is not like individuals (*ashkhāṣ*) un-

[246] *Ibid*, pp. 45-46.

[247] *Ibid*, p. 46. Herein, Avicenna says: *"wūjūb al-wūjūd lā yakūn ilā li-wāḥid."*

der species (*anwāᶜ*). Its necessity of being is only for It and not shared with anything other than Itself. The Necessary Existent due to Itself is a unity.[248] Unlike Necessary Existence due to Itself, the necessary existence due to what is other than itself is conditioned by temporality. The necessary existent due to something other than itself is temporal in the sense that it exists "during a certain time" and "not in another" (*laysa dā'iman bal fī waqtin duna waqtin*).[249]

Only the Necessary Existent due to Itself is one and simple, everything else is a composite (*murakab*). The Necessary Existent is One (*fard*) that is a *causa sui*. The Necessary Existent due to Itself implies perfection, absoluteness, infinity, and simplicity. The Necessary Existent has nothing that measures up to It ontologically. It is unlike all there is, It is unlike the categories, and It is one and simple.[250] The Necessary Existent is not divided neither in quantity nor in any other sense.[251] And, Its unity is presupposed in reality, in conception, and in the mind.

Avicenna says:

> Its (i.e. the Necessary Existent) existence does not follow from a quiddity (*māhīya*) other than existence, since It has no quiddity, nor a genus (*jins*), nor a *differentia* (*faṣl*), nor a definition (*ḥad*), nor a counterpart (*nad*), and is detached (*bāri'*) from matter (*mādda*) and has no opposite (*ḍid*). As for the following accidents (*aᶜrāḍ*) of quality (*kayf*), quantity (*kam*), place

---

248 *Ibid*, p. 47.

249 *Ibid*, p. 47

250 Salem Mashran, *al-Jānib al-Ilāhī ᶜinda Ibn Sīnā* (Damascus: dār quṭayba, 1992), p. 77.

251 Avicenna, *Kitāb al-Ishārāt wal-Tanbīhāt*, ed. by Suleiman Dunia (Cairo: dār al-maᶜārif, 1960), III, p. 65.

> (*ayn*), situation (*waḍᶜ*), and other, these are away from It, and It is one since It has no part and therefore has no similar (*mithl*).[252]

The identity of the Necessary Existent due to Itself does not depend on parts, since It is not a composite nor is It divisible or subject to partition. It is that which is encountered as "there is," "*il y a*," "*huwa*," and "*wāḥid aḥad*" (One). It does not imply composition, neither in a material quantifiable sense, nor in a logical or mental sense, It has no composition in Its nature nor in terms of attributes, quiddity, or existence.[253] All Its attributes are led back to Its knowledge (*ᶜilm*). The Necessary Existent is not like the Neoplatonist "One" in being "beyond being." And emanation also implies the emanation of knowing (*ᶜilm*) and perceiving (*idrāk*). To bring back all the attributes to knowing and perceiving is also a way of stressing the importance of unconcealing. The happening of truth is linked to knowing by unveiling, knowing by *kashf*. With the Necessary Existent there is unity between the intellect, the intelligible, and intellection. It is a unity of knower, known, knowledge, a unity of perceiver, perceived, and perception. On Avicenna's view, the Necessary Existent that is simple does not admit *differentia* (*faṣl*) and It is One.[254] And this is more the case since no *differentia* occurs in the essence of a universal.[255] This difficulty arises due to the account that takes existence not to be distinct from essence in the case of the Necessary Existent, since it is the case that on Avicenna's account, the Neces-

---

252 Avicenna, *Kitāb al-Hidāya*, ed. by Mohamad ᶜAbdou (Cairo: maktabat al-qāhira al-ḥadītha, 1874), pp. 262-263. Also see: Mashran, *al-Jānib al-Ilāhi ᶜinda Ibn Sīnā*, 1992, p. 99.

253 Also refer to: Salem Mashran, *al-Jānib al-Ilāhi ᶜinda Ibn Sīnā* (Damascus: dār quṭayba, 1992), p. 102.

254 Refer to the English Translation of Avicenna's views in: Avicenna, *Dānish Nāma (Metaphysica of Avicenna)*, ed. and trans. by Parviz Morwedge (New York: Columbia University Press, 1973), p. 54.

255 *Ibid*, pp. 54-55.

sary Existent is the one whose existence is not other than Its essence.[256] Avicenna says "that whose essence (*māhīya*) is other than existence is not the Necessary Existent due to Itself."[257] This account implies that the existence, of that whose essence is other than existence, is an accidental existence (*wūjūd bil-ᶜaraḍ*). The contingent being is contingent due to itself yet it exists due to an external cause. The Necessary Existent, unlike the existent beings, is that which is not united with any cause, Its existence is due to Itself and not to anything other than Itself. The cause of the existence of a contingent entity is either due to its essence (*dhāt*) or due to something else. According to Avicenna, "the essence of the Necessary Existent is not the cause of Its existence."[258] This is evidently the case due to at least two arguments. The first argument advances that the Necessary Existent has no cause, nor is It united with a cause. The second argument holds that the Necessary Existent is the one and only *Existent* whose essence is existence, and that It is that which possesses no other essence than existence.[259] Given that this is the

---

256 I wonder whether such an account still takes existence to be subordinated to essence, given that existence qualifies in different degrees and reaches the highest level of its determination in becoming itself the only essence of the Necessary Existent. Thus it is that which elevates and venerates essences, that the highest level of the determination of essence is for essence to become existence. As if essence is of a lesser determination whenever it is the essence of that which possesses an essence other than existence. Essence becomes perfected in terms of its purification from all essences that are other than existence, the existent which does not possess an essence that is other than existence is the Necessary Existent, all other existents are those who possess an essence that is other than their existence.

257 Avicenna, *Danish Nama (Metaphysica of Avicenna)*, ed. and trans. by Parviz Morwedge (New York: Columbia University Press, 1973), p. 55.

258 *Ibid*, p. 55.

259 Even if the Necessary Existent is that whose essence is existence, and is that which possesses no other essence than existence, It is still that which has the possibility of having a multiplicity of characteristics, without entailing that It has a multiplicity of essences. Regarding this point, refer to *section 26* of the translation of Avicenna's views in: Avicenna, *Dānish Nāma (Metaphysica of Avicenna)*, ed.

case, the Necessary Existent will then have another cause for Its existence than Its essence. Yet, the Necessary Existent is not united with any cause since It exists due to Itself. Avicenna also holds that a substance is that which has an essence, and that one does not then know whether that essence exists unless it is realized in a subject.[260] Thus, a substance, which is that which has an essence, cannot be known to exist unless it is realized in a subject. Consequently, Avicenna concludes that whatever is of such a nature is that whose essence is other than its existence. Therefore, that which has no essence other than existence is not a substance. This shows that the Necessary Existent due to Itself, is not a substance (*Jawhar*, οὐσία [*ousia*]). And this also entails that whatever possesses an essence other than existence, i.e. contingent existents, may be a substance (*jawhar*). If it were the case that existence is external to the essence of categories, then the Necessary Existent is not any category, and this is asserted as such in terms of saying that the essence of the Necessary Existent is Its existence. Its existence is Its essence, and Its essence is Its existence.[261] Avicenna explicitly holds that there is no genus, no *differentia*, no cause, no change, or divisibility in the case of the Necessary Existent. The account that takes the Necessary Existent to be indivisible, is an account that is based on the unity of the Necessary Existent, whereby there is no other Necessary Existent than the Necessary Existent.[262]

On Avicenna's view, existents are associated with innumerable causes. They all "have causes, and causes are infinite series."[263] Yet, these causes return to a "primary" (*awal*) cause. They all return

---

and trans. Parviz Morwedge (New York: Columbia University Press, 1973), pp. 57-59.

260 *Ibid*, p. 55. Herein, Avicenna gives the example of a substance that has an essence such as materiality, spirituality, humanity, etc.

261 *Ibid*, p. 57 (This will be considered in Chapter 5).

262 This specific account has been addressed in the course of our discussion in the earlier part of this section.

263 *Ibid*, p. 59.

to the Necessary Existent. Yet, one may also argue that there exists some sort of circular causation that entails a return of contingent beings to themselves. However, Avicenna claims that such account entails that one thing is both the effect and the cause of something else. And on Avicenna's view, this leads to an absurdity. Therefore, he concludes that, "all effects and contingencies return ([Persian] *rasand*) to the one Necessary Existent."[264] Avicenna gives expression to an Emanationist scheme that asserts that in the first (*al-awal*) realm of being "only one being can be realized from the Necessary Existent."[265] The gradation in being reflects the levels of reality where the more complete in its beingness and existence is that which is closer to the Necessary Existent. This gradation represents the intensity in the participation in being of all beings. Everything is thus related to the Necessary Existent. And, everything exists due to its relation to the Necessary Existent. An existent is one sort of entity in relation to the Necessary Existent and it is another sort of an entity in relation to itself.

VI- Contingent Being (*mumkin al-wūjūd*)

Avicenna defines contingency in terms of necessity and impossibility. At least this is what he attempts to do in *Kitāb al-Shifā'* and in *Kitāb al-Najāt*. The logical investigations of the modalities of necessity, impossibility, and contingency prepare the ground for the consideration of being in the metaphysics. The investigations of the senses of contingency in Avicenna's Logic (whether in *Kitāb al-Shifā'* or in *Kitāb al-Najāt*) are meant to elucidate the various meanings that the term *mumkin* holds. Avicenna, attempts to distinguish the meaning of *mumkin* as possible from the meaning of *mumkin* as contingent. The meaning of *mumkin* as "that which is possible" is what is implied by the common sense rendering of "*mumkin*."

264 *Ibid*, p. 59.

265 *Ibid*, p. 76.

On a common sense reading of *mumkin*, it is said that the non-*mumkin* (*ghaīr mumkin*) is the non-possible, and this entails that the non-*mumkin* is what is impossible (*ghaīr mumkin*, or *mumtani*ᶜ). The philosophical and logical meaning of *mumkin* as "that which is contingent" does not entail that the non-*mumkin* (*ghaīr mumkin*) is that which is impossible. The non-*mumkin* as "that which is non-contingent" implies that the non-*mumkin* is either necessary (*wājib*) or impossible (*mustaḥīl*, or *mumtani*ᶜ). The philosophical and logical meaning of *mumkin* as contingent entails that what is non-*mumkin* (i.e. non-contingent) is either necessary or impossible. And, Avicenna's account of *mumkin* is taken from the standpoint of rendering *mumkin* as (the philosophical) "contingent" rather than rendering *mumkin* as (the common sense) "possible." After all, Avicenna attempts to draw a distinction between the common sense meaning of *mumkin* and the philosophical meaning of *mumkin*.[266] The definition of each of the three modalities of necessity, contingency/possibility, and impossibility, involves the use of the other modalities. In this sense, the impossible is therefore that which necessitates nothingness in the sense that it is nothing (*al-muḥāl wājib al-*ᶜ*adam*), and the nothingness of that which is impossible is necessary. The impossible is that which cannot exist, it is that which is *mumtani*ᶜ, in the sense that it does not exist and cannot exist. The necessary is that which is impossible for it not to have existence or being. And, that which is necessary is that which cannot not be (*al-wājib huwa al-lazi laysa bi-mumkin an lā yakūn*). The contingent is that which is neither necessary nor impossible for it to be or not to be. The contingent (*mumkin*) is neither necessary nor impossible.[267] Moreover, in the first section (*maqāla*) of the Metaphysics part of *Kitāb al-Najāt*, Avicenna holds that every being is contingent due to

---

266 Avicenna, *Kitāb al-Shifā', Metaphysics II*, ed. by G. C. Anawati, Ibrahim Madkour, Saᶜid Zayed (Cairo: al-hay'a al-ᶜāmma lil-kitāb, 1975), p. 35.

267 *Ibid*, p. 35.

itself, and if a being is not as such, then it would not be. And, this is the case given that non-contingency implies that what is non-contingent is either necessary or impossible. Contingency is presupposed in the being of a being or else that being would be impossible if it were neither contingent nor necessary. A contingent being is made ready to be due to its contingency to be. To sum up, Avicenna says: "that which is impossible for it to be will not be, and that which is contingent (*mumkin*) for it to be, has its contingency [of being] prior to its existence/being" (*al-muḥāl an yūjad la yūjad, wal-mumkin an yūjad qad sabaqahu imkān wūjūdih*).[268] Avicenna then says that "we call the contingency of being a potentiality of being" (*naḥnu nussamī imkān al-wūjūd quwat al-wūjūd*).[269] And, the "elect learned" (*al-khāṣṣa*), and the philosophers are those who take the "*mumkin*" to be that which is "contingent."[270] On Avicenna's view, the first to be conceived out of the three modalities is that which is necessary, since on his view, that which is necessary is that which evidently has being; it is that which necessarily *is.* This entails that on Avicenna's view, one attests a convergence between affirmation (*ithbāt*) and being (*wūjūd*). On this view, one can say that: "To be necessary is to be."[271] Regarding impossible being, it has been mentioned above that it is that which cannot exist. Therefore, it is that which cannot result from a cause. As for the Necessary Being, Avicenna holds that, It "cannot be united ([Persian] *pai-*

---

268 Avicenna, *Kitāb al-Najāt, Metaphysics I*, ed. by Majid Fakhry (Beirut: dār al-āfāq al-jadīda, 1985), p. 255.

269 *Ibid*, p. 255.

270 French translation of the Arabic text of Avicenna's *Kitāb al-Ishārāt wal-Tanbīhāt* in: A. M. Goichon, *Le Livre des Directives et Remarques (Kitāb al-Ishārāt wal-Tanbīhāt)* (Paris: Librairie Philosophique J. Vrin, 1951), pp. 139-142.

271 Avicenna, *Kitāb al-Shifā', Metaphysics II*, ed. by G. C. Anawati, Ibrahim Madkour, Saᶜid Zayed (Cairo: al-hay'a al-ᶜāmma lil-kitāb, 1975), p. 36.

wand) with any cause (*sabab*)."[272] And we have already seen that the Necessary Existent is as such due to Its own nature and is not as such due to a cause. Being under the modality of necessity is being necessary without a cause. Unlike contingent existence, necessary existence is not necessary qua necessary due to a union with a cause. This is the case given that the existence of a contingent entity depends on the cause that brings it into realization. Yet, one wonders whether such contingent entity still depends on its cause after being realized. What is at stake is whether a contingent entity would still depend on its cause or any cause for its self-subsistence. So, can we say that on Avicenna's view, once a contingent entity is realized, this entity does not anymore need the cause that realized it? Avicenna says that, what has been made is still in need (*ḥāja*) of what he calls a "supporter" (*daranda*).[273] But what does he mean by "supporter"? Is it meant to be some sort of a cause or agent that contributes to the realization of a contingent entity and to the continuation of its subsistence? According to Avicenna one can draw a distinction between an "agent" (such as a maker) and a "cause." On his account, an agent is that which becomes a cause, in the sense that an agent acts like a cause at a given time (*waqt*).[274] This temporal nuance shows that an agent plays the role of a cause at a certain time without itself being a cause. This entails that the agent becomes a cause for a given temporal function while a cause is that which persists in its being a cause by virtue of persisting in playing the role of cause. But we encountered that a cause is what it is by virtue of its results. So, a cause persists in being a cause if and only if something persists in being its effect. Being a cause is distinct from becoming a cause by virtue of a temporal dimension. An agent is not the cause due to which an effect subsists. After all, in drawing the distinction between an agent and a cause,

---

[272] *Ibid*, p. 48.

[273] Avicenna, *Danish Nama (Metaphysica of Avicenna)*, ed. and trans. by Parviz Morwedge (New York: Columbia University Press, 1973), p. 50.

[274] *Ibid*, p. 52.

Avicenna attempts to stress on the claim that the persistence in existence of contingent entities depends on the persistence of what causes them. And this supports his earlier view that holds that the existence of everything depends on the relation with the Necessary Existent due to Itself.

The account that stresses on the dependency of an effect on a cause, invites counter claims that reflect Occasionalist views *vis à vis* creation, or it leads to dependency conceptions *vis à vis* Emanation. A conception of contingency in relation to causality relies on the continual intervention on the part of causes to support their effects. The countering tendencies in thought, that reject the causal nexus, might reflect some sort of an Occasionalist inclination similar to the philosophical tendency that one attests in al-Ghazālī's account. In his *Tahāfut al-Falāsifa* (The Incoherence of the Philosophers), Abū Ḥāmid al-Ghazālī (1058-1111) rejects the accounts of causal efficacy and denies contingency.[275] What is left for al-Ghazālī is an Occasionalist claim that depends on the continual intervention of the Sole Agent, God. On al-Ghazālī's view, the causal nexus blocks the way for any consideration of miracles. That in terms of causal efficacy and its chain structure, the miraculous divine intervention does not find a place. Al-Ghazālī also refutes, with innovative philosophical terms, the claim that there is a necessary link between a cause and its effect. His accounts in this regard are prototypical to what later figures in the work of David Hume. The *ashʿarī kalām* was also theologically impacted by al-Ghazālī's penetrating critique of causality. Yet, al-Ghazālī's Occasionalism (which finds an echo

[275] It might be debatable whether such denial of contingency reflects what one later encounters in Spinoza's denial of contingency and stress on Necessity, especially in his *Ethics*. What also is the case with al-Ghazālī, is that his Occasionalism reflects similar dimensions to what one encounters in the works of Descartes' disciple, the philosopher Malébranche. And al-Ghazālī's consideration of the causal nexus, in terms of an account of "habits," is reminiscent of what one also encounters at a later period in the works of Hume and in Kant's response to Hume.

in the work of Descartes' disciple Malébranche) attempts to overcome causality by demonstrating that the correlation between cause and effect is not necessary in terms of sense-experience or in terms of reasoning. Like what later appears in the work of Hume, al-Ghazālī has asserted that this correlation or recurrence of cause-effect sequences is a matter of custom (*ᶜāda*) or habit. This reflects that it is not the case that the effect happens due to a cause and through it (*bi-hi*). Rather what is observable is that the effect and cause are simultaneous, that they occur with one another. Al-Ghazālī thus denies the necessary connections between a sequence of events that according to our own logical reasoning and experience, we take to be a causal nexus. Instead of relying on innumerable agents in the sequential connection along the "great chain of being," from cause to effect, al-Ghazālī takes God to be the Sole Agent. Therefore, he rejects the Neoplatonist Emanationist schema that Avicenna reflects in his account of causality and its ordered sequential nexus. Regarding the dependence conception that figures in the Emanation scheme, this is best illustrated in the account of Emanation as a process that does not start at a given time and ceases after all the three *hypostasis* find their determination. The dependency conception, within the conception of Emanation, entails that everything that exists depends at every moment on the One for it to subsist in existence. Like it might be the case with the light metaphor, whatever is lit is always dependent on the source. In being and existence, everything is dependent on the One. Emanation understood this way is not anymore a mere process that starts from the source without implying subsistence. With emanation there is a continual dependence on the source in order that whatever is persists in being. This consideration, of the dependence of effects on causes in the continuation of their existence, also reflects a continuation conception of how a cause relates to its effect, and how all ultimately, through that "great chain of being," depend on the One. Occasionalism, continual emanation, or the subsistence of an effect by virtue of the subsistence of its cause, all of these incompatible schemes show that something is always dependent on what is other than itself in order for it to be. These major cosmological schemes, of Occasionalism, Continual Emanation, and Causality nexus, all figure as ways by virtue of which something persists due to what is other than itself. Therefore, an existent entity depends on what is other than it for it to be. This state of affairs is also attested in terms of the relation between Avicenna's account of causality and his conception of the relation between essence and existence. After all, Avicenna holds that, "the essence of an effect (*dhāt al-maʿlūl*) is not an actuality unless the cause exists."[276] This entails that the *dhāt* (essence, nature, or essential self) of an effect is not sufficient for that effect to be, that the *dhāt* of an effect simply does not imply its existence. Accordingly, one may deduce that the essence, nature, or essential self of an existent does not by itself bring that thing into existence. This account shows that existence requires the existence of something other than the essence, nature, or essential self of a thing in order for that thing to exist. An existential cause is what actualizes the essence, nature, or essential self of a thing. The role of an external existential cause (*ʿilat wūjūd*) in the process of actualization is primary. For the essence of an entity to be actualized, a cause must exist prior to it and act as its cause. And, the existence or the nonexistence, of a contingent being, depends on the existence or nonexistence of its existential cause. A contingent being in itself is realized, and therefore becomes an existent, if its cause exists. The existence of an existential cause turns a contingent being into a necessary existent due to what is other than itself. The nonexistence of an existential cause implies that the contingent being remains within its entrapping contingency. And, on Avicenna's view, what exists does so due to itself or due to what is other than itself as a cause. Only *wājib al-wūjūd bi-dhātihi* (Necessary Existent due to Itself) exists due to Itself; everything else exists due to the existence of existential causes. The necessary existent due

---

276 Avicenna, *Dānish Nāma (Metaphysica of Avicenna),* ed. and trans. by Parviz Morwedge (New York: Columbia University Press, 1973), p. 53.

to what is other than itself is a knowable entity. And, Avicenna holds that it is possible to know a contingent being from the "aspect that it is a necessity."[277] And what exists, exists as such necessarily. Therefore it is also the case that every existent has a cause.[278] And what is caused is knowable by virtue of its cause. Yet, Avicenna also holds that the causes of things are not "completely" known to us. Consequently, he holds that what we express in this regard is a mere opinion and not a certitude (*yaqīn*).[279] This entails that our awareness of causes is not complete, and that there might be causes that we are not aware of. Yet, there is something that we know and this is attested in Avicenna's assertion that "whatever exists is related to the Necessary Existent, since all things come necessarily from It. All things are due to the Necessary Existent and become necessary through their relation with It. Consequently all things are known by It."[280] To understand this passage, one has again to refer to Avicenna's accounts of causality and its relation to necessity. If an existent is necessary due to its cause, then this existent exists due to what is other than itself. And, we have seen above that the Necessary Existent due to Itself is not due to anything but Itself. It is what cannot but be. Even absence itself is a presence of some sort; It is as "there is," or "*il y a*," or "*hunālika*." And as Avicenna holds that "the being of that entity which has being is either necessary (*wājib*) in itself due to its own nature or is not necessary."[281] Unlike anything else, the Necessary

---

[277] *Ibid*, p. 63.

[278] Such claim is also reflected five centuries later in a similar account of reasons that one encounters in Leibniz's consideration of the "Sufficient Reason Principle." That for all there is, there is a sufficient reason for it to be what it is even though we do not know all the reasons.

[279] Avicenna, *Dānish Nāma (Metaphysica of Avicenna)*, ed. and trans. by Parviz Morwedge (New York: Columbia University Press, 1973), p. 63.

[280] *Ibid*, p. 64.

[281] Notice here that what is used is the term "nature" and not essence in reference to *dhāt*, or *dhātihi*. For the quotation, see: Avicenna, *Dānish Nāma*

Existent due to Itself is without cause. It exists due to Itself, and has no *māhīya* (quiddity).

VII- Additional Remarks on the Modalities of Being

In the second part of the Metaphysics book III of *Kitāb al-Najāt*,[282] Avicenna states that: "the Necessary Existent (*wājib al-wūjūd*) is an Existent whose non-existence entails impossibility (*muḥāl*)." And he adds that "the contingent existent (*mumkin al-wūjūd*) is an existent whose existence or non-existence does not entail impossibility (*muḥāl*)." On this account, the Necessary Existent (*wājib al-wūjūd*) is the One whose existence is a must, while the contingent existent (*mumkin al-wūjūd*) is the one whose existence or non-existence (*ᶜadamahu*) is not a must. The Necessary Existent, whose Existence is a must, is a Necessary Existent due to Itself (*wājib al-wūjūd bi-dhātihi*), or it is as such due to what is other than itself (*wājib al-wūjūd bi-ghaīrihi*). If the Necessary Existent is due to Itself (*wājib al-wūjūd bi-dhātihi*), then It cannot also be as such due to what is other than Itself. That which is a necessary existent due to something other than itself (*wājib al-wūjūd bi-ghaīrihi*) is a contingent being (*mumkin al-wūjūd*) due to itself (*bi-dhātihi*) while it is necessary existent (*wājib al-wūjūd*) due to what is other than itself (*bi-ghaīrihi*). Only what is a necessary existent can exist, and it is a necessary existent either due to itself or due to something else other than itself; while what is impossible due to itself (*muḥāl bi-dhātihi*) cannot exist. Contingent being either could have existence or not have existence. And, if a contingent being is a necessary existent, it is as such due to what is other than itself. And, its exis-

---

(Metaphysica of Avicenna), ed. and trans. by Parviz Morwedge (New York: Columbia University Press, 1973), p. 47.

282 Avicenna, *Kitāb al-Najāt, Metaphysics I*, ed. by Majid Fakhry (Beirut: dār al-āfāq al-jadīda, 1985), pp. 261-263.

tence or non-existence does not entail impossibility.[283] Avicenna then holds that the Necessary Existent due to Itself (*wājib al-wūjūd bi-dhātihi*) is "One" (*wāḥid*), "simple," and It is a "pure goodness" (*khaīr maḥḍ*) and "pure perfection" (*kamāl maḥḍ*).[284] After all, Avicenna holds that existence/being (*al-wūjūd*) is goodness (*khaīr*)." Accordingly, one could talk about the goodness of existence or being (*khaīrīyat al-wūjūd*) in the sense of saying that the Necessary Existent due to Itself is pure goodness and perfection.[285] Avicenna also stresses on the convergence between truth, being/existing, and goodness by saying that "there is no real/true (*ḥaq*) more real/true (*aḥaq*) than the Necessary Existent/Being (*wājib al-wūjūd*)."[286] The truest and most real is *wājib al-wūjūd* (The Necessary Existent). Avicenna then adds that the Necessary Existent due to Itself has no quiddity that matches up with It but Its own necessity of existence/being (*wūjūb al-wūjūd lā māhīya lahu tuqārinuhu ghaīr wūjūb al-wūjūd*).[287] He then asserts that:

> The first (*al-awal*) has no genus (*jins*), nor quiddity (*māhīya*), nor quality (*kayfīya*), nor quantity (*kamīya*), nor a place (*ᶜayn*), nor time (*mata*), nor a counterpart (*nad*), nor a partner (*sharīk*), nor a contrary opponent (*ḍid*), be It Exalted.., and that It has no definition (*ḥad*), nor does It have a demon-

---

283 *Ibid*, pp. 261-262.

284 *Ibid*, pp. 263-265. The Necessary Existent due to Itself is pure perfection, since It does not depend on anything else but Itself. It is that which is not depending on emanation or creation. See also: A. M. Goichon, *Le Livre des Directives et Remarques (Kitāb al-Ishārāt wal-Tanbīhāt)* (Paris: Librairie Philosophique J. Vrin, 1951), pp. 396-398.

285 Avicenna, *Kitāb al-Najāt, Metaphysics I*, ed. by Majid Fakhry (Beirut: dār al-āfāq al-jadīda, 1985), p. 265.

286 *Ibid*, pp. 265, 266.

287 Avicenna, *Kitāb al-Shifā', Metaphysics II*, ed. by G. C. Anawati, Ibrahim Madkour, Saᶜid Zayed (Cairo: al-hay'a al-ᶜāmma lil-kitāb, 1975), p. 350.

> stration (*burhān*), rather It is the proof of all that is,..., It is the originary principle (*mabda'*) of all and is not a thing among things [not an entity of entities].[288]

Avicenna then takes being to be what is good. He asserts that:

> The Necessary Existent is pure goodness (*khaīr maḥḍ*), and what is good in general is that which everything longs for, and what all longs for is being (*al-wūjūd*). Nothingness (*al-ᶜadam*) qua nothingness is that which is not longed for, rather it is longed for [i.e. nothingness] if being or perfection of being issues after it, consequently what is in reality (or in truth, *bil-ḥaqīqati*) longed for would be being; since being is pure goodness and pure perfection.[289]

If this is what Avicenna holds with respect to the Necessary Existent due to Itself, then he also holds that a contingent being is what could suffer from non-existing. And, this entails that a contingent being, which could become a necessary existent due to something else, is not pure goodness or perfection.[290] In his later work, *Kitāb al-Ishārāt wal-Tanbīhāt*, Avicenna mentions that, "Existing [or Being (*wūjūd*)] is being true (*ḥaq*)." That "being is truth" (*al-wūjūd ḥaq*).[291] He also objects to those who confuse being with being sensed. On his view, the existent is not always to be confused with what is sensible (*maḥsūs*).[292] Avicenna then remarks that the Necessary Existent due to Itself (*wājib al-wūjūd bi-dhātihi*) is being necessitated due to Itself in the sense that Its truth is self derived. In

---

288 *Ibid*, p. 354.

289 *Ibid*, p. 355.

290 *Ibid*, p. 355.

291 A. M. Goichon, *Le Livre des Directives et Remarques (Kitāb al-Ishārāt wal-Tanbīhāt)* (Paris: Librairie Philosophique J. Vrin, 1951), p. 353.

292 *Ibid*, pp. 351, 352.

this sense, the Necessary Existent due to Itself is also true due to Itself.[293]

An existent being is not impossible (*muḥāl*), since it is an existent. Yet, it is also a contingent being in itself while being [necessary] existent due to what is other than itself. And, its quiddity (*māhīya*) entails that it is neither impossible nor necessary. A necessary existent due to something else is caused by the Necessary Existent due to Itself (*wājib al-wūjūd bi-dhātihi*).[294] A necessary existent due to something else is caused.[295] The Necessary Existent is the cause of everything. It is that from which all existence emanates.[296] It is One, unique, and simple.[297] It is the intellect (*al-ᶜaql*), that which intellects (*al-ᶜāqil*), and what is intelligible (*al-maᶜqūl*).[298] It has no genus (*jins*), no definition (*ḥad*), no demonstration (*burhān*), no quantity (*kam*), no quality (*kayf*), nor quiddity (*māhīya*), nor does It have a place (*ayn*), nor a situation (*wadᶜ*).[299] It has no opponent contrary (*ḍid*), nor partner (*sharīk*), It is One

---

293 *Ibid*, p. 357.

294 *Ibid*, pp. 358-359.

295 *Ibid*, pp. 376-378, 380-384, 386-387.

296 Avicenna, *Kitāb al-Najāt, Metaphysics II*, ed. by Majid Fakhry (Beirut: dār al-āfāq al-jadīda, 1985), pp. 272, 273, 275, 283-285.

297 *Ibid*, p. 266.

298 *Ibid*, pp. 280-281.

299 The Necessary Existent due to itself has no quiddity (*māhīya*) and Its essence is Its Existence. And that which has no quiddity (*māhīya*) is that which cannot have a definition (*ḥad*). Since on Avicenna's view, in the Logic part of *Kitāb al-Ishārāt wal-Tanbīhāt* in: A. M. Goichon, *Le Livre des Directives et Remarques (Kitāb al-Ishārāt wal-Tanbīhāt)* (Paris: Librairie Philosophique J. Vrin, 1951), pp. 103-104. Also see Avicenna's *Kitāb al-Ḥudūd,* section 78 in: A. M. Goichon, Livre des Définitions (Cairo: Institut Français d'Archéologie Orientale du Caire, 1963). Therein, it is mentioned that: "A definition (*ḥad*) is an enunciation that indicates the quiddity (*māhīya*) of a thing."

(*wāḥid*) and indivisible (*lā yanqasim*).[300] Avicenna also adds that, the Necessary Existent due to Itself is not a genus (*jins*) nor is It a genus of substance (*jawhar*), nor is It a substance. The Necessary Existent due to Itself is neither in a subject (*mawḍūʿ*) nor is It a substance (*jawhar*).[301] On this view, the Necessary Existent due to Itself overcomes οὐσία (*ousia*). Therefore, under the ontological and logical modality of necessity due to itself, being overcomes *ousiology*. An οὐσία-based ontology would not account for *wājib al-wūjūd bi-dhātihi*. Under the Avicennian ontological and logical modality of necessity due itself, being cannot anymore be accounted for in terms of the Aristotelian *ousiological* ontology. And, if Avicenna overcomes the *ousiological* aspect of Aristotelian metaphysics, he does so while having a thorough understanding and grasp of the version of Aristotelianism that was available to him in his times. Avicenna explicitly indicates in his biographical counts, that he has read Aristotle's metaphysics "forty times" to the extent that he has memorized it. And, if ontologically one cannot fully reason about the Necessary Existent due to Itself, Avicenna does not stop short in his consideration of the question of being, he rather approaches the ontological issue from the standpoint of an existential

---

300 Avicenna, *Kitāb al-Najāt, Metaphysics II*, ed. by Majid Fakhry (Beirut: dār al-āfāq al-jadīda, 1985), p.288; A. M. Goichon, *Le Livre des Directives et Remarques (Kitāb al-Ishārāt wal-Tanbīhāt)* (Paris: Librairie Philosophique J. Vrin, 1951), pp. 362-367, 368, 369, 370.

301 A. M. Goichon, *Le Livre des Directives et Remarques (Kitāb al-Ishārāt wal-Tanbīhāt)* (Paris: Librairie Philosophique J. Vrin, 1951), pp. 367-369.

analytic of *al-nafs* (as *anima/Dasein* non-substance based self). This consideration of *al-nafs* is hermeneutic in the sense of being a processional and existential interpretation that is addressed in terms of epistemological considerations and meta-mystic insights that are mediated by an analytic of the existentiality of the being of *al-nafs* (examined in chapters 6 and 7 of this book).

CHAPTER 5
BEING AND ESSENCE

I- The Essence/Existence Distinction

Avicenna's distinction between essence and existence has been taken to be central to his metaphysics and to his ontology of being. Due to the influence that this distinction had on Thomism, and to a lesser extent on Maimonides' work, some Medievalists and Orientalists took Avicenna's distinction between essence and existence to be characterized by essentialism. A. M. Goichon's books: "*Léxique de la Langue Philosophique d'Ibn Sina,*" and "*Vocabulaires Comparés d'Aristote et d'Ibn Sina,*"[302] along with her interpretation of the Avicennian essence/existence distinction, all offered a great contribution to the translation, transliteration, and understanding of Avicenna's works. However the reception of Goichon's works has had a strong influence on subsequent Medievalists as well as Orientalist scholars. This impact on scholars, along with the stress on Avicenna's influence on Thomism, lead in some instances to an exaggerated stress on the centrality of the essence/existence distinction in Avicenna's metaphysics. This state of affairs eventually overshadowed other important aspects of Avicenna's ontology of being, and the metaphysical as well as logical analysis of being in terms of the modalities of necessity, contingency, and impossibility. The examination of Avicenna's metaphysics under the spell of all of these factors leads to an intellectually discomforting position that construes his ontology as essentialism. Consequently this led to the interpretation of his work as being that of a metaphysician that subordinates existence to essence. Such an interpretation has been even adopted by experts on Avicenna's work within the western scholarship, as

302 A. M. Goichon, *Léxique de la Langue Philosophique d'Ibn Sina (Avicenne)* (Paris: Desclée de Brouwer, 1938); A. M. Goichon, *Vocabulaires Comparés d'Aristote et d'Ibn Sina (Avicenne)* (Paris: Desclée de Brouwer, 1939).

well as among some Arabists. And, some scholars stress that Averroes (Ibn Rushd) and Mullā Ṣadrā are the metaphysicians of existence, while taking Avicenna to be the metaphysician of essence. John Caputo, who is a leading interpreter of Heidegger's thought, makes extensive references to the work of the Thomist scholar É. Gilson in the context of examining Aquinas' adoption of the Avicennian distinction between essence and existence. Caputo's discussion of the essence/existence distinction adopts the standpoint that Gilson reflects in the reading of Avicenna's metaphysics as being the staring point of a long standing essentialist tradition that culminates with Hegel's Logic. This line of argumentation already supplied Caputo with sufficient arguments that enabled him to readily stamp Avicenna's metaphysics with Heidegger's critique of the tradition. Caputo based himself on what the Thomist scholar Gilson offers in this regard, particularly in taking Aquinas' metaphysics to be the metaphysics of *esse*. Gilson's position may itself be questioned on the ground that its interpretation of Avicenna has been pervaded by Thomist inclinations. And this is the case, given that Gilson and other scholars construe Avicenna's metaphysics as being essentially the metaphysics of essence. Based on this, Caputo accepts the claim that Avicenna's ontology is essentialist.[303] Such readings lead to the conclusion that Avicenna subordinates existence to essence and consequently that his ontology is characterized by the oblivion of being. The question that ought to be raised in this regard is whether the position of secondary scholarly sources is accurate. This is the case, given that some of the scholars that propagate the claim that Avicenna is an essentialist, are after all scholars that have not consulted or studied the primary sources. They rather primarily rely on

[303] In the last section of this chapter, I will briefly introduce a reply to J. Caputo's and É. Gilson's claims while addressing Avicenna's thought of being in terms of Heidegger's critique of metaphysics. I will also link this reply to a brief investigation of the manner in which Caputo receives Heidegger's critique, and the way he uses this critique in terms of probing the extent of its applicability to St. Thomas Aquinas' philosophy.

secondary sources that mediate Avicenna's metaphysics through the Thomist scholarship. Having said that, the issue becomes more complicated in the light of considering Arabist or Medievalist scholars who do consult the primary Arabic sources, yet still hold that Avicenna is an essentialist. Such scholars remain under the influence of earlier translations, transliterations, and interpretations that were offered by prominent Orientalist scholars. And, those Orientalists addressed the essence/existence distinction in the light of broad philosophical concerns with Medieval Latin and Jewish philosophy, or by tracing the Aristotelian and Peripatetic influences on Islamic and Arabic philosophy. The Medievalists who consult primary sources, yet who are still under the spell of earlier Orientalist views, do not attempt to review some of their positions by going back to a closer examination of the texts and to a questioning reception of dominant translations and interpretations. There is a hermeneutic need to return to the primary texts and re-examine them in the light of new philosophical concerns. This is also needed in the light of questioning and adopting new methodological inclinations in translation and interpretation. And this becomes a pressing issue, given the seriousness of the philosophical consequences that might arise if we readily take Avicenna's metaphysics to be characterized by essentialism. The examination of Avicenna's ontology must account for the renderings of the terms *māhīya*, *dhāt*, and *wūjūd*, be it in Latin, English or French, or in terms of the Arabic/Persian semantic, syntactic, and grammatical structure and derivation. The translation nuances are determined by how these terms are philosophically used within the text and in the course of development of Avicenna's arguments. Such linguistic investigations would elucidate the philosophical interpretation of the essence/existence distinction in the light of addressing contemporary philosophical concerns, as the case might well be with the Heideggerian critique of classical ontology.

II- Being, Existence, Essence, and Existents

Avicenna had a thorough knowledge of the Aristotelian theory of categories, and he also was well versed in his philosophical consideration of substance (*jawhar*), and of essence and quiddity (*māhīya*). After all, he himself mentions in his biography that he has read Aristotle's metaphysics forty times and was able to recite it by heart. His distinction between essence and existence was also supported by his ontological and logical analysis of being in terms of the modalities. And his distinction between essence and existence is also undertaken in the context of a syntactic inquiry (*lafẓī*) in terms of which essence is taken to be prior to existents. And it is also conducted in terms of non-syntactic [actual] inquiries (*ghaīr lafẓī*) that consist of either a conceptualist investigation (*zihnī*) or a non-conceptualist investigation (*ghaīr zihnī*). In the case of an inquiry that is conceptualist (*zihnī*) the consideration of concepts and abstract non-existent entities shows that essence is taken to be prior to existence. In the case of a non-conceptualist (*ghaīr zihnī*) empirical or perceptual consideration of entities or experiences, existents are taken to be prior to essence. In this sense, and depending on the type of inquiry, Avicenna's approach is both essentialist and existentialist while taking these approaches to be compatible and complementary of one another.

Substance (οὐσία [*ousia*]), is an essence that is not in a subject, while an accident is an essence that subsists in a subject. This constitutes an Aristotelian account of substance and accidents according to which being gets divided. The principles of reality are matter and form, and these are not distinct. Form constitutes the material and formal causes of things. Matter is that which has a potentiality to be complete, while form is that whose completeness is realized in actuality. This entails that form is closer to being a necessary existent that is as such due to what is other than itself, while matter is more like a contingent being that is as such due to itself. And both matter and form do mark what we also attest with regard to the contingent being due to itself and the necessary existent due to what is other than itself. Form is a necessary existent that has been actualized due to what is other than itself, while matter is that which has potential realization and is therefore a contingent being that is what it is due to itself. It has been shown earlier that the Necessary Existent is an Existent whose nonexistence entails impossibility. It is impossible for the Necessary Existent not to exist. It is impossible for It not to be. This is not the case with contingent being, since its nonexistence does not entail impossibility, while the impossible is that whose existence is impossible. Even if contingent being is not necessary, its nonexistence does not entail its non-being, in the sense that its nonexistence does not entail that it is nothing. The Necessary Existent is that which is not granted existence. It is what exists due to Itself by virtue of possessing *no other essence but existence.* Given this state of affairs, and given that existence/being (*al-wujūd*) is goodness and perfection, then *essence reaches its highest determination in existence* and not the other way round. So, from the standpoint of ontology, one may advance the thesis that based on Avicenna's account of existence in relation to perfection and goodness his ontology is not completely characterized by essentialism. With Avicenna one does not attest an essentialist line of thought that finds the highest determination of being in essence (as is the case with the essentialist line of thought that finds its highest determination in Hegel's *Logic*). Some scholars like Goichon, Roland-Gosselin, and Gardet might think that existence with Avicenna becomes some sort of an accident of essence that has been received *ab extrinseco*. Yet, it is still the case that goodness and perfection of being point towards the high determination of essence in terms of existence. Louis Gardet observes that with Avicenna, "the fundamental principle is that everything that exists desires its perfection; some sort of an ontological love" (Gardet, 1952, p. 37). Such "ontological love" (*un amour ontologique*) is a mark of souls that are endowed with λόγος (*logos*), endowed with speech (*nufūs nāṭiqa*). Love cannot but be the trait of a living existent that is endowed with speech (*al-nafs al-nāṭiqa*). The soul endowed with *logos* is the one that is able to love. And, as Gardet adds, each existent is "animated by a natural longing (*ᶜishq*)" and "innate love" by virtue of which that existent tends to its "self-perfection" (Gardet, 1952, p. 37). This ontological love acts as a sufficient reason behind the existence of an intelligent being. Pointing towards this "loving" trait in living intelligent existents, Gardet writes that Avicenna's fundamental intuition is not to be mainly found in his emanationist cosmology or in his deterministic views of existence. It is rather the case that Avicenna's fundamental intuition is accounted for in terms of the [vital] flux (*élan*) of ontological love (*amour ontologique*) of every being that exists for its source and in the desire of every intellectual being to encounter its First Principle (Gardet, 1952, p. 67). This *ᶜishq* is more like a mystic love of the order of ἀγαπη (*agapē*) which is more intense than love as ἐρως (*eros*).

In a linguistic account, the Arabic term *māhīya* is composed of two terms: *mā* and *huwa*, or *mā* and *hīya*, the *mā* is used in a question form to ask about something. When one says in Arabic: "*mā huwa?*" The question is then rendered in English as: "what is it?" The term *huwa* is used in reference to a masculine entity while the term *hīya* is used in reference to what is feminine. "*Mā huwa*?" or "*mā hīya*?" are questions that ask about what makes something what it is. They are fundamental questions about what something is as opposed to what it is not. These questions of essence ask about "what is it to be?" (*to ti ēn einai*). These questions wonder about the *quid*/what/*mā* of something. They are questions about the quiddity of something, where quiddity (the Latin *quidditas*) fits well as a possible rendering of the Arabic term *māhīya*. The term "essence" has its roots in the Latin *essentia*, which is also linked to the root *esse* (to be). Essence is that which makes something what it is. And it does so by virtue of being the intrinsic fundamental self (*dhāt*) that constitutes the inward nature underlying the manifestations of a thing. The Arabic term *dhāt* might be more specifically rendered as "self," while *ṭabīᶜa* or *ṭabᶜ* may both be rendered as "the nature of something." Quiddity (*māhīya*) implies the essence of a thing or its essential self, in the sense that the quiddity of a thing is its "whatness" which also comprises its substance and qualities that make it up as being the thing it is. It is in terms of its quiddity that a thing is distinguished from another, since quiddity is what makes something what it is, and asking about the quidditative aspect of a thing, is asking about what is constitutive of the essence of that thing. Given this, if *māhīya* is rendered as quiddity, and *dhāt* is rendered as essence, essential self, or nature, then *māhīya* is constitutive of the *dhāt* of something. In the English translation of the *Dānish Nāma-i ᶜalāī*, we read that: "the being of a substance is due to its essence (nature, *dhāt*) while the being of being possible is due not to its essence (nature, *dhāt*) but to that thing which is its possibility of being."[304] In this passage, *dhāt* is mainly rendered as "essence" while "nature" is taken to be a possible alternative rendering.[305] In a similar fashion, the interplay in the rendering of *māhīya* and *dhāt* causes confusions that feed into the claims that take Avicenna's metaphysics to be a metaphysics of essence. A clarification of this nuance, between taking *dhāt* as essence or taking it either as nature or essential self, holds important consequences for our reading of Avicenna's ac-

---

304 Avicenna, *Dānish Nāma (The Metaphysica of Avicenna)*, ed. and trans. by Parviz Morewedge (New York: Columbia University Press, 1973), p. 46.

305 Goichon renders *dhāt* as essence and also says that *dhāt* may be rendered as by itself (*par soi*) and as the in itself (*en soi*), given that this rendering is taken by her to be a more general rendering than essence. She then renders *māhīya* as *quidditas* while giving it the sense of a secondary *ousia*. *Wūjūd* is rendered as *être* or *existence* [being or existence] and the *mawjūd* (*ens*) as that which exists [*ce qui existe*]; and she gives *wujida* the sense of that which was in the state of being "*il fut dans l'état d'être*." As for *inna* or *anna*, Goichon renders takes them to be a fact of being, or as a *mawjūd* (*ens*), and in a more general sense as "there is." Or as the *hypostatsis* of "*il'y a*" (there is, *hunālika*) which is linked to the Greek εἶναι (*einai*) and out of which is linked to the Arabic term *anīya*. See: A. M. Goichon, *Vocabulaires Comparés d'Aristote et d'Ibn Sina* (Paris: Desclée De Brouwer, 1939), pp. 1-2, 12, 33, 38.

count of essence and existence. The same holds true with regard to the rendering of *māhīya* sometimes as essence and at other times as quiddity. This is the case given that the Necessary Existent due to Itself (*wājib al-wūjūd bi- dhātihī*) does not have *māhīya* and It is what It is due to Its *dhāt*. Yet *māhīya*, as the quiddity of something, is also its essence. So, the Necessary Existent due to Itself is as such due to Its *dhāt* while being that which has no *māhīya*, i.e. has no quiddity or essence. It is therefore more likely the case that in the context of talking about the Necessary Existent due to Itself, the term *dhāt* occurring in the expression: "*wājib al-wūjūd bi- dhātihī*" would be rendered as "Its-Self," rather than being "Its essence." Given this interpretation, one might claim that in the case of the Necessary Existent due to Itself, the distinction between essence and existence is not central and consequently essentialism does not hold. To further elucidate the difficulties in translation, the term *wūjūd* itself is either rendered as existence or being, while another term like *ānīya* is also used in reference to existence and being. However, *ānīya* has a sense of *presence* since it is linked to *anna* which relates to *al-ishāra* (ostensive definition or pointing). Furthermore, the Persian term *hasti* provides another nuance that distinguishes between *wūjūd* (existence) and *hasti* (being). According to Jamil Saliba, *māhīya* is rendered as being that which asks about the whatness of something in the mind. And, *ḥaqīqa* (reality/truth) is that which asks about the whatness of something in the world. While, *huwīya* (identity) is that which asks about the whatness of something in terms of its distinction from another. And *dhāt* (self, or nature) is that which holds the whatness that makes something what it is.[306] Based on this rendering, *ḥaqīqa* (reality) and *huwīya* (identity) are less universal than *māhīya* (quiddity) and *dhāt* (self), in the

---

306 Jamil Saliba, *Al-Muᶜjam al-Falsafī*, Vol. II (Beirut: dār al-kitāb al-lubnānī, 1971), p. 315; Salem Mashran, *Al-Jānib al-Ilāhī ᶜinda Ibn Sīnā* (Damascus: dār quṭayba, 1992), p. 62.

sense that *māhīya* and *dhāt* apply to what exists and what does not exist, while *ḥaqīqa* and *huwīya* are more restricted to what exists. Regarding some broader views of essence and existence, the *ashᶜarī mutakalimūn* (exponents of *kalām*) held that existence and essence are the same for the Necessary Existent (*wājib al-wūjūd*), as well as contingent beings. This position is attested in al-Ashᶜarī's work as well as in al-Ījī's. According to the *muᶜtazilī kalām,* existence has the same meaning for the Necessary Existent as well as the contingent beings. While Avicenna holds that the Necessary Existent has no quiddity (*lā māhīya lahu*) and that Its existence is due to Its *dhāt* (Its-Self). This is the case, while the contingent being possesses an essence that is other than its existence, and is brought into existence by virtue of what is other than itself.[307] Being/existence (*al-wūjūd*) is not due to the essence or quiddity of things, since it is what happens to things and their essences. Existence is more like an advantageous happening or occurrence. Things are given or granted their existence not due to themselves but due to something else. There is a distinction that is drawn between the reality (*ḥaqīqa*) of something and its essence from one side, and the reality of that thing and its existence from the other side. This distinction entails a distinction between causes of essence (*ᶜilal māhīya*) and causes of existence or being (*ᶜilal wūjūd*). The contingent being is that whose existence is necessary due to an existential cause (*ᶜilat wūjūd*) that is other than itself. The cause of existence (*ᶜilat al-wūjūd*) implies the necessity of existence of something due to something else other than itself. In this sense, contingency prepares the ground for the necessity of the existential cause. The necessary existence of a contingent being is due to something other than itself, and this implies that the contingency of that being prepares the conditions for a necessary existence due to something other than the contingent being. In the

307 Salem Mashran, *Al-Jānib al-Ilāhī ᶜinda Ibn Sīnā* (Damascus: dār quṭayba, 1992), pp. 62-63.

case of a contingent being, and its necessary existence due to something other than itself, necessity is due to an active external cause of existence while contingency lays down the conditions for such a necessary existence due to something else. Necessity is that which acts as the main reason behind bringing something from potentiality into actuality. And, on Avicenna's account, it is not due to the nature or essence of something that the actualization of something takes place. It is not due to its essence or nature that something moves from potentiality into actuality. This in itself undermines the status of essence viz. existence. The move from potentiality into actuality is due to the necessity that follows from an active cause, that is external, and that brings something from potentiality into actuality. The necessary existence, of an existent being, is due to what is other than itself. A contingent being has to have an active cause of existence (*ᶜilat wūjūd*) that brings that being into existence as a necessary existent due to something other than itself. The claim that the distinction between essence and existence points to essentialism, is a claim that links Avicenna's work to a later development within Western Philosophy that culminates in Hegel's Logic. And, this claim sees essentialism as being a triumph of the "notion," "concept," and "essence," within some sort of a Hegelian emanationist scheme. Those who hold such a view simply think that Avicenna's distinction between essence and existence eventually is nothing other than the subordination of being and existence to essence. Those who hold this view refer to Avicenna through Latin translations and secondary sources that are entrapped in thinking about *wūjūd, māhīya,* and *dhāt*, in terms of the inner workings of the Latin renderings of *esse*, *existentia*, *quidditas*, and *essentia*, without going back to primary Arabic texts. With some of those scholars, the meditation on Avicenna's work mainly passes through Maimonides (Mūssa Ibn Maïmūn) or through Thomas Aquinas or Duns Scotus. Given this state of affairs, the distinction between *wūjūd* and *māhīya* should be considered in the light of Avicenna's metaphysics of necessity (*wājib, wūjūb*) and that of contingency (*mumkin, imkān*). And, this account is tied to

Avicenna's doctrine of the contingency of the world and to his conception of divine creation, where being is a *gift* that is granted to beings that participate in *being*. This conception, of a participation in being, takes the essence of beings, or their essential constitution, to be the limiting and constraining feature in their participation in being. In other words, the participation of beings in *being* is intense or limited by virtue of the *essentia* or quiddity of beings.

III- A Reply to the Essentialism Claim

In his book: "Heidegger and Aquinas, An Essay on Overcoming Metaphysics," John D. Caputo says, in the context of quoting Étienne Gilson, that being (*Sein*) has been reduced by Platonism to unity, and by Aristotelianism to substance (οὐσία, [*ousia*]). And in the essentialist tradition from Avicenna to Hegel, "being becomes essence."[308] Caputo then adds that [the Avicennian] "essentialism" reaches its high levels with Duns Scotus who is the "foremost logicist and essentialist philosopher of the High Middle Ages."[309] Adopting a strict Heideggerian agenda, Caputo holds that the understanding of being in terms of essence and existence "belongs to the oblivion [of being] in the Heideggerian sense." And this hints to the oblivion of being as it may be detected in the essence and existence distinction. Accordingly, this critique is directed to Avicenna's distinction be-

---

[308] In objection to Gilson's accounts, one may refer to what Parviz Morewedge advances. Professor Morewedge holds that the "scarcity" in the availability of material, for the Western Scholarship in the area of Near Eastern philosophy, and the "underlying interest in a particular religion," both underlie the works of some scholars. And, these scholars address the works of Near Eastern Philosophers (like Avicenna) in terms of studies that investigate what is reminiscent of the Aristotelian or Thomist works. In Gilson's case, the Thomist interests are coupled with a background in "Catholicism," and both influence the manner Gilson approaches the work of Avicenna. See: Avicenna, *Dānish Nāma (The Metaphysica of Avicenna)* (New York: Columbia University Press, 1973), pp. 2-3.

[309] John D. Caputo, *Heidegger and Aquinas: An Essay On Overcoming Metaphysics* (New York: Fordham University Press, 1982), pp. 2, 32-33, 102.

tween essence and existence. On Caputo's interpretation of Heidegger, the oblivion of being is characterized by the oblivion of the "*difference*" which opens up the unthought ontological difference between being and beings.[310] On this account, what remains to be thought is the *Ereignis* (the event of appropriation) which diverges from the Aristotelian *ousiology*. Thinking about *Ereignis* is thinking about that which sends, grants, and gives being. It is a thinking that calls for thinking about the granting rather than thinking about the granted. It stresses on giving rather than stressing on the gift. In other terms, it calls for a thinking that thanks, commemorates, and recollects. This thinking displays "openness to [the] mystery" of the self-withdrawing sending of being. The appropriate response of *Dasein*, to the grace of the gift of being, is thanking. This is taken to be a thinking that moves in the direction of a mystical Love that is without "reasons," as to defy Leibniz's Principle of Sufficient Reason.[311] If philosophy from Descartes on, has meant "subject-ism," i.e. "The unleashing of the demand of the ego for conformity to its own a priori prescriptions." Then, according to Caputo, what is needed, "instead of philosophy," is a "thinking" which learns from the "mystical poet" how "to let beings be,…, without why." On this account, to think is to let beings be. It is to let being "lie forth."[312] In this regard, the objection to Aquinas (as advanced by Caputo), which may also be extended to Avicenna, is that a "causal-ontological" account of things emerges from a philosophy of "*actualitas*" that is based on a "Roman language of production." According to Caputo, such state of affairs is touched by the Heideggerian objection to the metaphysics that attends to the *realitas*, *causalitas*, and *actualitas*, while neglecting the "unconcealment process" that

---

310 *Ibid*, pp. 3, 4.

311 John D. Caputo, *The Mystical Element in Heidegger's Thought* (New York: Fordham University Press, 1986), pp. 27, 29.

312 *Ibid*, pp. 76, 80.

consequently falls into oblivion.[313] What eludes Heidegger's critique of metaphysics is a mystic tendency that overcomes the confines of the propositional logical truth and tends towards the truth of an ineffable face-to-face encounter; a truth that is accordingly beyond ratiocination, and is of the order of a "mystic union." If this is what Caputo advocates as being what eludes Heidegger's critique,[314] then Avicenna's philosophical mysticism of the Visionary Recitals consequently eludes Heidegger's critique. Based on Gilson's reading of the "reduction of being," to *unity* or *idea*, to *ousia* , or to essence, Caputo's account of Avicenna's distinction between essence and existence reflects an objection to the claimed "primacy of essence" over existence that such distinction (supposedly) propounds. Caputo, Gilson, and H. A. Wolfson, are among those scholars who hold that on Avicenna's view, a created substance must, in order to be created, have had "existence super-added to its essence."[315] On this account, existence figures as being an "accidental (*per accidens*) addition" to the created *ousia* (substance) that is not anymore an actual *ousia*, but is rather reduced to being a possible *ousia*. However, given this consideration, Caputo still concedes that Avicenna did "insist" on the "uniqueness of existence." Yet, it is still the case, that according to Caputo's and Gilson's [incomplete] reading of Avicenna, essence is

---

313 John D. Caputo, *Heidegger and Aquinas: An Essay On Overcoming Metaphysics* (New York: Fordham University Press, 1982), p. 6.

314 *Ibid,* pp. 10, 11.

315 Harry Austryn Wolfson says that Avicenna, and his "Jewish followers, as [Moses] Maimonides," maintain that "existence is an accident super-added to the essence." If Gilson addresses this Avicennian distinction in relation to Aquinas and Catholicism, Wolfson addresses it in relation to Spinoza's Philosophy in particular and Jewish philosophy in general; see: Harry Austryn Wolfson, *The Philosophy of Spinoza* (New York: Meridian Books, The World Publishing Company, 1961), I, p. 125.

still that which has primacy over existence.[316] Both Caputo and Gilson, do not address the intricacy and originality that Avicenna's ontological account of being holds. Caputo does not make any reference to Avicenna's ontolological and logical use of the modalities of being in relation to his essence/existence distinction. Caputo readily based himself on Gilson's account in order to consider Avicenna's metaphysics as being the "metaphysics of essence." And, this paves the way for him to easily take Aquinas' metaphysics to be the "metaphysics of existence." As if it were the case that it was a matter of convenience to draw a distinction between Aquinas and his Avicennian source of inspiration. Caputo makes this move towards Avicenna in an effort to question why (in his own terms) Heidegger did not account for the (Avicenna/Averroes) "Arab interlude." Yet even if Caputo is able to recognize the importance of attending to Avicenna's contributions in relation to "the matter to be thought" (*Sache des Denkens*), i.e. being, nevertheless he did not have access to the original texts. And he did not consider Avicenna's work through the Avicennian scholarship. His account of Avicenna was mediated through the works of Gilson who considers Avicenna's work in terms of its links to Thomism. And Thomas Aquinas' reception of the Avicennian essence/existence distinction could be traced mainly in *S. Thomas Aquinatis opusculum De ente et essentia.*[317] Therein, Aquinas holds that "whatever does not belong to the concept of essence [*essentia*] or quiddity [*quidditas*] comes from outside it and makes up a composition with essence." He then adds that, "every essence or quiddity can be known without anything being known concerning its being [*esse*]." Consequently, he concludes

316 John D. Caputo, *Heidegger and Aquinas: An Essay On Overcoming Metaphysics* (New York: Fordham University Press, 1982), p. 109.

317 Regarding this text, see: Thomas Aquinas, *S. Thomas Aquinatis opusculum De ente et essentia*, ed. by C. Boyer (Rome: Gregorian University, 1933); Thomas Aquinas, *On Being and Essence*, trans. by A. Maurer (Toronto: The Pontifical Institute of Medieval Studies, 1949).

that, "it is obvious that being is other than essence or quiddity," yet he also adds that this would be the case unless there is "something whose quiddity is its being." And like is the case with Avicenna, Aquinas holds that "there can only be one such being, the First."[318] Given this interpretation of the Avicennian distinction between essence and existence, Aquinas then asserts that anything other than that whose essence is Its existence (being), it is necessary that such thing should have its being other than its quiddity or nature or form. This would be the case given that this thing is not caused by its form or quiddity or else it would be its own cause and would bring itself into existence. Yet, it is rather the case that every thing whose being is other than its nature should have its being from another. This view of being as a granting act would be deduced from Aquinas' reading of Avicenna.[319] From this brief passage among many others, one still attests that what Aquinas is advocating does not divert from the Avicennian heritage, yet Caputo is still able to receive Thomism as "existentialism" while seeing Avicennism as "essentialism."

John Caputo holds that the line of "essentialist metaphysics" passes from Avicenna, to Duns Scotus, Suárez, Descartes, and influences the whole of the Rationalist movement, up to Hegel. Caputo also extends his Gilsonian support to touch upon Kant by saying that the philosophy of essence and concept is the place in which the ontological argument could flourish. He also holds that Kant's claim, that existence is just a positing mode of a subject, "has its roots all the way back in Avicenna." This is the case given that this Kantian account does not take existence to be an essence, therefore arguing in favor of the essence/existence distinction. However, Gilson and Caputo take what they call the Avicennian essentialist line, to be a line that culminates in Hegel, "the high priest of the concept and es-

[318] See the translated excerpts in: James J. Walsh, "On Being and Essence," in *Philosophy in the Middle Ages*, ed. by Arthur Hyman & James J. Walsh (Indianapolis: Hackett Publishing Company, 1986), p. 514

[319] *Ibid*, p. 515.

sentialism" with whom "logic has eaten up all reality," and "existence disappears under objective thought."[320] Caputo's incomplete account of Avicenna, is also reflected in the failure to make a reference to Avicenna's mystic Visionary Recitals, which irrefutably elude the claims of essentialism and elude Heidegger's critique of metaphysics. Caputo holds that what is needed is an "integrated philosophy of essence and existence, in which *being* primarily signifies existence without eliminating essence, in which *being* means "that which is" (to inflect the old formula slightly differently).[321] Avicenna seems to be a philosopher who achieves this task without turning being into something other than being. With Avicenna, being is neither reduced into an entity nor is it reduced into an essence. Based on taking the first being to be that which is "existence only," Caputo holds that Aquinas is by that "the author of the wholly un-Aristotelian thought of an act which is not form, of an act which actualizes form itself," where God is subsisting *esse*, pure *esse*, *esse* only.[322] This account reflects the extent of Caputo's inaccessibility to Avicenna's works. Since what has been advanced above, in relation to Aquinas, is none other than a paraphrasing of what is learned from the Avicennian corpus. The account stated above is evidently the account that Avicenna advances in relation to the Necessary Existent due to Itself (*wājib al-wūjūd bi-dhātihi*). The overcoming of the Aristotelian *ousiology* is attested with Avicenna's account of the Necessary Existent which is not substance (*ousia*), nor genus, nor species, nor does It have definition, description, quantity, quality, or place. The Necessary Existent due to Itself is pure goodness, and pure perfection.

---

320 John D. Caputo, *Heidegger and Aquinas: An Essay On Overcoming Metaphysics* (New York: Fordham University Press, 1982), pp. 109-112.

321 *Ibid*, p. 113.

322 *Ibid*, p. 124.

And this is so given that existence/being (*wujūd*) is perfection.[323] If what Caputo quotes from Aquinas is meant to be an indication that Aquinas "has left the Greek world behind," then this is also the case with Avicenna the originator of the views that allow for such an overcoming to take place. Caputo then quotes from Aquinas: "that alone is able to be understood by our intellect which has quiddity which participates in *esse*. But the quiddity of God is *esse* itself, whence He is beyond understanding."[324] This is evidently what Avicenna advances in relation to *wājib al-wujūd bi-dhātihi* (Necessary Existent due to Itself), which is beyond all beings, and who mystically exceeds our intellect that is only at home with beings and cannot comprehend the Necessary Existent due to Itself. On Caputo's reading, all of this would entail that the philosopher who holds such views is getting closer and closer to Heidegger's thought of being.[325] Another issue that is to be addressed is related to what in Arabic is called *tashkīk al-wujūd*, which expresses the hierarchy in the chain of beings that "participate" in being. And, this hierarchy is based on a variation in degrees of intensity in the "participation" in being.[326] According to *tashkīk al-wujūd*, all beings are participants in being. And, such a Neoplatonist Islamic doctrine of the "participation in being" (which Aquinas also adopts) is taken by Caputo to be in accord with Heidegger's distinction between being and beings. Being is pure perfection and beings participate in that perfection. On this account, we do not say that "being is" we rather say that "a being is." And in this sense, we draw an ontological distinction between being and beings. In this account, the Necessary Existent (which is without

---

323 Refer to what has been advanced in the previous chapter "The Ontology of Being," on the Necessary Being (*wājib al-wujūd*).

324 John D. Caputo, *Heidegger and Aquinas: An Essay On Overcoming Metaphysics* (New York: Fordham University Press, 1982), p. 131.

325 *Ibid*, p. 131.

326 The notion of *tashkīk al-wujūd* will be elaborated later in chapter 7 of this book on "The Authenticity of Being."

definition, without genus, species, or description) is pure perfection that is not in need of anything extraneous to It. All of these accounts are taken by Caputo to be in conformity with what Heidegger seeks regarding the thought of being.[327] Herein, the *tashkīk* participation doctrine reveals Neoplatonic tendencies that loosen up the Aristotelian ousiological metaphysical language. The Necessary Existent due to Itself (*wājib al-wūjūd bi-dhātihi*) is pure being (pure *esse*) according to Its own idea; and this might be taken by Caputo's reading to be an initiation of an "*einaiology*" in the face of "*ousiology*."[328] The Necessary Existent due to Itself (*wājib al-wūjūd bi-dhātihi*) is that which is "self-withdrawing." It is what one encounters in Heidegger's account of the "self-withdrawing" of being. And as Caputo holds in his book, *The Mystical Element in Heidegger's Thought*, such self-withdrawing *being* reflects an account of a thinking that avoids ontology in the name of thinking about the primordial granting that figures in the mystery of the sending and self-withdrawing of being. And this is seen by Caputo as being what Nietzsche, Heidegger, and Derrida have attempted to do.[329] Given that these views are originally those of Avicenna, yet echoed by Aquinas. And, given that these views elude Heidegger's critique, and get close to the Heideggerian thought of being. Then it seems that within Caputo's own text, the claim that Avicenna's metaphysics is that of *essentia* seems altogether to be refuted based on accounts that Caputo advances with regard to Aquinas' views which echo what originally appears in Avicenna's works. Yet one cannot request that Caputo covers all of these grounds, since he did not have a sufficient knowledge of Avicenna's work in order for him to make such significant links. After all, it seems that Caputo's text contains the claim that Avicenna's

327 John D. Caputo, *Heidegger and Aquinas: An Essay On Overcoming Metaphysics* (New York: Fordham University Press, 1982), pp. 131-133.

328 *Ibid*, pp. 135, 136.

329 John D. Caputo, *The Mystical Element in Heidegger's Thought* (New York: Fordham University Press, 1986), p. xx.

metaphysics is that of essentialism, while at the same time offering what implicitly constitutes the basis for the refutation of this claim of essentialism. In all of this, Avicenna's thought gets very close to Heidegger's thought of being without the need to refute or overcome metaphysics as first philosophy. In Avicenna's works, thought and philosophy live side by side along with mysticism. The metaphysical language neighbors the poetic and mystical language of thought. This is a polemical Avicennian achievement that avoids the utopian refutation of those indispensable elements of the conventional metaphysical tradition, while humbly moving towards the beyond through a mystic and poetic language. This is how Avicenna enacts what teaches us how to attend to "the matter to be thought" (*Sache des Denkens*); i.e., *al-wūjūd*: being.

CHAPTER 6
THE EPISTEMOLOGY OF BEING

I- The "Suspended Person Argument"

Avicenna's famous "Suspended Person Argument" (also known as the "Flying Man Argument" or the "Floating Man Argument") appears at the onset of his *De Anima* part of the Physics of *Kitāb al-Shifā'*. In the first chapter (*faṣl*) of the first *maqāla* (part) of the *De Anima* book of the *Ṭabīʿīāt* (Physics) of *Kitāb al-Shifā'*, Avicenna presents what was called the "Suspended Person Argument." And, this argument supports the affirmation (*ithbāt*) of the existence (*wūjūd*) of *al-nafs* (which normally may be translated into self or soul), while not being based on an account of substance or metaphysical considerations of subjectivity. The "Suspended Person Argument" (or what has been known as the "Floating Man Argument") points towards an experiential field whereby the self or subject is not a substance or a static unity. What is rather described is a self/soul field of experiences that is self-generated from an experiential process (Almost similar to what one encounters in the notion of "prehension" of Alfred North Whitehead). The self-generated experiences are not those of a static self-same state, they rather describe a vector. In this sense, the self is not a self-same substance; it is rather a potentiality-for-being-itself (almost like what characterizes the authenticity of being in *Dasein*'s being-in-the-world). *Al-nafs* is experiential, existential, and its being is stamped with the mark of becoming. And this account of selfhood, or its experiential *Anima/Dasein* dimension, is to be considered in terms of reflecting on the hermeneutic notion of *al-ta'wīl* that represents a return back to the ground of the self as a return to *al-awal* (as primordial *nafs*). And this is similar to what one encounters in Maurice Merleau-Ponty's consideration of the primordial subject that is beneath the subject, whereby being is already being oriented.[330] Avicenna's consideration of the encounter of being through an existential analytic of the existence of *al-nafs* (*anima/Dasein*) is hermeneutic and at the same time it is meant to show something that is not explicitly said. Avicenna's account of *al-nafs* is not based on subjectivity. And the "Suspended Person Argument" presents a version of depicting how *al-nafs* (loosely as *anima*, or soul-field) is the limit of the world. That *al-nafs* does not thus exist as a metaphysical subject. In a manner that is akin to what one finds in L. Wittgenstein's *Tractatus Logico Philosophicus*,[331] *al-nafs* is not an individual that exists somewhere in the world where it would be noted and contained as is the case with a substance based conception of subjectivity. And Avicenna's mystical accounts of *al-nafs* (as they will be addressed in the subsequent chapter) take the mystic journey and union into consideration. In this sense, Avicenna's accounts of *al-nafs* are undertaken in terms of a processional and existential "blending," "evolving," and "uniting," which all cannot be attributed to substance (*ousia*), given that substance only admits generation and corruption. Whenever *al-nafs* is considered, what is meant is not a metaphysical self or subject nor is it a substance. It rather designates an experiential field that converges into an existential mode of being in the world without answering to the question of the quiddity of what converges the experience as "experiencer." After all, the "experiencer" is not a static self nor a metaphysical subject nor a substance. In the "Suspended Person Argument" what is encountered primarily in this immediate experience is being. In this sense, the "Suspended Person Argument" asserts the ontological emphasis on the primacy and immediacy of the primordial encounter of being.

---

330 Maurice Merleau Ponty, *Phénoménologie de la Perception* (Paris: Éditions Gallimard, 1945), pp. 293-294.

331 Ludwig Wittgenstein, *Tractatus Logico Philosophicus*, trans. by C. K. Ogden (London: Routledge & Kegan Paul, 1988), 5.542(1), 5.631(1), 5.632, 5.633, 5.641(3).

The "Suspended Person Argument," that is presented herein, is translated into English from the original Arabic text of the *De Anima* part of *Kitāb al-Shifā'* and it reads as follows:

> One of us has to consider (*yatawaham*) that one has been just created in a stroke, and that one has been thus created fully developed and perfectly complete (*kāmilan*), yet [created] with one's vision shrouded [or veiled] (*ḥujiba baṣarahu*) from watching [perceiving] (*mushāhadāt*) external entities created falling [floating] (*yahwa*) in the air or in empty space (*al-khalā'*) in a fall not buffeted by any felt air that buffets it [i.e. the Person in question]; its limbs separated and not in contact nor touching one another. Then let it contemplate (*yata'amal*) whether it would affirm the existence of its own self. It would not then doubt the affirmation that its self is existent (*mawjūda*), yet not affirming the existence of any of its limbs nor inner bowels, nor heart, nor brain, nor any thing of the external things. Rather it was affirming the existence of its-self without affirming that it had length, breadth, or depth. And if it were possible for it, in such a state, to imagine (*yatakhayal*) a hand or any other limb, it would not then imagine it to be part of its-self nor to be a condition of it [i.e. its-self existence]. And you know that what is affirmed is distinct from what is not affirmed, and what is implied is distinct from what is not implied. Therefore the *nafs* [self, soul], whose existence the person has affirmed, is its [the person's] characteristic identity that is not identical to its body nor to it limbs [whose existence] it did not affirm. Therefore, the attentive (*al-mutanabih*) [to this situation] has a means of realizing (*yatanabah*) that the affirmation of the existence of its-self (soul, *al-nafs*) is distinct from the body and something that is quite a non-body [i.e. that the mind/soul (*al-nafs*) is distinct from the body (*jism*)]; this is known through self-consciousness and if one was distracted from it, one needs to knock one's baton [as to be alerted to it].[332]

---

[332] This argument appears in the following references: Avicenna, *Kitāb al-Shifā', al-Ṭabīᶜīyāt, Kitāb al-Nafs (De Anima)*, ed. by I. Madkour, G. Anawati, and S. Zayed (Cairo: al-hay'a al-miṣrīyah al-ᶜāmma lil-kitāb, 1975), p. 13; Avicenna, *Avicenna's De Anima (Arabic Text)*, ed. by F. Rahman (London: Ox-

It should be noted that the "suspended person" in question is genderless and is not a metaphyical subject or self, yet for translation purposes it would have been extremely difficult to account for the argument without a reference to a person. Yet, the person in question will disappear in the background of the reduction (*epoché*) and what is addressed is *al-nafs* (not as a self, nor as a subject, nor as a substance, but more like *Dasein*).

Before introducing his "Suspended Person Argument" in the *De Anima* of *Kitāb al-Shifā'*, Avicenna mentions that the affirmation of the existence of *al-nafs*, by way of *tawahum* (*consideration* of the situation at hand), is even noticeable by those who are not educated in such a way as to understand it. The *tawahum* (prehensive-consideration) shows the self-evidence and immediacy of the convergence between the affirmation of existence (*wūjūd*) and thinking. It also shows the distinction between the affirmed existence of the mind and the non-affirmed existence of the body as implied by the "Suspended Person Argument." The immediacy and self-presence of consciousness is asserted by the "Suspended Person Argument" and in other sections of the *De Anima*. At the onset of the first chapter (*faṣl*) of the first part (*maqāla*) of the *De Anima* part of *Kitāb al-Shifā'*, Avicenna mentions that the aim is to affirm (*ithbāt*) the existence of *al-nafs* qua *nafs* (soul-field). Avicenna then says: "the first thing that we need to talk about is the affirmation (*ithbāt*) of the existence [being] (*wūjūd*) of that thing which is called (*yusama*) soul (*nafsan*), then we address what follows that, and say that we perceive bodies (*ajsāman*) that feel and move by virtue of will (*irāda*)."[333] Given this priority in the subject matter of the *De Anima*, the first thing to be addressed is none other than the notion

---

ford University Press, 1959), p. 16; Lenn E. Goodman, *Avicenna* (London: Routledge, 1992), pp. 155, 156.

333 Avicenna, *Avicenna's De Anima (Arabic Text)*, ed. by F. Rahman (London: Oxford University Press, 1959), p. 4

of the soul, self, or mind as the expression *al-nafs* entails. This is also expressed at the onset of the *De Anima* part of *Kitāb al-Shifā'*. Therein, Avicenna holds that what makes a substance what it is, as composite substance, is the bringing together of form (*ṣūra*) and matter (*mādda*). And form is the soul (*al-nafs*) while matter is the body and its limbs (*al-jism wal-aᶜḍā'*).[334] And given that the knowledge of forms has primacy over the knowledge of matter, the examination of the soul (*al-nafs*) ought to be prior to the examination of the body (*al-jism*). And this entails that the affirmation of the existence of *al-nafs* has to be addressed before the consideration of bodies.

On the affirmation of the existence of the soul (*al-nafs*), one reads in *Kitāb al-Najāt* that "it is impossible for the soul (*al-nafs*) to be prior to the body."[335] Before its embodiment, or its acquisition of a body, *al-nafs* (soul-field) is solely a quiddity (*māhīya*). However, this does not entail differentiation between one soul and another. *Al-nafs* is created whenever the appropriate [matching] body is created for its use. Its personal identity and individuation is associated with the corporeity it uses. However, the soul "does not die with the death of [its] body" nor "does it admit [self] corruption."[336] And, the soul would not have existed unless it had been associated with a body. Yet, this does not entail that what was associated with the soul, in the causing of its existence, would be associated with it indefinitely. It happens that the body factors in the causing of the existence of *al-nafs*. Yet this association, of *al-nafs* (soul-field) with the body, reaches a rupture through the death of the body that admits

---

334 Avicenna, *Kitāb al-Shifā', al-Ṭabīᶜīyāt, Kitāb al-Nafs (De Anima)*, ed. by I. Madkour, G. Qanawati, and S. Zayed (Cairo: al-hay'a al-miṣrīya al-ᶜāmma lil-kitāb, 1975), p. 1.

335 Avicenna, *Kitāb al-Najāt*, ed. Majid Fakhry (Beirut: dār al-'āfāq al-jadīda, 1985), p. 222.

336 *Ibid*, pp. 222-223.

corruption, while the soul endures that bodily death, since the soul is originarily incorruptible (*la taqbal al-fasād*). If it were the case that the body figures as a requirement or a condition that is associated with the existential causing of the soul, this does not mean that the body is itself the existential cause of the existence of *al-nafs*. Nor does it mean that the body will be indefinitely associated with the existential causes that allow the soul to subsist in existence. One could conjecture that the body dies yet the soul does not. This is what may be derived from Avicenna's account. The body is not an existential cause of the existence of *al-nafs*. What [existentially] causes the soul (*al-nafs*) to exist is utterly immaterial. And the same holds with regard to subsisting in existence. This is moreover asserted as being the case due to the soul's simplicity which does not admit composition; and that which is not composed of form and matter is of the order of entities that do not admit [corporeal] corruption (*fasād*).[337]

The initial sketching of the "Suspended Person Argument" is not restricted to the first chapter of the first section of the *De Anima* of *Kitāb al-Shifā'* nor is it restricted to what appears in *Kitāb al-Najāt*. The reformulation of the "Argument" also appears in the seventh chapter of the fifth section of the *De Anima* of *Kitāb al-Shifā'*. In the *De Anima* V7 Avicenna tells us that some have held that "*al-nafs* is its-self (essential self: *dhāt*)." He then adds that this *nafs* (soul-field) is the origin of all its own actions. And the *nafs* uses its own powers of perception to act as the basis of distinct actions and powers (*qiwa*).[338] In an indication to his stress on the unity of self-consciousness, Avicenna says "that the one (*al-wāḥid*) thing (*shay'*) in which all of these powers (*qiwa*) gather, is that which everyone of us sees as one's own self (*dhāt*)...and that thing (i.e.

---

[337] *Ibid*, pp. 224, 226, 230.

[338] Avicenna, *Avicenna's De Anima (Arabic Text)*, ed. by F. Rahman (London: Oxford University Press, 1959), pp. 250-252.

nafs/soul-field) cannot be a body (*jisman*)."[339] Avicenna would then argue that what gathers all the powers of the self cannot be the body. This is not the case given that every body would be a gatherer of powers and this would entail the perfection of the body (*kamāl al-jism*) which itself (as a perfection *qua* perfection) is not a body. Therefore what gathers (*al-mujami*ᶜ) is a not a body. Avicenna adds "that which is not a body (*laysa bi-jism*) could be the source (*manba*ᶜ) of powers (*al-qiwa*), whereby some of them [i.e. the powers] emanate from it [i.e. the source] instrumentally while others [emanate] as its characteristics."[340] And he meant by that, that some of the powers of the soul emanate from the soul as instrumental functions, while other powers are more closely linked to the soul as its characteristics. Yet, even kinaesthetic movements that are bodily functional movements find their source in the soul and not in the body. This account is presented in terms of showing the self-sufficiency of a united self-consciousness in which the powers are not emanating from the body. And this shows that the relationship of these powers to the body is that of reception or acceptance (*al-qubūl*). Returning to a reiteration of the "Suspended Person Argument," Avicenna says, in the *De Anima* part V7 of *Kitāb al-Shifā'*, that:

> I am myself even if I do not know that I have a hand, or a leg, or any limb of these limbs; [and as it was mentioned in another context], I rather think that these [limbs] are what follows from me (*tawābi*ᶜ*ī*), and I [also] believe that they are my functional instruments that I use in fulfilling certain needs, and without these needs I would not need these limbs- I am therefore I as I (*anā anā*) and [I am] not these limbs. And to return to what has been mentioned earlier by us, we therefore say, if a human being (*insān*) was created at a stroke with separate limbs, and he did neither see his limbs nor did he touch them, nor did

339 *Ibid*, pp. 253-254.

340 *Ibid*, p. 254.

> these limbs get in contact, nor did he hear a sound, then although he would not know of the existence (*wūjūd*) of all his limbs, he would still know of the existence of his I-ness (*inīyatahu*) as being one while not knowing all [that is other than it, i.e. his I-ness]. And that which is unknown by itself is not the known, and these limbs are in reality not more than being like clothes that, due to their long standing attachment (*mulāzama* [association]) to us, became for us like our own parts (*ajzā'*). And if we imagine (*takhayalnā*) ourselves, we do not imagine ourselves as being naked, rather we imagine ourselves as having clothed bodies (*ajsām kāsiya*). And the reason behind this is due to the long standing attachment (*mulāzama* [association]). However we got accustomed to abstract and do away with clothing in such a way that we did not accustom ourselves to do [away] with limbs. Consequently we thought that limbs are parts of ourselves in a more ascertained way than in thinking that clothes are parts of ourselves.[341]

Avicenna then adds that if it were the case that there exists a bodily limb in such a way that I take it to be "I," then whatever that limb is (be it my brain, heart, or bowels) it is accidentally (*per accidens*) "I" (*yakūn bil-ᶜaraḍ anā*).[342] Arguing for the unity of the soul, Avicenna's holds that "the soul is one" (*al-nafs dhāt wāḥida*), and the faculties (*qiwa*) of the soul lead back to one unified soul that gathers them.[343] Avicenna also holds that "it is impossible for a [bodily] limb to live without being associated to a spiritual power;" i.e. no body lives without a soul. Plants, animals, and humans all do not live without souls. And a soul that exists in association with a body is not brought into existence due to the body, rather it is brought into existence by means of a substance (*jawhar*) that is a

---

341 *Ibid*, p. 255.

342 *Ibid*, p. 256.

343 Avicenna, *Kitāb al-Najāt*, ed. Majid Fakhry (Beirut: dār al-'āfāq al-jadīda, 1985), pp. 228, 229.

non-bodily form, i.e. *ṣūra*.[344] According to Avicenna's account in the Metaphysics part of *Kitāb al-Najāt*, the preoccupation of the soul (*al-nafs*) with its body (*badan*), causes the soul to fall into self-forgetfulness.[345] The preoccupation with the body is a source of self-alienation, which is emphasized as self-oblivion that arises due to the oblivion of the soul's own "Beloved One" (*maᶜshūq*) towards which the soul tends in its quest for self-perfection. In its preoccupation with its corporeity, the soul is oblivious of itself, it is oblivious of the call to its self-perfection, and more so, it is oblivious of the "Beloved One" (*maᶜshūqahā*) towards which it tends. This gives expression to the mystic love (*al-ᶜishq*) that cannot be expressed in a metaphysical language. It is an experience of a longing for a union with the Exalted One.

In *Kitāb al-Ishārāt wal-Tanbīhāt* (The Book of Directives and Remarks, also known as the Book of Hints and Pointers), Avicenna hints (*yushīr*) to the affirmation of the existence of the human soul (*al-nafs al-insānīya*) in terms of an intuitive perception of being.[346] Avicenna remarks:

> Reflect upon yourself and examine if, while being in good health, even under other states [of mind], according to which you grasp things with a sound intellect, [examine] if [under other states] you are unaware of your self existence and that you do not affirm it [i.e. would you not be able to affirm your existence?]. I am not of the opinion [that holds] that this happens with an attentive observer. Even with the one who is asleep or drunk, the depth of his own self is not separate from him [that his self-awareness is not lost], even if his self-representation is not continually present to his memory [i.e. that one is not continually aware of the existence of one's own self].

---

344 *Ibid*, p. 230.

345 *Ibid*, pp. 330, 332.

346 Avicenna, *Kitāb al-Ishārāt wal-Tanbīhāt*, ed. Sulayman Dunia (Cairo: dār al-maᶜārif, 1960), Remark I (1st *Ishāra*), Group 3 (3rd *Namaṭ*).

> And if you imagine (*tatakhayal*) that your own person has been created since the beginning as endowed with a sound intellect and disposition, that we suppose in this situation and disposition that you cannot see or touch your limbs or [bodily] parts which are separated and suspended for a moment in thin air. You find your own self unaware of all things but the certitude of its own being (*wūjūd*).[347]

In the remark that follows the one stated above, Avicenna speculates about the perception of the *nafs* by itself. He thus says:

> By what means do you grasp your own self at this moment [the one stated above] or before and after this moment? What would be that which is in you that grasps? Do you find that what grasps as such is one of your five perceiving senses by intuition? Or would it be the intellect and another faculty (*quwa*) that is other than your senses or analogous to them? If it were your intellect and a faculty that is other than your senses [by virtue of which you perceive], would you then perceive due to an intermediary or without an intermediary? I do not think that at this moment you need an intermediary. This is certainly not one [i.e. not an intermediary]. Rather you grasp your own self without being in need of any other faculty nor any intermediary. Rather it is either by your [five external] senses or by your internal [sense], without intermediary.

In other words, and as the Remark (*ishāra*) that follows hints: "*al-nafs* is not perceived by the senses."[348] And Avicenna also adds in the following remarks that *al-nafs* is not solely perceived by

---

347 The Arabic text appears in: Avicenna, *Kitāb al-Ishārāt wal-Tanbīhāt*, ed. by Sulayman Dunya (Cairo: dār al-maᶜārif, 1960). The French translation in: Avicenna, *Livre des Directives et Remarques*, trans. by A. M. Goichon (Paris: Librairie Philosophique J. Vrin, 1951), pp. 303-304. Also refer to an English passage that appears in: Lenn E. Goodman, *Avicenna* (London: Routledge, 1992), p. 157.

348 Avicenna, *Livre des Directives et Remarques*, trans. by A. M. Goichon (Paris: Librairie Philosophique J. Vrin, 1951), pp. 305-308.

the intermediacy of its own acts. Since he argues that one could say that "I could affirm my own existence by the inter-mediacy of my own action." However, from the standpoint of the "suspended person," it is not possible for that person ["experiencer"] to attest "its" own act, movement, or anything of that order. And even if that act is attested or felt, it is still attributed to *al-nafs* of the suspended person, by saying that it is "its" own act, which also presupposes the priority of "its" intelligence. Therefore, one's actions are not sufficient to affirm one's own existence, or the existence of one's "I-ness." Then, Avicenna remarks that *al-nafs* is neither corporeity nor temperament. In this, Avicenna is pressing a pre-suppositional account of the processional unification of self-consciousness that is not mediated by corporeity, materiality, or actions. On this view, self-consciousness is not dependent on anything else but on the convergence of the affirmation of being with thinking. Self-reflexivity differs from self-consciousness in the sense of constituting the knowledge of something about one's own self. It is not reduced into mere introspection and it underlies my knowledge that I know that I exist. The suspended person is able to know that she or he exists and that whose existence is affirmed is none other than her or his own self. Yet, knowing that what exists is one's own *nafs*, is not taking place through a perception of appearances, nor is it mediated by representation, nor is it a knowledge that depends on anything other than the *nafs* itself. What underlies and grounds the knowledge that *al-nafs* of the "suspended person" exists is none other than the knowledge of the presence of this *nafs* by virtue of its presencing. This knowledge by presence may be inferred from Avicenna's postulation of the "Suspended Person Argument" (The elaboration of *al-ʿilm al-ḥuḍūrī*, or "knowledge by presence," is what figures later in the philosophical accounts of Suhrawardī). On Avicenna's account, knowledge, the known, and the knower, all converge in the self-affirmation of the suspended person's existence. The suspended person knows that "it" exists, and this person knows that "it" is the one that exists and no other entity or being exists. This marks the convergence between knowing about being and thinking. Self-identity is then affirmed by virtue of self-presence to one's own self. Yet this self-presence is also marked by procession in the sense that being is becoming. It does not entail self-sameness or substantial unity. Presence already points to absence, and self-presence already points towards *otherness* or alterity. In this sense, the convergence of being and thinking is also the site of the granting of the gift of being. Revolving around one's center of being, is itself a whirling commemoration of one's own being. In all of this, consciousness does not depend on the positing of a body. It is affirmed in its being while even being presupposed in a state of disembodiment. The Avicennian *nafs* is not a constitutive transcendental subject (as might be the case with a Husserlian account). Avicenna's account of *al-nafs* also differs from the echo of this account in Descartes' *Cogito*, which itself is subjected to the Kantian objection that appears in *The Critique of Pure Reason*.

Avicenna's *De Anima* constitutes a part of his natural philosophy and his *Ṭabī ᶜīyāt* (physics). This does not entail that the study of *al-nafs* is undertaken from the standpoint of physics. What this rather implies is that the consideration of *al-nafs* is undertaken from the side of its relationship to the body. The intersubjective consideration of *al-nafs* reflects an interest in its embodiment. And, Avicenna does tell us that one of the originary characteristics of a human being is that this being lives in a society. And as a social being, a human being needs other humans without turning that need into a mark of imperfection. Avicenna would take such need for others to be a mark of the nobility of the human condition. He thus stresses on the intersubjective dimension that plays a role in the constitution of a person and a subject.[349] In a social intersubjective

[349] *Avicenna Latinus, Liber De Anima Seu Sextus De Naturalibus IV-V*, Édition Critique de la Traduction Latine Médiévale par Simone Van Riet, introduction sur la doctrine psychologique d'Avicenne par G. Verbeke. Ouvrage publié

realm, humans are in a world that is shaped by their own labor. They are in a world that is being transformed in response to rising needs, and such change focuses on the self-perfection of individuals. Avicenna might well hold the view that a human being is a being that incessantly transcends itself and transgresses its own limits. On his account, the human condition points towards "the principle of unlimited evolution" (*le principe d'une évolution illimitée*).[350] Avicenna holds that *al-nafs* acquires its individuality due to its association with a body. However, it survives the death of the body without losing its individuality. Avicenna also holds that *al-nafs* does not pre-exist the union with the body.[351] The "Suspended Person Argument" describes a reductive situation in which one is created already as an adult without having passed through any previous stages of growth. Therefore, the argument excludes the consideration of memory, and the suspended "person" is thrown in an empty space that is not in the realm of sensible entities. Reductively, this suspended person is disembodied and does not receive any sensible impressions. The suspended person has no visual, auditory, or tactile experiences. Dismembered and suspended in empty space, with no sensible impressions, experiences, or perceptions, the suspended person does not have knowledge of anything (At least this is an Aristotelian assessment of this person's possibilities of having any knowledge). The suspended disembodied human being floats in a void without having any contact with the sensible world. So one wonders whether that being is able to have the knowledge of anything at all. Nevertheless one finds that on Avicenna's account the suspended and disembodied person does indeed have knowledge of existence as encountered in *al-nafs* (*tamen sicret se esse*).[352] This account en-

---

avec le concours de la Fondation Universitaire de Belgique (Leiden: E. J. Brill, 1972), épi.13*-14*, vol. IV, V.

350 *Ibid*, p. 25*.

351 *Ibid*, pp. 32*-35*.

352 *Ibid*, pp. 36*-37*.

tails that the primary encounter with being or existence does not rest on sensible experience or sensory perception. And this also entails that corporeity and organismic members are not constitutive of subjectivity. As Peter Heath quotes Michael Marmura, one reads that the awareness of the self of itself proves the existence of an "I-ness," some sort of ego that is independent of physical perception and therefore is an immaterial self-sufficient rational soul that is also a [some sort of] substance.[353] The "I" is therefore conceived as being the spiritual center of a human being, and this "I" is immediately present to itself.[354] This immediacy entails that the profound and deep center of the self does not get dislocated and separated from the self. It is rather always present and available to it (Given that no psychological disorder is implied). Such an account would then subject Avicenna to similar criticism that Descartes' *ego cogito* argument might have received (whether by Leibniz or by Kant). The "I" is *al-nafs*, it is the center of being of a field of processional existential experiences. After all, the body is indispensable to the soul's spiritual journey, while at the same time acting as an obstacle to the completion of that journey. The body allows the journeying self to be displaced from one place to another as well as being indispensable for growth and progress until it turns into an obstacle that is placed in front of the journey of the spirit in its contemplative and spiritual development. Therefore, sensible knowledge is required in the course of the cognitive development and growth of *al-nafs*. Yet the self has to disengage itself from such knowledge when it is ready to

---

353 Peter Heath, *Allegory and Philosophy in Avicenna (Ibn Sina), with a translation of the book of the Prophet Muhammad's Ascent to Heaven (Mi ʿraj Nama)* (Philadelphia: University of Pennsylvania, 1992), p. 56. Also refer to: Michael Marmura, "Avicenna's 'Flying Man' in Context." *The Monist*, 69, 3, 1986, pp. 383-395.

354 *Avicenna* Latinus, Liber De Anima Seu Sextus De Naturalibus IV-V, ed. by Simone Van Riet (Leiden: E. J. Brill, 1972), p. 37*.

receive the higher knowledge of intelligibles.[355] If the human being is great due to the greatness of the spiritual *nafs*, this gift manifests an intervention or givenness that stretches beyond the confines of the self.[356]

II- "Suspended Person Argument" & "*Cogito* Argument"

Avicenna's consideration of bodies in the "Suspended Person Argument" accounts for the relationship between the body and the mind. And it does so while focusing on the immediacy of the primary encounter of being in *al-nafs*. The "Suspended Person Argument" pictures a convergence between thinking and being, and the positing of a body that a Kantian would presuppose is legitimate. However, one is not able to see what sort of a body is implied, and whether this body has lost its limbs, or has some of the limbs lost, or whether it is deformed, or just having enough limbs to survive. The Kantian line of argumentation does not sufficiently support what the positing of the body entails, since the positing of the body is still an abstract request of embodiment. What the Kantian request shows, is that the self is never imagined or posited without positing a body. Abstracting the conception of the self from what does not enter into its conception stresses on the independence of the self for the affirmation of its existence. In René Descartes' Second Meditation, and based on the grounds of doubt that are laid in the First Meditation, the mind is taken to be "free" to suppose the nonexistence of all things, while distinguishing "without difficulty" what belongs to itself from what belongs to its body. In the Second Meditation, Descartes "demonstrates" how in doubting all things, it was "impossible" for the mind (self) to doubt its own existence. In the First Meditation, Descartes reflects his distrust of the senses that "occasionally deceive us," yet he remarks that "it is prudent never to trust completely those

355 *Ibid*, pp. 46*-47*.

356 *Ibid*, pp. 72*-73*.

who have deceived us even once."[357] In the Second Meditation, he remarks that "anything which admits of the slightest doubt I will set aside just as if I had found it to be wholly false; and I will proceed in this way until I recognize something certain, or if nothing else, until I at least recognize for certain that there is no certainty."[358] It is evident from the way this hypothesis is placed, that Descartes will after all stumble on something certain, since the path he is about to take, already shows were it leads to. After all, his own self (his "I") will give the verdict whether there is something certain or not. And, this self will even state that there is no certainty and does so in terms of a contradictory judgment that "for certain there is no certainty." Having said to "himself" through his doubt exercise, that he has no senses nor a body, what follows is that he is not bound to the body. Then he moves on to say that there is nothing in the world while still asking himself whether it follows that he does not exist; i.e. whether his "I" does not exist as well. Descartes would say that: "I am, I exist, is necessarily true whenever it is put forward by me or conceived in my mind."[359] He then attempts to understand what this "I" means; he therefore assesses whether his "I" is his limbs, actions, or whether it has to do with his nutrition or movement (Like what one finds in reference to the actions of the animal soul in Avicenna's *De Anima*). All of these conjectures were denied the status of being what determines the affirmation of the existence of one's own soul. In asking the question: "what then am I?" Descartes' reply is that I am "a thing that thinks." It is therefore this "I" that doubts or affirms everything. It is this same "I" that is given from the onset the status of being that which sets for its own self the path of doubt, and at the same time from the onset gives itself the status of the judge

---

[357] René Descartes, *Meditations on First Philosophy with selections from the Objections and Replies*, trans. by John Cottingham (Cambridge: Cambridge University Press, 1994), p. 18.

[358] *Ibid*, p. 24.

[359] *Ibid*, p. 25.

that affirms or doubts. Descartes finally reaches his conclusion that: "it is not possible that I who am thinking am not something," the result that follows is "namely that I exist." What he then repeats in the Third Meditation is that "I am certain that I am a thinking thing." Descartes then says "let whoever can do so to deceive me, he will never bring it about that I am nothing, so long that I continue to think I am something."[360] As long as one continues to think that one is something, one namely exits. This reflects a strict convergence between thinking (that I am something) and being or existing (as something). As if it were the case that, under such circumstances of doubt and deception, if I keep uttering to myself that I am something, in the sense of thinking to myself that I am something, then no deceiver can tell me that the case is otherwise. The thinking nature is mine, and it is also what I am. We reach here another version of the immediacy of self-presence that has been reached by way of doubt rather than by way of supposition or by way of hypotheses (as it might be the case with Avicenna's "Suspended Person Argument"). To add to the immediacy of self-consciousness and to its independence from external objects, bodies, limbs, and materiality, Avicenna goes further in pointing to the "immateriality of thinking." In *Kitāb al-Ishārāt wal-Tanbīhāt*, Avicenna presents an *ishāra* (pointer or directive) that argues for the immateriality of all intelligent substances. And he argues from the standpoint of the indivisibility of the intelligible and the divisibility of the corporeal and material.[361] In another part of *Kitāb al-Ishārāt wal-Tanbīhāt*, Avicenna then argues in support of his directive that points to the intelligibility of immateriality. He holds that all intelligent beings are intelligible. And in a more general sense, he adds that all immaterial beings are able to have knowledge, and that this ability to know also implies that an

---

360 *Ibid*, pp. 33, 35, 36.

361 Avicenna, *Livre des Directives et Remarques*, trans. by A. M. Goichon (Paris: Librairie Philosophique J. Vrin, 1951), pp. 333-334.

immaterial being may also have self-knowledge.[362] As Lenn E. Goodman holds, Avicenna's Floating Man Argument is a celebrated "*Cogito ergo sum*" argument in which Avicenna neither follows Plato nor the Neoplatonists. The "Suspended Person Argument" would be "ancestral" to Descartes' *Cogito* argument and to contemporary "Brain in a Vat" conjectures or thought experiments of the Analytic School in Philosophy (one at least could mention Philosophers like Saul Kripke, Robert Nozick, and Derek Parfit among other exponents of that school).[363] Yet it will not be conducive to an account of *al-nafs* in terms of static subjectivity or substance. One could speculate whether Kant's critique of Descartes' *Cogito* argument might also be extended to touch upon Avicenna's "Suspended Person Argument" as it is advanced in *Kitāb al-Shifā'* (the *De Anima* part) and in *Kitāb al-Ishārāt wal-Tanbīhāt.* In reference to the original synthetic unity of apperception, Kant holds that "it must be possible for the 'I think' to accompany all my representations; for otherwise something would be represented in me which could not be thought at all, and that is equivalent to saying that the representation would be impossible, or at least would be nothing to me."[364] And, it was mentioned above that on Descartes' view, no one would deceive me, or bring it about that I am nothing "so long that I continue to think I am something." This continual accompaniment of the Cartesian "I think" is ruled out from the Kantian account. Since Kant does not presuppose a continual accompaniment of "I think." He rather carefully states that "it must be possible for the "I think" to accompany all my representations," and this differs from the Cartesian continual accompaniment of "I think." The representation "I think" is an original pure (Kantian) apperception that is possible for

---

362 *Ibid*, pp. 337-338.

363 Lenn E. Goodman, *Avicenna* (London: Routledge, 1992), pp. 155-157, 178-179 note 50.

364 Immanuel Kant, *Critique of Pure Reason*, trans. by Norman Kemp Smith (New York: St. Martin's Press, 1965), B131-B132.

it to accompany all other representations. Its unity, as apperception, represents the Kantian "transcendental unity of self-consciousness" which acts as the source of a priori knowledge.[365] The unity of apperception gathers all my representations in such a way that they are mine without continually asserting "I think" in the Cartesian fashion. With Avicenna, the unity of the *nafs* is none other than one's own *nafs*. It is this unity that is unique in me, that is me, in which all representations, actions, temperaments, and faculties gather. The problem with the *Cogito* argument (Cartesian) is that the only empirical assertion that is certain is that "I am." This radical idealist tendency is problematic if accounted for from the standpoint of Kant's critique. On this idealist view, one assumes that the immediate experience is an introspective experience from which all other external experiences are derived. Kant's objection is based on his view that one is conscious of one's self based on a "determination in time."[366] Now, if Avicenna accepts this positing of consciousness in terms of temporality, he still does not escape from being hit by Kant's critique, since (on Kant's analysis) being temporal entails that what is temporal is linked to what is sensory and external. On Kant's view, consciousness in time is "necessarily bound up with the consciousness of the [condition of] possibility of this time-determination." Therefore consciousness in time is necessarily bound up with "the existence of things outside it," as being the condition of this time-determination.[367] Yet in all cases, Avicenna does not concede to an account that takes consciousness to be temporal as such, though it is implied from his argument that there is a processional self-unfolding movement which could be characterized as being temporal yet not reliant on external perceptual experiences. In the meta-mystic construal of the travelling *nafs*, the process of change is also what char-

365 *Ibid*, B132-B133.

366 *Ibid*, B275-B276.

367 *Ibid*, B276.

acterizes the *nafs* rather than characterizing the *nafs* in terms of substance (*ousia*). Temporality is eventually marking the individuality of the Avicennian *nafs*, yet this is not fully the case with the abstract introspective state of affairs that one encounters in relation to the "Suspended Person Argument." Avicenna would agree with both Hume and Kant that the "I think" is not something that is seen or perceivable, as Kant also holds that the proposition "I think" does not contain a perception of an existent. On Kant's analysis, the "*Cogito* ergo sum," is a "tautology" since the *cogito* "asserts my existence immediately." To say that "I am simple," or that "I, as thinking being, am substance," or to say that "I am a simple substance," all do not amount to saying anything (And this is also what is entailed from Avicenna's account of *al-nafs* apart from a consideration of substance). As if they were "empty expressions" that do not tell us anything whatsoever. Such abstractions do not tell us, in *concreto*, what consciousness is. Yet Kant concedes that the only use of such a talk is to enable us to state that the soul is distinct from matter.[368] That is to say that the "soul is incorporeal," which after all is Avicenna's aim. However, this does not entail that one can do much with such a distinction between the soul and matter, between the mind and the body. Nevertheless one cannot still say that, on Kant's account, we have been able to say what consciousness is. Kant would say that the representation of myself, as thinking being, belongs to inner sense, while representations marking extended beings belong to outer sense.[369] Kant would not want to accept that a distinction between matter and thought would be a sufficient justification for conducting an introspective thought experiment like that of Descartes' *Cogito* argument. Arguing from the standpoint of Transcendental Idealism, Kant would assert that material external objects are mere appearances and that they are nothing but "a species of my

---

[368] *Ibid*, A347, B405, A356-A357.

[369] *Ibid*, A371.

representations." Therefore, external objects would be nothing apart from my representations. On this view,

> Matter, therefore, does not mean a kind of substance quite distinct and heterogenous from the object of inner sense (the soul), but only the distinctive nature of those appearances of objects - in themselves unknown to us - the representations of which we call outer as compared with those which we count as belonging to inner sense, although like all other thoughts these outer representations belong only to the thinking subject.[370]

It was mentioned above that in *Kitāb al-Ishārāt wal-Tanbīhāt*, Avicenna uses one of his pointers (*ishārāt*) to remark that all immaterial beings are able to have knowledge, and that this ability to know also implies that an immaterial being may also have self-knowledge.[371] Such claim amounts to a clear convergence between thinking and being (or existing) that one finds a later version of it in Descartes': *cogito, ergo sum.* Based on Kant's account in section B423 of the *Critique of Pure Reason* even if one accepts that the (empirical) proposition "I think" already contains in it the proposition "I exist," this does not entail that one has to accept the claim that "everything which thinks, exists." What Kant is cautioning about is that such claims would entail that whatever "thinks" is therefore a Necessary Existent. And given Avicenna's remark in *Kitāb al-Ishārāt wal-Tanbīhāt*, immaterial beings think, since they have knowledge, and they even may have self-knowledge. "Everything which thinks, exists" would then be a proposition that precedes and grounds the proposition that "I think, therefore, I exist." Since thinking entails being or existing based on the proposition that "everything thinks, exists." Yet Kant takes this entailment to be necessary. And he accordingly objects to it on the ground that it turns

---

370 *Ibid*, A385.

371 Avicenna, *Livre des Directives et Remarques*, trans. by A. M. Goichon (Paris: Librairie Philosophique J. Vrin, 1951), pp. 337-338.

everything that thinks into a necessary existent. And, in addressing Avicenna's modalities of being, such claim is ontologically unjustifiable. It is a claim that cannot hold by itself and it thus requires further ontological analysis and explication. Avicenna's ontological consideration of the modalities of being seems to be in tune with what later figures in Kant's objection to statements that take "everything that thinks" to be a necessary being or existent. Given this affinity, between Avicenna's view and Kant's objection, one might add that in Avicenna's consideration, one finds an account of Necessary Being that is more detailed than what is advanced by Kant. Avicenna's consideration of necessity is more specific, in the sense that the modality of necessity is qualified in terms of being a necessity due to itself or a necessity due to something else that is other than itself. What the "Suspended Person Argument" shows is that being can be primarily encountered, and that being is thus encountered due to a convergence of thinking with being which already points to a self-unfolding of being through an experiential and existential mode of being. The convergence of thinking and being reveals an unfolding of being through an existential mode of being that is none other than that of a human being (And this might well be the case with Heidegger's view of *Dasein*). The question of being is then turned into a wondering about "what it is to be" as if one says: "what does it mean for me that I am?" "What does it mean for me that I exist?" This is the sort of wonder that the "Suspended Person Argument" might entail by way of accounting for the meaning and truth of being. The reality of being is therefore reflected through a return to this reality *via* the being of a human being whose consciousness is revealed as being independent, and where bodily limbs are revealed as being needed for a particular mode of being that is that of being-in-[a material terrestrial]-world. On this account, ontology, as the study of being *qua* being, is then mediated through an analytic of the modes of being of a human being (as an analytic that approximates Heidegger's existential analytic of *Dasein*). It is also the case that with Avicenna, the human being is revealed as being the "entity" that is to be ontologically [*not-ontically*] interrogated. In the ontological account of the modalities of being, Avicenna encounters being conceptually and analytically. With the "Suspended Person Argument," Avicenna reveals that being and thinking are convergent while self-presence already points to a granting otherness. On this account, being is encountered in selfhood, being is encountered in the *anā* (I), and in this sense being is existentially experienced. The *nafs* is found in the site of being as *anā* (I).

III- *Al-Wahm*

In the third *namaṭ* (group) of the *De Anima* of *Kitāb al-Ishārāt wal-Tanbīhāt*, Avicenna classifies the inner senses into common sense, imagination (*mutaṣawira*, or *khayāl*), and inner sense of prehension (*wahm*). He then adds a fourth inner sense that is "cogitative" when used by reason, and "imaginative" (*mutakhayīla*, like *fantasia*) when used by *wahm* (Inner sense of prehension, or estimation). And an additional faculty that recollects and gathers is that of memory (*al-dhākira*, or *al-ḥāfiẓa*). In the *De Anima* of *Kitāb al-Najāt,* Avicenna adds that, *al-wahm* (inner sense of prehension) is served by a common sense and imaginative potentiality that is anterior to it, and it is also served by memory (*al-dhākira*, or *al-ḥāfiẓa*) that is posterior to it.[372] In the *De Anima* sixth part (*maqāla*) of *Kitāb al-Najāt*, Avicenna holds that the soul (*al-nafs*) is of three sorts, it is vegetative, animal, and human. Regarding the human soul, its perception is based on external and internal perception.[373] The faculties that perceive from within do rely on inner senses (*ḥawās bāṭina*) in their inner perception. Yet, some of the inner faculties perceive the "forms" (*sūwar*) of sensible entities (*al-maḥsūsāt*), while others perceive the "meanings" (*ma*ᶜ*ānī*) of sen-

---

[372] *Ibid*, pp. 317, 322, 323. Also see: Avicenna, *Kitāb al-Najāt*, ed. Majid Fakhry (Beirut: dār al-'āfāq al-jadīda, 1985), pp. 202, 206-207.

[373] *Ibid*, pp. 197, 198.

sible entities.[374] The distinction between perceiving the form of an entity, and the perception of its meaning, is due to the fact that the perception of the form is simultaneous between the inner *nafs* (soul, mind) and the "apparent" sense datum (or sensation). This is the case, given that the perception of the "meaning" of the sensible entity happens directly to the soul. In the case of the perception of the form of a sensible entity, what is perceived by the soul is mediated by (external) sense data that are relegated to the soul. In the case of meaning, its perception is immediate by the soul. To illustrate this point, Avicenna uses the example of the sheep (*al-shāt*) and the wolf (*al-dhi'b*). According to him, the form of the wolf is first perceived by the senses of the sheep. Then the form [wolf] is perceived internally by the animal soul of the sheep. As for the meaning of the form "wolf," it is perceived by the soul without being mediated by the senses. The sheep perceives the meaning of the form wolf as "opponent" or "contrary" and therefore it perceives that this meaning necessitates its own escape.[375] Accordingly, the perceived meaning brings about action.

In the *De Anima* of *Kitāb al-Najāt*,[376] Avicenna presents a subdivision of inner perception into four types that are correlated with the four inner senses. He holds that perception is sensory (*idrāk bil-ḥiss*), imaginative (*idrāk bil-mukhayīla*), prehensive (*idrāk bil-wahm*), and intellectual (*idrāk bil-ᶜaql*). Regarding perception by means of the senses (*al-idrāk bil-hiss*), it does not take place unless matter is related to form, or else, form will not be perceived by sensory perception. Sensory perception (*al-idrāk bil-ḥiss*) cannot abstract (*yujarid*) form from matter without retaining the auxiliaries of matter (*lawāḥiq al-mādda*) such as quantity, quality, place or situation. Perception by means of imagination (*al-idrāk bil-*

374 *Ibid*, p. 200.

375 *Ibid*, p. 201.

376 *Ibid*, pp. 208-209.

khayāl) is able to perform a better abstraction of form from matter. Yet such abstraction (*tajrīd*) is not complete or full, since imagination is not able to abstract form from the auxiliaries of matter (*lawāḥiq al-mādda*), and the imaginative form will still occupy a place, it would also still have certain qualities. Perception by means of the inner sense of prehension (*al-idrāk bil-wahm*) leads to a high level of abstracting form from matter. The abstraction by *al-wahm* (prehension), is far more successful than the one performed by imagination or the common outer sense. *Al-wahm* gathers the meanings that are not material in essence while accidentally being meanings that happen to be associated with material entities. The meanings that are grasped by *al-wahm* accidentally (*bil-ᶜaraḍ, per accidens*) happen to be in matter. In that sense, the abstraction of form from matter is not complete since the derived meanings are still accidentally linked to the auxiliaries of matter. *Al-wahm* has therefore a partial accidental link with material entities, and meaning itself is still seen as being accidentally linked to material auxiliaries that suggest these meanings. However, a bodily form always requires a subject or matter (*hayūlī*) to be in; and this entails that the abstraction of bodily form from matter is not possible, at least a full and complete abstraction is not.[377] While Avicenna advocates this view in the First *maqāla* (section) of the Metaphysics (*ilāhīyāt*) of *Kitāb al-Najāt*, he still shows that in perception, there are varying degrees of abstracting form from matter that take place depending on the sort of perception that takes place. The degree of abstraction becomes more successful as one moves from sensory perception, through imaginative, and prehensive perception. And the possibilities of the highest levels of abstraction are opened up with the Intellectual or Rational perception (*al-idrāk bil-ᶜaql*). After all, Avicenna holds in the second *maqāla* (part) of the Metaphysics of *Kitāb al-Najāt*, that "all that is abstracted from matter is intelligible

[377] *Ibid*, pp. 239-242.

(*maᶜqūl*)." The abstraction of form from matter is not complete, yet imaginative or prehensive perceptions elevate the degrees of abstracting forms from matter in such a way that such abstracted forms inflame imagination and set to it to a creative wake. This happens while prehension discloses significant meanings out of the imaginative creativity. The abstracted forms that are envisioned, without being sensed in their corporeity, are imaginative forms that may bear the poetic meanings of creative day dreaming that oneirically stretch the limits of what is offered by sensory perception. Unlike intelligence (*al-ᶜaql*), *al-wahm* is not able to have a complete abstraction (*tajrīd*) from matter (*al-mādda*). *Al-wahm* is bound up with its material context and the practical circumstances of that context. *Al-wahm* is also associated with sensible imagination in the service of the pragmatics of practical reason (*al-ᶜaql al-ᶜamalī*). In Avicenna's *De Anima* sections of *Kitāb al-Shifā', Kitāb al-Najāt*, and *Kitāb al-Ishārāt wal-Tanbīhāt*, *al-wahm* is considered to be an internal sense (*ḥiss bāṭinī*) that figures in a kind of perception that is that of the inner sense of prehension (*idrāk bil-wahm*). A. M. Goichon and Parviz Morewedge both take *al-wahm* to be an original category that is absent in Greek epistemology.[378] This inner sense of prehension (*al-wahm*) performs a creative process of abstracting form from matter in such a way that it sets imagination into a higher level of play while providing it with significant meanings that induce actions. However, *al-wahm* (as an inner sense of prehension) does not merely act in relation to an act-oriented imagination. The meanings that are reflected through *al-wahm* do have further practical consequences. Avicenna's use of *al-wahm* in the case of the sheep escaping the wolf is one instance of how *al-wahm* leads to useful actions. As Parviz Morewedge points out, the notion of *al-wahm* also figures in the works of al-Fārābī, al-Rāzī, al-Ṭūsī, al-Ghazālī,

---

378 Parviz Morewedge, *Essays in Islamic Philosophy, Theology, and Mysticism* (Oneonta: State University of New York, 1995), pp. 139, 140.

and Suhrawardī. Yet as Parviz Morewedge, A. M. Goichon, H. A. Wolfson, and F. Rahman, point out, the epistemological and philosophical account of *al-wahm* was elaborated in an original way by Avicenna who could be taken to be a "key Muslim philosopher of *wahm*."[379] According to Morewedge's interpretation of the use of *al-wahm* in the Metaphysics part of the *Danish Nama (Metaphysica of Avicenna)*, *al-wahm* is a "conceptual type of imagination" that is used in the description of "a lower bound of a phenomenal extension of a conceptual image." Morewedge's interpretation is used in reference to Chapters 8 & 4 of the *Ilāhīyāt* (Metaphysics) of Avicenna's *Danish Nama*, wherein Avicenna examines the conditions of a bodily substance and its division. Parviz Morewedge interprets *al-wahm* as being an "awareness" of the "transcendental" conditions of "phenomena." He also gives an illustration of such interpretation in terms of accounting for Avicenna's consideration of time as being "*tawahumī*," i.e. as being the object of *al-wahm*. In that sense, time exists internally in the mind not externally in the world. And, on this account, *al-wahm* is used in relation to synthetic *a priori* judgments, and what is *tawahumī*, like time, is taken to be a form of intuition.[380] *Al-wahm* and imagination are in the service of "practical reason" (*al-ᶜaql al-ᶜamalī*). *Al-wahm* detects and receives meanings from the sensible entities in the world, by abstracting the meaning of the forms from matter. The meanings, that *al-wahm* receives from sensible entities, are practical act-oriented significant meanings that induce useful actions (like the sheep escaping the wolf due to *tawahum*, i.e. to the act of *wahm*, or inner sense prehension). Therefore, *al-wahm* entails the use of judgements that are based on meanings inferred from sensible entities. *Al-wahm*, is an active imaginative process that allows the self to receive meanings from entities that in their turn allow the self to conduct itself properly amidst beings in the world.

---

379 *Ibid*, pp. 141, 412.

380 *Ibid*, pp. 142, 143, 144.

Being shared with animals, *al-wahm* is the highest inner sense in animals, and it is above sensible imagination and sensation in humans while being below the spheres of intelligence (*al-* ᶜ*aql*). *Al-wahm* is the highest animal inner sense and is second after reason in the rational beings that are endowed with speech (*al-nufūs al-nāṭiqa*). According to Parviz Morewedge's interpretation, *al-wahm* may itself be a form of evaluative "internal ability to use logical reasoning and to associate ideas." On such interpretation, and in reference to Avicenna's account of reflective reasoning, *al-wahm* may be taken to be another "faculty" after the intelligence that is capable of reasoning. This is the case given its role in relation to practical reason. After all, *al-wahm* may be seen as a faculty that associates a particular with a universal. It is a faculty that reflects an association of ideas based on generalization. The received meaning of animosity, as associated with wolves, is practically associated with a particular problematic concrete event that arises on the occasion of an encounter between the sheep and a wolf. *Al-wahm* is a particularization of what is general, and it is a concretization of what is universal in the service of the pragmatics that lived circumstances require. On Parviz Morewedge's view, *al-wahm* is clearly illustrated in terms of an "organism's adaptation to a problematic situation." In this context, Morewedge illustrates his account of *al-wahm* in terms of relating it to Deweys' pragmatist conception of "habit" (In art as the successful performing of a task without reflection). Morewedge also links *al-wahm* to G. H. Mead's notion of "significant gestures" that clarify "a family minded behavior." Morewedge presents *al-wahm* as being a "pragmatic prehension" that is to be "explained in a behavioral context." On his account, *al-wahm* would be translated in English as "the pragmatic process of prehension." Accordingly Morewedge reflects the pragmatic and utilitarian features of *al-wahm*.[381] This rendering of *al-wahm* into English is based on Morewedge's objection and "re-

---

[381] *Ibid*, pp. 150-153, 157, 159, 169.

jection" of six theories of *wahm* that are to be found in the translation of "*al-wahm*." Morewedge presents some arguments against some translations of *al-wahm* as they are offered by the contemporary scholarship of Avicenna's *De Anima*. Morewedge first objects to F. Rahmans' rendering of *al-wahm* as "nervous response." And, his objection is based on the account that takes *al-wahm* to be "a generalized pattern of behavior" that is supposed to be a "normatively successful behavior." And it is also supposed to be unlike the "passive response" which is not as generalized and which may not always lead to a successful behavior, since a response might sometimes cause harm. Regarding R. Hammand's rendering of *al-wahm* as "instinct," Morewedge refutes this rendering on the basis that instincts might be harmful. And, *al-wahm* is after all supposed to be successful. One can talk about a "death instinct," while there is no relevance in saying that one has a "death *wahm*." As for S. H. Naṣr's use of "apprehension" to express *al-wahm*, Morewedge says that "apprehension" involves a "conscious awareness" and "intellectual capacity" that are "absent in the animal soul." Moreover, "apprehension" does not necessarily imply that an activity is taking place, while *al-wahm* involves active agents. Based on the same reasons that lead to his objection on the use of "apprehension," Morewedge also refutes M. Iqbal's use of the term "conception" in translating the term "*al-wahm*." "Imagination" also disqualifies as being an appropriate rendering of *al-wahm* since it is used for *takhayul*, *khayāl*, *muṣawira*, and all refer to imagination not to *al-wahm*. Finally, Morewedge objects to the use of the most common rendering of *al-wahm* as "estimation," which is mainly used by Wolfson, Goichon, Rahman, and Afnan. And here, Morewedge takes estimation to be a rendering that is influenced by the Latin Scholastic use of *estimatio* as a *terminus technicus*. However, Morewedge's main objection is not based on the tracing of the roots of estimation to Latin Scholasticism, rather he holds that *estimatio* reflects "deliberation" and consciousness which are not presupposed by *al-wahm*.[382] And he also adds that estimation does not necessarily imply action, and this is not the case with the action-oriented *wahm*. Herein, *estimatio* as syntax may not have reference to pragmatic norms. Based on all these six objections, Morewedge advances his carefully examined rendering of *al-wahm* as "The Pragmatic Process of Prehension."[383] This interpretation of *al-wahm* reveals how the translation of the Arabic or Persian terms is carefully rendered in such a way as to reflect the interpreters' hermeneutic positions. The focus on intentionality, temporality, meaning, and the pragmatics of *al-wahm*, all reveal a line of interpretation that attempts to lift the reading of Avicenna's philosophical views from the confines of scholarly interpretations that keep the Avicennian texts bound to their Medieval context. Using estimation in rendering *al-wahm* already reflects a predisposition to address *al-wahm* through the Latin conception of *estimatio*. Such a reading already undertakes a line of interpretation that confines the Avicennian concepts within the limits of Medieval philosophy. By rendering *al-wahm* as "The Pragmatic Process of Prehension,"

---

382 There is a sense by which the expression *tawahum* may be rendered according to distinct meanings. *Tawahum* is the act of having a *wahm*, it is being prehensive. Yet in contemporary Arabic, *tawahum* may be taken to be derived from either the root term *wahm* (as indicated above) or it may be derived from the root term *al-ham* (which designates a concernful worry about a concrete practical situation). *Al-wahm* itself has the contemporary meaning of imaginative illusions or myths (*khurāfāt*). In both cases, *tawahum* as having *wahm* is neither a *tawahum* by having a *wahm* as myth or illusion, nor is it a *tawahum* by having a "*ham*" (as concernful worry about a concrete practical situation. *Al-wahm* that we are addressing is considered from the standpoint of classical Arabic that is not affected by colloquial or contemporary uses, and moreover, the use of *al-wahm* in the context of our discussion is restricted to the philosophic use not the common sensical one.

383 Parviz Morewedge, *Essays in Islamic Philosophy, Theology, and Mysticism*, 1995, pp. 154-156, 169.

Morewedge attempts to carefully address Avicenna's philosophical works in relation to phenomenology. *Al-wahm* is therefore treated in such a way as to reveal phenomenological dimensions of intentionality, meaning, and the pragmatics of perception. *Al-wahm* is therefore lifted from the field of mental deliberation and it is taken to be a faculty that is phenomenological and intentional in character. In all of this, *al-wahm* (as a pragmatic process of prehension) reflects an epistemological account of knowledge that takes knowledge to be pragmatic and intentional while also being contextual and temporal. Such accounts of *al-wahm* reveal the epistemological emphasis on perception and its phenomenological dimensions.

CHAPTER 7
THE AUTHENTICITY OF BEING

I- The Visionary Recitals

The entire account of a philosophical interpretation of visionary meta-mystical texts is perhaps questionable given the problems that arise if one takes into consideration the "private language" argument that Wittgenstein pointed at in the *Philosophical Investigations*,[384] and some Analytic philosophers are still debating. Another difficulty viz. the symbolism of visionary texts may be raised in terms of the development in semiological studies and in accounts that one finds in E. Cassirer's consideration of symbolic forms. These problematic issues may need an investigation of their own. However, the consideration of a possible interpretation of Avicenna's Visionary Recitals would be addressed while knowing that some hermeneutic issues are unsolvable and unverifiable. If it were indeed the case that what one faces with the Avicennian visionary recitals is a version of a "private language," or a "private" experience or impression, then there is no obvious way to verify the interpretive assumptions about these recitals. One might think that he or she understands the significance and the meaning of a word by attaching a meaning that is not right. Or one could block interpretation on the basis of claiming that what is at issue is "private" and no one else would understand it but the one to whom this "private language" belongs to. In this sense, any philosophical interpretation of meta-mystic writings may be quite problematic given the developments in the philosophy of language, in theories of interpretation (German Hermeneutics, and Deconstruction), and in semiology. Yet, based on a hermeneutic history of mystic writings, a possible reconstruction of the mystical re-

[384] Ludwig Wittgenstein, *Philosophical Investigations*, trans. by G. E. M. Anscombe (New York: Macmillan Publishing Co., Inc., 1968), sections 269, 272, 275.

citals might give some insights about how these recitals ought to be addressed, and how these recitals ultimately inspire the reading of Avicenna's philosophical works. This is also the case, given that meta-mystic issues do figure in Avicenna's *Kitāb al-Ishārāt wal-Tanbīhāt*, which is a book of knowledge that is not less complex and philosophical than *Kitāb al-Shifā'*, or *Kitāb al-Najāt*.

The Avicennian Visionary Recitals[385] do reflect a profound preoccupation with the authenticity of being in the world. The relation of the self to the cosmos reflects a cosmological encounter with being. The self is understood in terms of the universe in which it finds itself. The Trilogy of Avicenna's Visionary Recitals constitute a "cycle" that situates Avicenna's conception of the human condition in relation to the cosmology that he elaborated in his monumental work *Kitāb al-Shifā'*. The Visionary Recitals turn the cosmology into a personalized and lived existential experience that attempts to reflect the authenticity of the philosophical account. The cycle of the trilogy consists of the Recital of Ḥayy Ibn Yaqẓān, the Recital of the Bird, the Recital of Salmān and Absal. According to Henry

385 To refer to the Recital texts, see: August F. Mehren, *Traités Mystiques d'Avicenne* (Amsterdam: Philo Press, 1979). In Mehren's *Traités Mystiques d'Avicenne*, one finds the following mystical treatises translated into French and followed by the Arabic text: *Ḥayy Ibn Yaqẓān* Recital, Part I, pp.10-19; Traité Mystique at-Thair (*al-ṭayr*, l'oiseau, the recital of the bird), Part II, pp. 27-32; The third Part consists of: i- Traité sur l'Amour (*risāla fī al-ᶜishq*), Treatise on Love (pp. 1-15); ii- Traité sur la nature de la prière (*risāla fī māhīyat al-ṣalawāt*), a treatise on the nature of prayers (pp. 16-24); iii- Missive sur l'influence produite par la fréquentation des lieux saints et les prières qu'on y fait (*kitāb fī maᶜna al-ziyāra wa kayfīyat ta'thīriha*), a book on the meaning of the frequenting of sanctified sites and its influences (pp. 25-27); iv- Traité sur la délivrance de la crainte de la mort (*risāla fī dafᶜ al-gham min al-mawt*), a treatise on the deliverance from worrying about death (pp. 28-32); The Fourth Part consists of a Treatise on Destiny (*risāla fī al-qadar*, Traité sur le Destin), pp. 1-12.

Corbin,[386] the Recital of Ḥayy Ibn Yaqẓān may be accounted for as being the Recital of "Occidental Exile" (*L'Exil Occidental*). The cycle of the trilogy represents a personal experience that depicts Avicenna's own world-picture, his "*Imago mundi*," which also represents his perception of his being-in-the-world. His *Imago mundi* is also the picture of his own *modus essendi*; that his world-picture is also the picture of his own personal mode of being. Therefore the trilogy is to be interpreted as consisting of personal accounts of being-in-the-world while at the same time unveiling one's being-in-the-world as being in "exile" away from home. Consequently, the Recitals trilogy opens itself up to the beyond. And it does so in anticipation of a future in which one's own possibilities are reconfigured in terms of transmuting the world into a world of symbols. The recitals give expression to the interdependence between one's own origin and place of return, and one's being-in-the-world and its quest of self-realization. With the recital, being is *being oriented.* It is a being that is like a vector of potentiality-to-be and anticipation by way of an oriented mystic journeying. *Al-nafs* tends to be united with the Necessary Existent due to Itself through a delineation of the mystic return. And, in *Kitāb al-Ishārāt wal-Tanbīhāt*, Avicenna holds that the only way in which one can point (*yushīr*) to the Necessary Existent due to Itself is by way of *al-ᶜirfān al-ᶜaqlī* (mystical intelligence).

As Henry Corbin puts it, the task that lies ahead is to understand and touch what made the past once possible and allowed it to have a future.[387] To grasp what in the past still has a future constitutes a hermeneutic approach to the recitals. And such reading seeks to re-collect what allows the past to have its future. This hermeneutic interpretation of the recitals calls for an "Oriental philosophy"

---

386 Henry Corbin, *Avicenne et le Récit Visionnaire (Tome 2): Étude sur le Cycle des Récits Avicenniens* (Tehran: Société des Monuments Nationaux de l'Iran, 1954), p. 7.

387 *Ibid*, pp. 9-12.

whose past unveils possibilities of having a future. This constitutes a call to liberate the past and allow it to have a future. The one who lives the Avicennian cosmology differs from the one who only attempts to study and comment on that cosmology. And, as Corbin eloquently puts it in *Avicenne et le Récit Visionnaire*, "the oriental philosopher that professes the traditional philosophy lives in the Avicennian cosmos...for the orientalist, it is rather the cosmos that lives in him."[388] The oriental philosopher lives Avicenna's cosmology, while the modern scholar integrates Avicenna's cosmos within herself or himself. In this regard, the Visionary Recitals form the cycle of a trilogy that depicts a journey by virtue of which the "integration" of Avicenna's cosmos within one's own self becomes possible. Yet, integration presupposes some sort of exile that takes place prior to it. Integration is preceded by an "alienation" from what is to be re-integrated. Falling precedes ascension, and the return back home is preceded by exile. The call is that which summons the self to be brought back to where it belongs, to where it came from. Ascension is a retrieval of the self from its alienation and exiling captivity. However, liberation and ascension require orientation. And, one reading of the visionary recitals shows that orientation is derived from that which orients. Orientation is a quest of the Orient that orients. And, the first recital of the trilogy is the Recital of Ḥayy Ibn Yaqẓān which "teaches the fundamental orientation" ("*enseigne l'orientation fondamentalle*").[389] And this may reveal the recital of Ḥayy Ibn Yaqẓān as being itself a scene of orientation or instruction."[390] The recital of Ḥayy Ibn Yaqẓān opens up the eyes of the

---

388 *Ibid*, p. 17. Herein, Henry Corbin says: "*Le philosophe oriental professant la philosophie traditionnelle vit dans le cosmos avicennien...pour l'orientaliste, c'est plutôt le cosmos qui vit en lui.*"

389 *Ibid*, p. 19.

390 This way of reading the recitals as "scenes of instruction" as "teachings" is also what Stanley Cavell for example proposes with regard to the reading of Wittgenstein's *Philosophical Investigations*.

soul to its estrangement and alienation. It orients in the sense of awakening the self to its human condition as being that of "exile." In a similar fashion to what nine centuries later figures in the Heideggerian call of conscience, the call of the recital also awakens the self to its homelessness. The recital calls the self from its alienating thrownness and absorption in its everydayness concerns. Orientation becomes a hermeneutic interpretation of one's modes of being-in-the-world. It is an interpretation of one's "*imago mundi*" (world picture), and an "*interpretatio mundi*." Orientation mediates one's own interpretation of one's being-in-the-world through an interpretation of one's own world. In orientation, the soul is awakened to experiencing itself as a stranger (*gharība*) in this world. Yet, such awakening of the self to its own estrangement and alienation is also an awakening of a quest for home. The estranged and alienated homeless self, by virtue of its recognition of its condition, sets itself into a search for the origin of its provenance. It already sets itself to search for what orients it towards its way back home. Being awakened to its own alienation, the self is set for a return back home. The call that awakes the self to its homelessness is also a call that calls back home. And, according to Corbin's reading of Avicenna's recital of Ḥayy Ibn Yaqẓān, the soul of the gnostic discovers where it is, where it comes from, and where it ought to return to, by virtue of being awakened to its own estrangement.[391] The awakened self is that which hears the call that brings it to its awareness of where it is, where it came from, and where it returns. It is this spatial recognition that characterizes the orientation of an awakened self. And orientation draws distinctions between where one is, where one came from, and where one returns.

[391] Corbin says: "It is in its awakening to the sentiment of being a stranger, that the soul of the gnostic discovers where it is, and pressing at the same time where it comes from and where it returns" ("c'est en s'éveillant au sentiment d'être une étrangère, que l'âme du gnostique découvre où elle est, et pressant à la fois d'où elle vient et où elle retourne"). See: Henry Corbin, *Avicenne et le Récit Visionnaire (Tome 2): Étude sur le Cycle des Récits Avicenniens* (Tehran: Société des Monuments Nationaux de l'Iran, 1954), p. 22.

The recital of Ḥayy Ibn Yaqẓān is also a recital about one's own place in the world, one's origin (ἡ ἀρχη *archē*, *maṣdar*), and one's destination. If where one is now is the place of estrangement, the place of exile and un-homeliness, then one is also aware of where one is originally from and where one eventually would hope to return to. The recital that orients does call for a return back to one's place. It is a recital of recollection and re-gathering that brings the self out from oblivion and forgetfulness. The recital is then a recital of place and recollection that constitutes the meaning of orientation. The self that hears the call of guidance, is the self that is also awakened to the uniqueness of its own self-experience away from the absorption in the world of the "they-self" (what Heidegger calls *das Man*). The self is thus called to its individuality and self-gathering from its absorption in the everydayness world of estrangement. The self is therefore awakened to the reality that shows its world of familiarity as being the world of oblivion and alienation. Orientation is therefore an alienation of the self from its alienating world of "collective norms and common rules."[392] The self discovers itself as being a stranger and as being solitary in a world that was altogether too familiar. This awakening is accompanied by a "visualization" of the soul's own guide. And, according to Corbin, the soul's guide is the soul's "perfect nature" that takes its visionary appearance from the figure of Gabriel (*Jibrīl*, *Jibrā'īl*), the Holy Spirit (*al-rūḥ al-quds*), or the Intellect (νοῦς *noûs*, *al-ʿaql*).[393] Orientation is also an initiation to the futural way back to the origin where the end meets the beginning. In this, the self recognizes its existential dependence on what is other than itself. The self is awakened to its human condition whose existence is due to the Necessary Existent (*wājib al-wūjūd*). In this sense, the visionary side of Avicenna's concern with being encounters his ontological side at the same site where the oriented vision takes place. The ontological considerations of being find their place within

---

392 *Ibid*, p. 22.

393 *Ibid*, pp. 23, 26-27.

the symbolic account that locates the self within the cosmological topology. The self is thus located between the place of exile, where the self is thrown into existence, and the other place towards which its futural journey leads to, as the originary place of its provenance and the continual source of its being. Orientation is then a recollection of the origin and a thanking for the granting of being. Eventually, orientation is an invitation to a futural journey that leads the self back to where it belongs. And, this journey is also an ascension and elevation of the self towards the source of its being across time. Given that the source of being is the origin towards which the futural return tends to. In orientation, the guide summons the self to follow. Calling those who want to hear: "if you want it, follow me." And, those who hear the call are invited to a pilgrimage journey to the Orient, a voyage towards the realm of pure forms where the physical universe is represented in symbols. The Ḥayy Ibn Yaqẓān recital is thus an initiation into the journey. It is an invitation to the Orient (*mashriq, sharq*). The Recital of the Bird is the recital that tells us that the journey is undertaken in the form of a mental ascension in the company of the Guide. And the third recital of Salmān and Absal completes this cycle of the trilogy by showing how the gnostic journeying-self encounters its "Angelic" definition while anticipating the homological ἐκστασις (*ecstasis*) of the return of no return as death (*mawt*).

II- The Recital of Ḥayy Ibn Yaqẓān

Based on Avicenna's disciple al-Juzjānī, it is said that the Recital of Ḥayy Ibn Yaqẓān has been written when Avicenna was held in detention in the fortress of Fardajān by the *wazīr* of Hamadhān. The recital itself was an invitation to a flight from exile, and it may be an expression of Avicenna's personal experience in prison. After all, one may interpret the Recital of Ḥayy Ibn Yaqẓān as being an invitation to leave one's own prison. On this reading, the Recital of Ḥayy Ibn Yaqẓān is taken to be the story of an invitation to the Orient offered by a caller named: *Vivens filius Vigilantis*. The recital starts with a first person narration. Amidst being settled in the city, the place of politics and social undertakings, and in the company of friends, the narrator had the vision of an old sage. The sage appeared amidst the dealings of everyday companionship, and this sage was surrounded by divine glory. His name was Ḥayy (*Vivens*) and his lineage: Ibn Yaqẓān (*filius Vigilantis*). His homeland is *Bayt al-Maqdis* in Jerusalem (*al-Quds*). The narrator was immediately attracted to this sage, and was summoned to address that divine figure. The sage is well versed in *ʿilm al-firāsa* (the science of physiognomy). He is able to read the faces of the narrator's companions, as if moving in the form of a *ta'wīl* that reveals the hidden (*bāṭin*) that underlies what is apparent (*ẓāhir*). The initial encounter with the sage is turned into an exegesis of companionship. "Amidst them lies your misfortune," "do not let them take you over," and "it is you who ought to have the upper hand," "that your authority surpasses theirs," thus spoke the sage. Given that *ʿilm al-firāsa* (physiognomy) may be interpreted as being a form of *ta'wīl*, one may also find interpretations of *ʿilm al-firāsa* that do not take it to be a form of *ta'wīl*. In another approach to the interpretation of the Recital of Ḥayy Ibn Yaqẓān, both A. M. Goichon and Aḥmad Amīn do not account for *ʿilm al-firāsa* (the science of physiognomy) in terms of *ta'wīl* (hermeneutic exegesis).[394] On Goichon's view, physiognomy is a science that reveals the mysteries that remain hidden for other sciences. Goichon herein asserts that physiognomy is to be accounted for in terms of linking it to syllogistic logic.[395] In another context, Aḥmad Amīn takes a similar position to that advocated by

394 *Ta'wīl* is a form of hermeneutic exegesis that educes the hidden truth that lies behind appearances. This exegesis is applied to texts as much as to the self. In the following chapter 8 on language and being, *ta'wīl* is addressed in the light of considering the hermeneutic tradition in Islamic doctrines and how this is addressed in relation to Avicenna's philosophical work.

395 Avicenna, *Le Récit Visionnaire de Hayy Ibn Yaqẓān*, trans. by A. M. Goichon (Paris: Desclée de Brouwer, 1959), pp. 40-41.

Goichon. Amīn asserts that physiognomy (*al-firāsa*) and its science (*ᶜilm*) are none other than logic (*al-manṭiq*). Amīn holds that with *ᶜilm al-firāsa* one knows what is hidden through the knowledge of what is apparent, therefore one deduces conclusions from premises, as is the case with a syllogistic structure.[396] On Goichon's reading, the active intellect (*al-ᶜaql al-faᶜāl*) appears as the figure of the sage whose name is Ḥayy Ibn Yaqẓān. And, this "intellect" emanates from pure intelligence that does not know sleep. The sage summons that the soul is at the risk of being brought down to a level that is below itself due to its bad companionship that is limited to the sensible realm.[397] In order to undertake the journey, the separation from the companions has to happen. Yet, this separation will take place when the time of its "fixed term" comes. It is in solitude that the journey will be initiated and the response to the invitation to the voyage will take place. The separation from what keeps the self in estrangement is required. And, on Goichon's view the separation from the body in the return (*maᶜād*) is what is required. This is taken to be the case, given that the "soul would not be liberated but at death."[398] The journey starts in solitude and the invitation to journey is itself presented in a personal vision. The self encounters its own guide who topologically unveils the occident as the realm of materiality, and reveals the orient as the source of light (*al-nūr*). This topological division of the universe reflects a Neoplatonic and Illuminationist (*ishrāqī*) account of emanation. Based on the "Light metaphor," one could say that the orient is the source of light, while the occident is the place of darkness. And this also shows that an orientation towards the orient presupposes a dis-orientation from

---

396 Avicenna, *Ḥayy Ibn Yaqzān*, ed. by Aḥmad Amīn (Cairo: dār al-maᶜārif bi-miṣr, 1952), p. 18.

397 Avicenna, *Le Récit Visionnaire de Hayy Ibn Yaqzan*, trans. by A. M. Goichon (Paris: Desclée de Brouwer, 1959), pp. 10-11.

398 *Ibid*, p. 65. Therein, Goichon says: "*l'âme ne sera libérée qu'à la mort.*"

what leads to the occident. In this sense, the realms of light and darkness interplay. And the same holds viz. unconcealment and concealment. The mystic journey itself gives expression to the "great [cosmological] chain of being." The world of familiarity is exited in order that the traveller (*al-musāfir*) ascends towards the sun (*al-shams*) which cannot itself be seen, though it is in itself the source of all seeing. The light, that lights all that is seen, is itself forbidden to sight. The light of the *light* veils the *light,* a beauty veiled by its proper beauty.[399] After all, Ḥayy Ibn Yaqẓān says that "this is how the sun, when it veils itself a little is thus revealed a lot more; while when it emanates an intense shining [*tajalī*], it is hidden to the sights. Its light is then the veil of its light."[400] And, this may be written in allusion to the following Qur'anic verse of *Surat al-Nūr*: "Light on Light (*nūr ᶜala nūr*), God orients to His own Light" (Qur'ān, 35:24).

III- Orientation

As mentioned above, the Ḥayy Ibn Yaqẓān Recital may be taken to be an invitation to a journey to the Orient that is extended by a sage who appears in a personal vision. This sage calls the soul to encounter the invisible world. The caller (*al-dāᶜī*), who calls to the voyage to the Orient, practices *ᶜilm al-firāsa* (physiognomy). He is able to perform a reading of the apparent physiognomy of the face that unveils what the soul veils of its hidden truths. As Henry Corbin would interpret it, the sage's ability with physiognomy reading mani-

---

399 *Ibid*, pp. 173, 189. As the French translation of the Ḥayy Ibn Yaqẓān recital reads as follows: "*Le soleil se refuse au regard, et c'est pourquoi sa lumière est le voile de sa lumière*" (The sun refuses itself to sight, and this is why its light is the veil of its light).

400 *Ibid*, p. 277 (Goichon's French translation of a passage of Ḥayy Ibn Yaqẓān recital reads as follows: "*Ainsi le soleil, s'il se voile un peu se révèle beaucoup plus; mais lorsqu'il émet un intense rayonnement il est caché aux regards. Sa lumière est alors la voile de sa lumière*").

fests an "exemplification" of *ta'wīl* that reveals the hidden truth behind the apparent face.[401] This *ta'wīl* exegesis plays between the realms of darkness and light in the soul. Being like the world in which it is, the soul itself is also topologically divided into an oriental side and an occidental one. Like the world, the self has its own orient (as the realm of its light) and its own occident (as the shadowy realm of its darkness). Like the composite body that reflects the insertion of form and matter, the oriental and the occidental inclinations of the soul are themselves torn between the oriental intelligibility of forms and the occidental sensibility of matter. *Ta'wīl* is the hermeneutic process by virtue of which the *bāṭin* (esoteric) is uncovered from underneath the *ẓāhir* (exoteric). It is the movement of *ḥaqīqa* (truth) as it is unconcealed from behind the *majāz* (metaphor). It is the return of what has fallen gracefully and thankfully in *tanzīl* (Divine Revelation). And *ta'wīl* is also the procession that makes use of all spheres of science to lead the self on the path of truth. In this sense, and as Louis Gardet observes, sensible knowledge is a "pretext" or some sort of a guise that allows the human soul to encounter itself as "being towards the light" that comes to it from the *dator formarum* (*wāhib al-ṣūwar*).[402] By *ta'wīl*, the text becomes a trace of the exegesis of the soul in its journey to the Orient as the place of truth. All the knowledge acquired by the self is recollected and gathered in a textual register that is open to the hermeneutic move of

---

401 Henry Corbin, *Avicenne et le Récit Visionnaire (Tome 2): Étude sur le Cycle des Récits Avicenniens* (Tehran: Société des Monuments Nationaux de l'Iran, 1954), pp. 179-180

402 Louis Gardet, *La Connaissance Mystique chez Ibn Sina et ses Présupposés Philosophiques* (Cairo: Publications de l'Institut Français d'Archéologie Orientale du Caire, 1952), p. 14. Therein, Gardet writes: "*Ainsi, ce n'est point à partir de la connaissance sensible que se forme la connaissance intelligible. La connaissance sensible n'est que l'excitant, le prétexte, pou l'âme humaine, de se trouver vers la lumière qui lui vient du 'donateur des formes', et donc vers les intelligibles.*"

ta'wīl.[403] The interpretive process builds itself by way of passing through logic, physics, and metaphysics. Eventually, this process leads us to a personal story-telling or poetic reciting of the soul's journey. Thus, Avicenna's mysticism finds its "justification" in the great metaphysical, noetic, and cosmological schema in his system, and no comprehension of his mystical views is possible without them.[404] In this sense, the recital re-enacts the experience of journeying by way of transmuting beings into symbols. Language is thus turned into the trace of the soul's self-exegesis. And the soul's self-exegesis is the soul's journey to the orient. The recital seeks *al-ḥaqīqa* (truth). And, the language of the recital is a poetic language that seeks to bring the soul back home in language. Orientation is therefore a bringing home of the self in language. Goichon also tells us that one reads in the recital of Ḥayy Ibn Yaqẓān that the soul, that seeks the intellectual path, asks the guide to orient it. However, Goichon's interpretation relies on an account that takes logic to be that which guides the soul to the source of light and forms. On Goichon's reading, it is logic not poetry that leads to the orient. Logic leads us to the light and orients us away from the path that leads to an occidental realm of matter that is none other than a desert of ruins that has been relinquished by the migrating forms.[405]

IV- The Mystic Ascension and *al-Miʿrāj*

The ascension through the Seven Heavens (*al-samawāt al-sabʿ*) to the *Throne (al-ʿarsh*) found its echoes in the mystical journey of the gnostic. *Al-Isrā'* is the night journey that the Prophet

403 Regarding a further elaboration of *ta'wīl*, see chapter 8: "Language and Being."

404 Louis Gardet, *La Connaissance Mystique chez Ibn Sina et ses Présupposés Philosophiques* (Cairo: Publications de l'Institut Français d'Archéologie Orientale du Caire, 1952), p. 67.

405 Avicenna, *Le Récit Visionnaire de Hayy Ibn Yaqzan*, trans. by A. M. Goichon (Paris: Desclée de Brouwer, 1959), pp. 11-12.

Muḥammad took from the sacred place of prayer (*al-masjid al-ḥarām*) to the furthest place of prayer (*al-masjid al-aqṣa*) in *bayt al-maqdis* (the house of sanctified) i.e. Jerusalem, *al-Quds* (Qur'ān, *surat al-isrā'*: 17:1, and 19:1, 53:1-18). Herein, the ascent (*al-miʿrāj*) to Heaven took place on a white beast called *al-Burāq*. And the Prophet ascended in the company of the angelic messenger *Jibrīl* (Gabriel); referred to as "*Jibrīl ṣāḥibī*" (Gabriel my Friend, my companion). Ascension became then linked to a poetic and lyrical tradition that attempted to re-enact the *miʿrāj* (Prophetic ascension) by way of a hermeneutic cosmological *ta'wīl* that expresses a mystic setting out in a serious journey. *Tanzīl* as descent by emanation (*fayḍ*) is followed by *miʿrāj* as ascension. Procession by *tanzīl* (descent) is followed by reversion as *miʿrāj* (ascent). If descent as thrownness is alienating, the ascension is a de-alienating return (*maʿād*) of the soul that beholds to the Beloved (*al-maʿshūq*) it seeks. The soul tends in self-perfection toward the Necessary Existent (*wājib al-wūjūd*). The soul is in quest of truth. And, in being towards the Necessary Existent, the soul is in the mode of being-toward-truth (*al-ḥaqīqa*). The self that undertakes the mystic journey is a self that attends to truth by transmuting its world of sensible entities into a world of symbols and signs that attend to its beholding of truth. In this state of affairs, everything is transmuted into signs (*āyāt*) of divinity.[406] The scripture and beings become signs and points of anchorage that stabilize the world. Those who attend to

---

406 In a phenomenological approach to Islam, some scholars start by addressing this transmutation in terms of accounting for phenomena and then going deeper within the "layers of the human response to the Divine" until one reaches the "*Numinous*" core of the religion or its "*deus absconditus*." In this sense, everything serves as an *āya* (sign) of the Divine. Such approach has been conducted in the works of A. Schimmel and Friedrich Heiler. For further elaboration on this approach, refer to: Annemarie Schimmel, *Deciphering the signs of God: A Phenomenological Approach to Islam* (Albany: State University of New York Press, 1994), p. xii.

the immersion in the mundane world of everydayness (*al-ḥayāt al-dunyā*), content with what they have, are those who miss the divine signs (*hum* ᶜ*an al-āyāt ghāfilūn*, in allusion to the Qurā'nic *āyāt* of *Surat Yūnis*: 10:7, 10:92). Since truth (*al-ḥaq*) is sent to those who are able to be lead to it, and they are being led to it for the sake of their selves. Those who are oriented towards truth lead their lives towards it, those who are disoriented are those who are alienating themselves (Qur'ān: *Surat Yūnis*: 10:108). Those signs (*āyāt*) are recited, and those who hear are those endowed with listening (*sama*ᶜ), and those who see are endowed with vision (*baṣar*). The ones that hear are those who speak (*nāṭiqūn*). And hearing is the characteristic of those endowed with speech, with *logos*. Hearing is an aspect of *al-nafs al-nāṭiqa* (the speaking soul). Those who strive toward their Lord, in strife, will meet Him (Qur'ān, *Surat al-Inshiqāq*: 84:6). And, humans are created with strife and labor (*inā khalaqna al-insān fī kabad*; Qur'ān, *Surat al-Balad*: 90:4). Ascension itself is a journey of strife in quest of the Beloved. In all of this, the *said* points to what is missing in the *saying*, as well as that which is thought points to what remains unthought in thinking. The *said* points to silence, it points to what remains hidden, unsaid, and unthought. This is where figures the role of hermeneutics and *ta'wīl* in unveiling veiled meanings. What is ineffable is also what is encountered in experiencing something that has been seen or heard yet that cannot be said. If Heidegger considers the categories of being to be spheres of meaning,[407] then *ta'wīl* (hermeneutic interpretation) is to be granted a high value as being the hermeneutic exegesis that seeks these hidden meanings.

If *Dasein*'s existential movement is that of being-towards-death, Avicenna's self-perfection [existential] movement is that of

[407] At least this is what John D. Caputo holds with regard to being in his reading of Heidegger. Caputo explicitly says: "Being is meaning.." See: John D. Caputo, *Heidegger and Aquinas: An Essay on Overcoming Metaphysics* (New York: Fordham University Press, 1982), p. 32.

being towards the Necessary Existent. This state of affairs describes a hermeneutic circle that starts with being and terminates with being. And it is as such without being a vicious circle, since the beginning and the end are not the same. The movement, from being and towards being, is that of self-perfection. Such movement goes across "The Great Chain of Being." It gives expression to an existential movement by *tashkīk* that "suggests a movement of being," from the less determinate level of being to the more determinate level of being. And, in *Kitāb al-Ishārāt wal-Tanbīhāt*, Avicenna remarks that "every being seeks its own proper self-perfection." Every being has its own self-perfection either by love or by will. And, every being wills its own proper perfection.[408]

Al-tashkīk expresses an "evolutionary" and "self-unfolding process of being" according to which a "contingent being is the shadow of Absolute being."[409] *Al-tashkīk* may be a concept that is more associated with Mullā Ṣadrā than with Avicenna. Yet what *al-tashkīk* implies is also encountered in Avicenna's account of the existential movement of self-perfection where the self-perfecting self passes in its existential movement through lower modes of being and therefore rises as that self which guards the cosmos. The existential movement of self-perfection, is a cosmological movement that configures the relation between the self and the world, where the self is worldly in the sense of gathering the world in its movement through the grades of being while preserving and recollecting what it passes through. This account points to the unity of being that acts as the principle of identity and difference. *Al-tashkīk* classifies beings in terms of their "intensity of being" and "completeness of being,"

---

408 Avicenna, *Livre des Directives et Remarques*, trans. by A. M. Goichon (Paris: Librairie Philosophique J. Vrin, 1951), p. 481. This account finds its echo in Spinoza's notion of *Conatus* (endeavor) in his *Ethics*.

409 Alparslan Açikgenç, *Being and Existence in Ṣadrā and Heidegger* (Kuala Lumpur: International Institute of Islamic Thought and Civilization [ISTAC], 1993), pp. 37-38, 60, 76.

whereby the differentiation between a being and another is reflected in the "intensification" (*ishtidād*) of being, or the "weakening" (*taḍāʿuf*) of being.[410]

V- The Recital of the Bird

If the Recital of Ḥayy Ibn Yaqẓān constituted the invitation to a pilgrimage towards the Orient, the Recital of the Bird (*Risālat al-Ṭayr*) tells us that the gnostic has started the pilgrimage. Yet, some might interpret the pilgrimage journey as being a mental ascension that analogically seeks to approximate the prophetic ascension (*al-miʿrāj*) from *Bayt al-Maqdis* in Jerusalem. The ascension of the gnostic might itself be read as being a *ta'wīl* (hermeneutic interpretation) of the prophetic *miʿrāj*. And, this *ta'wīl* of the prophetic *miʿrāj*, in the ascension of the gnostic (*ʿārif*), puts the soul of the gnostic into an exegesis.[411] This is the case given that the *miʿrāj* is the ascension to heaven from *bayt al-maqdis,* while the *isrā'* is the night journey to *bayt al-maqdis* (*al-quds*, Jerusalem). Awakened by the angel Gabriel the Prophet was conducted to the winged beast called *al-Burāq,* and the Prophet journeyed together with Gabriel to *bayt al-maqdis.*[412] Some interpret this journey as being a vision in a dream, while others maintain that it happened to the soul and the body. The Recital of the Bird might itself be interpreted as being a hermeneutic interpretation of the prophetic *miʿrāj*. And, in setting itself free in the journey to the orient, the soul is eschatologically brought back to a homological encounter with the primordial and

---

410 *Ibid*, pp. 131, 135, 137.

411 Henry Corbin, *Avicenne et le Récit Visionnaire (Tome 2): Étude sur le Cycle des Récits Avicenniens* (Tehran: Société des Monuments Nationaux de l'Iran, 1954), pp. 191-193.

412 *The Encyclopaedia of Islam*, ed. by M. Th. Houtsma, A. J. Wensinck, T. W. Arnold, W. Heffening, and E. Levi-Provencal (Leiden: E. j. Brill Ltd, 1927), vol. II, p. 553.

originary source of its being. It is the gnostic *ᶜārif* (the one endowed with mystic knowledge) who undertakes this voyage to the orient. The mystic voyage to the orient overcomes what the metaphysical, physical, or logical discourse is able to achieve. The journey is a pilgrimage that no philosopher or metaphysician is able to undertake. The mystic vision takes place between sleep and wake (*mā bayna al-nawm wal-yaqẓa*). In solitude and in departing from the realm of everydayness and its concerns, the trained *ᶜārif* hears the call to unveil one's own self in a personal elevating experience that is not of the order of the sensible realm. The reception of the call that summons to journey reflects a readiness and willingness to hear that call. The self is herein drawn away from the everyday world of estrangement. The call summons those who are able to hear when their senses are weakened. The call summons in silence. It calls those who hear not by their ears but by the depth of their souls. It is not a call that brings philosophers by their ears, as to draw them near by the power of argument. It is rather a call that summons the solitary souls in silence. It calls for the light, for the orient that grants being. The call is not heard by those absorbed in the world of everyday concerns, rather the call summons those who are abstracted from that world, those who depart from that world of alienation and therefore do not receive the call through their senses. The call summons between the state of wake and of sleep. It summons between consciousness and unconsciousness away from the distraction of everyday concerns. It calls the soul from its side of light. It calls the soul from its oriental side to heed, thank, and commemorate being.

In the mystical journey, the sensible world and its beings are subject to a transmutation into a world of symbols. Even the physical representation of the voyage in terms of places and scenes is itself what is *ẓāhir* (exoteric) that veils the *bāṭin* (esoteric) truth or reality that underlies it. The symbolic representation of the topological character of the mystic journey is itself subject to *ta'wīl* as an exegesis of what the apparent in the representation veils as hidden reality and truth.[413] The bird (*al-ṭayr*) is a symbol of the soul set in its flight of liberation. The bird with its wings lifts up the self in spite of the burden and heaviness of its corporeity. The bird with wings lifts the heavy body from its corporeal materiality, sending the self in an ascending spiritual voyage against the risk of falling. The wings allow the self to lift itself from its fall and thrownness into existence. The novice bird, the untrained and novice *ᶜārif* (the gnostic), is faced with the risk of falling; the wings of the soul will have to develop, to grow, to spread. The fall, as a thrownness into existence, is a perpetual grounding that pulls the self to the ground of its everyday concerns. And, everydayness resists an ascension that draws the self away from its captivating and comforting familiarity. Without wings, no ascending celestial procession can be put into practice. This is why Ḥayy Ibn Yaqẓān tells that the invitation to the voyage has its set time. Ascension calls for the re-gathering of what has fallen into oblivion in everydayness.[414] The winged soul approximates the angelic figure of the guide who is an image of the soul's self-perfection. How could the soul not take wing and speed away into the "unseen" when it hears the call of return? As Jalāl al-dīn Rūmī expresses it *"Fly, fly O bird, to you have escaped from the cage and your feathers and wings are outspread...Journey away from the brackish water towards the water of life: return to the high table of the soul from the porter's lodge...Off, off! For we too, O soul, are arriving from this world of separation to that world of union."*[415]

[413] Henry Corbin, *Avicenne et le Récit Visionnaire (Tome 2): Étude sur le Cycle des Récits Avicenniens* (Tehran: Société des Monuments Nationaux de l'Iran, 1954), pp. 205-206.

[414] *Ibid*, p. 210. *"La catastrophe de sa [l'âme] naissance terrestre en a aboli les traits de sa mémoire, vien ici-bas ne les lui rappele."*

[415] Jalāl al-dīn Rūmī, *Mystical Poems of Rūmīl, first selection, Poems 1-200*, trans. by A. J. Arberry (Chicago: The University of Chicago Press, 1968), poem 167.

VI- φίλια (*philia*) and the Authenticity of Being

If the invitation to the mystic journey was extended to a solitary self, this does not entail that Avicenna stresses on solitude and individuality while disregarding the relation of the self with the other. One way of reading his mystic recitals would be to illustrate some accounts that he advances viz. friendship and brotherhood. In the Ḥayy Ibn Yaqẓān recital, the guide appears in a vision to the narrator that will be initiated to the journey. The guide by a hermeneutic exegetical move attempts to decipher the hidden reality behind the faces of the narrator's companions; the *ta'wīl* (hermeneutic interpretation) of their physiognomy is itself an attempt to disclose from their apparent faces the reality that lurks behind them. And this is done in such a way as to show that their friendship is not a genuine friendship. This attempted *ta'wīl* of companionship is set in the context of preparing the self to receive its invitation to undertake the mystic journey. The self ought to face the fact that it is distracted by companions who draw it to the ground of its everydayness. In order to be a *winged* self that undertakes its path of voyage, the self ought to be solitary. In this regard, the self is called upon to detach itself from the world of its self-estrangement. The self ought to be separated from companions whose friendship is not a genuine friendship. The account of φίλια (*philia*), as it may figure in the physiognomy reading that Ḥayy Ibn Yaqẓān performs, is an account of the disorientation that a non-genuine *philia* may bring. Ḥayy Ibn Yaqẓān implicitly says that the "companions who are around you, never moving away [from you], are bad companions."[416] Ḥayy then says that one of the companions is a liar, that he is talkative, that he embodies what is false and is a fiction maker. Yet, this companion is still the secret eye that "illuminates," and he is thus a source of dependence despite all the perplexity that surrounds his stories. As for the second companion, the one who is on the right, he is violent with an uncontrollable

---

[416] *Ibid*, p. 163. "*Ces compagnons qui sont autour de toi, jamais ne s'écartant, sont des mauvais compagnons.*"

anger. He is "like a lioness whose calf has been killed." As for the third companion, the one on the left, he is unmannered and indecent like a "pig" that has been hungered and then released to feed itself on garbage. "These are the companions that are attached to you and nothing can separate you from them but journeying to a land that those who are like them cannot touch its soil." Thus spoke the sage guide. The time to emigrate has not yet come, since the separation from bad companions ought to precede it, and the self that is destining itself to journey ought to assert its authority over its context and be resolute. Three bad companions, one distorting truth, one violent, and one harming beauty; each badly affecting the conditions for the occurrence of truth, peace, love and beauty. Ḥayy Ibn Yaqẓān calls for the genuine friendship in the company of one's guide in the mystic journey. Genuine friendship is that which accompanies the self in the realization of the truth of its self-perfection. Genuine friendship is the friendship of truth. Genuine friendship thus calls to journey in the company of the guide. And, as one feels towards a friend what one feels towards one's own self, the feeling that the self has towards its guide is a feeling of the genuine friendship of an oriented companionship. Being oriented in the company of the guide is being *amicably* disposed towards oneself and towards one's own guide to the orient. Another account of genuine friendship figures in the introduction to the Recital of the Bird. There, the narrator stresses on "brotherhood" before telling the story of the journeying gnostic. In this sense, brotherhood is taken to be a kind of friendship that assembles those who are in search of what enables them to be contemplative of true realities through inner visions. Those friends are brothers who purified the depth of their hearts from doubt, and thus formed a "society of brothers" that is gathered by a divine vocation. Those are the "brothers of truth" (*ikhwat al-ḥaq*) who communicate their secrets to one another (This may itself be akin to what one encounters with the "Bretheren of Purity" order, *ikhwān al-ṣafā'*). They are the brothers of truth who lift the veils that hide the depth of their own hearts, so that in trust they will guide one another in their quest for self-perfection.[417] Brotherhood implies common parenthood and shared lineage and provenance. Brothers who recognize their brotherhood are also those who recognize that they come from the same origin and source. To be awakened to one's own source and origin, to be awakened to the orient as one's own source, is to be awakened to a lineage that is shared with everything. Yet, only those endowed with *logos,* and who as such are themselves awakened to their source as the orient, consequently may assemble in the brotherhood of truth. The brothers of truth are brothers by virtue of being awakened to the truth of their provenance and to the recognition of that truth as being the truth of their birth. Unlike camaraderie, brotherhood is not chosen, it is recognized as being the link that one is thrown into at birth. Brotherhood cannot be transgressed, it could be denied, it could be hidden and one being unaware of it, yet it persists from the time of one's own birth. It is the truth of one's own lineage and provenance. Those who recognize the orient as the source of all being, those who recognize it as the origin of their being since birth, are those who are endowed with intellect and are able to recognize their brotherhood in truth. Those who have the vision of their Ḥayy Ibn Yaqẓān are already on the path of recognizing their shared brotherhood of truth. They are those who regard the orient as their common source and origin, and see it as the place of their truth. Orientation, towards the orient that orients, implies that companionship, guidance, brotherhood, and friendship; all are set in quest of the orient. The bothers of truth are called five times into an initiation to the journey. The caller is the narrator who could also be Avicenna himself calling his brothers of truth *five times* before initiating the story that recounts the journey.[418] A story that is itself a trace of the journey.

---

[417] *Ibid*, p. 216.

[418] Called five times as if those brothers in faith were called to their daily prayer.

The first call summons the brothers of truth to open their hearts and unveil their secrets so that they aid one another on their journey to self-perfection. The second call summons: "brothers of truth, retreat, retreat in such a way that in 'solitude' you will reveal your hidden being and veil your apparent being." It is solitude that unveils your concealed being and veils your apparent being; like a movement of *ta'wīl* that makes your underlying hidden being appear while veiling your apparent being. This call, of an unveiling veiling, is the call that renders the apparent occult and the occult apparent. It is a movement of giving and withdrawing, of unconcealing and concealing.

The third call summons the brothers of truth to leave behind their old skin like the snake leaves behind its old skin. The caller summons the bothers to take their path like the "ant" that does not make itself heard or noticed. Yet the brothers have to be like the "scorpion" that carries its arm at the edge of its tail, since it is from behind that "the demon" sneaks to surprise the human soul. The caller calls the brothers to absorb the "poison" as a Platonic *pharmakon* that carries both cure and death. A poison that in the third Visionary Recital of Salmān and Absal would be what Absal swallows in the final mystic death. The caller therefore calls for a mystic death that is both cure and poison. "Absorb the poison, and be awakened to your death," and "Love death;" thus calling the self to its authenticity of being-towards-death. "To stay alive: 'be always in flight'," thus summons the caller. "Be always in flight," be like birds not taking for themselves a "settling nest," since it is in the nest that birds are caught. The call is that of resisting the attraction of the estrangement world of familiarity which threatens to dispossess our souls of their wings. The call is a call of vigilance as to not let the self be taken by surprise. The self is summoned to be vigilant and insomniac like bats, since bats are said to be "the best of all birds." They fly concealed by the veils of the night. They are vigilant when all are asleep, and the night and sleep constitute the time when visions and divinations take place. The fourth call that reaches the brothers of truth, is a call of courage to face "tomorrow." It is a call to be resolute in facing the responsibility of self-perfection. After all, the caller says that "the most coward" is the one who is always late in attending to one's own proper self-perfection. And, the fifth call to the brothers of truth is a call to control one's desires instead of drifting around in the attempt to fulfill them. This call summons the self to assume the position between the Angelic figure of its self-perfection, as the figure that does not have organs of corruption, and the beastly animal that does not have faculties of comprehension. The call is then that which summons the self to tend towards its Angelic self-perfection and to control the desires that cause its devolution towards a mere organism, towards a beastly animal. The self has the blessed potentiality for rising by virtue of having νοῦς (*noûs, al-ᶜaql*) as an analogical capacity to the one that the Angel carries.[419]

It might be the case that those who have realized in themselves the response to the five calls are now of the rank of birds. They are thus endowed with wings and are about to release them in their mystic flight of liberation in the company of the messenger. The journey is liberating. It releases the captivated oriental side of the self that has been subordinated by the everydayness of the occidental side of theoretic and practical undertakings. The flight to the orient is then a liberation from the captivating world-picture that subordinates the orient to the occident; as it might well be the case in subordinating the intelligible to the sensible, the invisible to the visible, the hidden to the apparent. The liberation in the mystic flight is a releasing of the self from being captivated by monopolizing modes of revealing truth. With the journey, the self undertakes the path of seeking truth in a personal experience that is ineffable in the language of logic, physics, or even metaphysics. The liberation in the journey

---

[419] Regarding the narration of these calls that figures in the initiation to the Recital of the Bird, refer to the French translation in: Henry Corbin, *Avicenne et le Récit Visionnaire (Tome 2): Étude sur le Cycle des Récits Avicenniens* (Tehran: Société des Monuments Nationaux de l'Iran, 1954), pp. 216-217.

consists of breaking away from systems that subordinate truth to correctness, systems that subordinate infinity to totality. The journey is a personal path taken in the company of one's own image of self-perfection, heading towards the orient as the source and truth of one's own being. The recitals attempt to bring the self and language back home by way of a mystic inclination in poetry that seeks to turn language itself into the language of truth, the language of the truth of being, the language of being.

Under the threat of captivity, birds find their comfort in a genuine companionship. And, before resigning to a fate of captivity some birds managed to liberate themselves. Those who were still captive were left behind to suffer from the deepest sorrow, anxiety, and pain. The liberated souls set an example for those who are still captive. Every soul has to be resolute and take its destiny upon itself. For "how would the sick heal another?" Even after its flight, the soul is still threatened by the fall. The soul should not be distracted from its journey where veil after veil is unveiled. When the last *veil of veils* is unveiled, the beauty of the Lord blurs all like a light that veils the light. And the journeying souls are not fully released *walking in the company of the Messenger of the King.*[420] Having recited what the flight of the bird leads to, the narrator is faced with doubt. Some of the companions say that "it is your reason that has flied." Yet, flying to the orient is never the flight of a "Man of Reason." The flight to the orient is not the journey of the masters of arguments who profess dogmas. As Corbin would say, the voice of the criticizing brothers is the voice of those who once criticized mystics like Proclus and Suhrawardī.[421] The Recitals are not to be approached or accounted for solely by the theoretic means of philosophers or masters of reason. A philosopher cannot undertake the flight that is undertaken by the gnostic *ᶜārif.* The theories of *Kitāb al-Shifā'* altogether cannot account for what a mystic journey means

[420] *Ibid*, pp. 217-221.

[421] *Ibid*, p. 222.

or what the detachment from one's own cage is meant to be. Reaching the Kingdom of all kingdoms, reaching the Divine Throne, the Light of all lights, that is what the journeying soul anticipates in its mystic voyage of no return. The mystic death is an anticipation of death as the return of no return.

VII- The Recital of *Salmān wa Absal*

The Recital of Salmān and Absal is the last recital of the trilogy. It is the recital that accounts for the final destination in the journey where Salmān typifies the self that seeks (*taṭlub*) the gnostic rank of Absal (*al-maṭlūb*, the one that is sought). Unlike *Kitāb al-Najāt* and *Kitāb al-Shifā'*, *Kitāb al-Ishārāt wal-Tanbīhāt* does appeal to *ahl al-ʿirfān* (those endowed with mystic knowledge) and to the practice of the gnostic *maqāmāt* (mystic stages).[422] The central theme that characterizes the recital is the mystical death of the gnostic *ʿārif* (the one endowed with knowledge) as it is suggested in the mystical death of Absal who also represents "the degree of advancement" in the gnostic mystical rank or station (*maqām*).[423] Absal and Salmān are two Angels, the former celestial and the latter terrestrial. The death of Absal is an invisible disappearance in the visible world (It is thus put by Corbin's interpretation based on his translation of Naṣīr al-dīn Ṭūsī's abridged version of Avicenna's recital of *Salmān wa Absal*). The absence of Absal is mysterious in the sense that he is absent while still being present (*ghā'ib ḥāḍir wa ẓāʿin muqīm*); he is on his way while still being in place.[424] Turning away from the world of metaphor to the real world is being oriented towards facing true being face to face. The self that reaches the final veils contemplates itself contemplating. And the last veil is

---

422 *Ibid*, pp. 237-238.

423 *Ibid*, pp. 263-264.

424 *Ibid*, p. 277. ***"Il est absent tout en étant présent, il est en route tout en restant en place."***

that mystery that is none other than this contemplation. The terrestrial angel Salmān retreats from administering and controlling things, Salmān retreats from seeking the success and the ambition of governing, and of ranks and distinctions, Salmān retires, and Absal dies the mystical death of a return (*ma* ^{C}*ād*) of no return. What remains is contemplative life for the retreating Salmān who has been brought to this contemplative life by the celestial guide Absal whose death turned Salmān into a sage or terrestrial angel.[425] And, in reference to the death of Absal, one could refer to an eloquent insight that one finds in the commentary on the French translation of the *Avicenna Latinus* (*liber De Anima*) where it is said that the death of Socrates has become the symbol of true philosophy.[426] "The philosopher learns to die, to detach oneself from the sensible world, in order to have access to the true authentic reality, the world of ideas. He [i.e the philosopher] transcends corporeal appearances in order to realize an encounter at the level of the soul that is at the level of the 'I' of another person."[427] On this view, one wonders whether the being of human beings does indeed belong to the world or whether the being of humans is from the onset reflected in being-in-the-world unauthentically. Death has a constitutive role in the existential self-movement of Heidegger's account of *Dasein*'s being-towards-death. Death also characterizes Avicenna's account of the soul's being-towards-the-Necessary-Existent. Both accounts reveal the mode of being-in-the-world as also being an existential movement towards death. Avicenna and Heidegger do not merely determine selfhood in terms of metaphysical accounts of subjectivity or substance. With

---

425 *Ibid*, pp. 277-279.

426 Avicenna, *Avicenna Latinus Liber De Anima Seu Sextus De Naturalibus I-II-III and IV-V*, Édition Critique de la Traduction Latine Médiévale par Simone Van Riet, introduction sur la doctrine psychologique d'Avicenne pure G. Verbeke. Ouvrage publié avec le concours de la Fondation Universitaire de Belgique (Leiden: E. J. Brill, 1972).

427 *Ibid*, p. 5*.

Avicenna and Heidegger, the self is accounted for in terms of an existential process or movement that reflects authenticity, self-perfection, anticipation, and resoluteness. Avicenna accounts for the self in terms of process ontology. And his cosmology differs from the Heideggerian cosmological utopia that attempts to fully overcome accounts of substance and subjectivity without showing how they would not be anymore indispensable.

Avicenna dedicates the ninth group (*namaṭ*) of *Kitāb al-Ishārāt wal-Tanbīhāt*[428] to the gnostic mystics, and to the Recital of Salmān and Absal. Avicenna holds that those who know (the mystics; *al-ᶜārifīn*) are already destined to lead their lives like saints. In the context of addressing the stages of knowledge (*al-maqāmāt*) that the gnostic mystics hold, Avicenna holds that the Recital of Salmān and Absal is to be considered an allegory that represents "you" [or me]. Accordingly, Absal is allegorically taken to be the degree of your secret mystic science or knowledge *ᶜirfān*.[429] The ascetic (*al-zāhid*), the pious (*al-ᶜābid*), and the one that knows (*ᶜārif*) are in harmony when truth is presented for unveiling (*al-kashf*). However, the *ᶜārif* (the one that knows) seeks truth for the sake of truth, since truth is taken by the *ᶜārif* to be the source of happiness. The *ᶜārif* is a *murīd* (a seeker) that wills and wants truth.[430] The *ᶜārif* has the mode of being-towards-truth, where truth is the Necessary Existent (*wājib al-wujūd*). It is in this sense that the gnostic notion of will is to be understood; will is being-towards-truth. The light of truth (*nūr al-ḥaq*) rises over the *ᶜārif* then submerges him/her with a soft lightening that lights up and at the same time withdraws. In being-towards-truth, the *ᶜārif* "gathers" truth as it is unveiled in beings. After all, the *ᶜārif* "sees truth in everything."

---

428 Avicenna, *Livre des Directives et Remarques (Kitāb al-Ishārāt wal-Tanbīhāt)*, trans. by A. M. Goichon (Paris: Librairie Philosophique J. Vrin, 1951).

429 *Ibid*, pp. 484, 485.

430 *Ibid*, pp. 487, 489, 491.

Things grant a place for the gathering of truth whose signs are reflected in these things. In being-towards-truth, the *ᶜārif* is in place while journeying, the *ᶜārif* is present while being absent. The *ᶜārif* thus departs from the world of illusion in quest of the world of truth. In a personal mode of being-towards-truth, the *ᶜārif* is "a mirror of truth," and is also the "trace of truth."[431] In the Tenth *namaṭ* (group) of *Kitāb al-Ishārāt wal-Tanbīhāt*, Avicenna presents some accounts of how hidden realities are known. He advances an account of the unveiling of the veiled through dreams (*aḥlām*) or visions that bring about imaginative external images without having a corresponding sensible external cause or agent. Such dreams, visions, and revelations do require a hermeneutic exegetical *ta'wīl*.[432] And, in sufism, the traveller (*al-musāfir*) transcends from one *maqām* (temporal stage) to another, and does so by a shift from a *ḥāl* (state) to another. The aim in this processional movement of the self-unfolding of one's being is to transcend and ascend from one *Weltanschauung* to another. In this sense, the future towards which the traveller tends is already imbedded in the present. The potentiality-for being is already a futural past that characterizes the present.

VIII- Symbolism

Al-ta'wīl, as heremeneutic interpretation, may also be an interpretive exegesis of the self. In this sense, *ta'wīl* hermeneutically posits the individuality of the subject as a contemplative agent that seeks self-realization and perfection (*kamāl*). On this reading, *ta'wīl* is taken to be a self-interpretation that consists of homologically bringing the self back to its primordial originary selfhood. In this sense, *al-ta'wīl* represents a constitutive transmutation process that turns the world of sensible entities into a world of symbols and

---

431 *Ibid*, pp. 493-498.

432 *Ibid*, pp. 506, 510-512, 517.

meanings.[433] Therefore, *al-ta'wīl* is a process that integrates and interiorizes the world in terms of transforming it into a setting that is to be deciphered and decrypted. And *ta'wīl* does so by virtue of transforming the self along with the universe it sets itself to transmute.

The self, in its exegesis of the world of symbols, already practices its own self-exegesis. The self does so by detaching itself from its natural attitude and developing another attitude towards the world. And, in the case of the recitals, that attitude is none other than the attitude of the gnostic mystics. The transmutation of the sensible physical world, and its "restitution" in a world of symbols, necessitates a radical transmutation of perception. And this is undertaken with the hope that the interpretation of the icons and symbols would not fall below the level of the symbol and back to the realm of immediate sensible entities. Everything in the world is thus reinterpreted in terms of new meanings, signs, and icons, that aim at what underlies the apparent and exoteric. And, as Henry Corbin says, the symbol is silent, it does not say something while at the same time it does say something. The symbol, thus enunciates what only itself would say; it is a mediator because it is silent.[434] The symbol is phonetically silent, yet it conveys what is inherent to it as its own meaning and signification with its own allegorical rules that require a particular inclination to undertake its decrypting in *ta'wīl*. And *in ta'wīl*, the intelligible forms are perceived in terms of symbols. And this perception is mediated by the inner senses rather than being a perception mediated by the outer senses. To undertake *al-ta'wīl* along the mystic path is to undertake hermeneutics away from the

---

433 Refer also to chapter 8 "Language and Being" where the notion of *ta'wīl* is discussed in the context of addressing philosophical issues related to contemporary European hermeneutics.

434 Henry Corbin, *Avicenne et le Récit Visionnaire (Tome 2): Étude sur le Cycle des Récits Avicenniens* (Tehran: Société des Monuments Nationaux de l'Iran, 1954), pp. 300-302.

context of great didactic disciplines. After all, the mystic path is undertaken by the *ᶜārif* (the gnostic) and not the rational scientist or philosopher.

Unlike what Henry Corbin holds, A. M. Goichon thinks that the Ḥayy Ibn Yaqẓān Recital is:

> Not a symbol, not an allegory, nor a *ta'wīl*, nor a *ẓāhir* recital, presenting a literal evidence, nor a *bāṭin*, esoteric, a recital in the hidden sense, nor an archetype, according to the diverse hypotheses that we could envisage and that Mr. Corbin examines, nor [is it] a recital of an initiation that could not be given or recounted but by symbols, nor [is it] the proper spiritual novel of the author, nor an encounter with the Archangels, nor the world of the imaginable.[435]

Goichon presents the Recital of Ḥayy Ibn Yaqẓān as being a summary of Avicenna's doctrine of knowledge that is given in the guise of images whose sources are carefully selected and precisely pointed out from the philosophical and scientific texts of Avicenna. Goichon would rather consider the recital in its literal meaning as *qiṣa* (i.e. as a talk, a case, a speech, a narrative, a tale, a story, or even a biography). In this, Goichon would avoid the issues of *ta'wīl* and orientation by not interpreting the recitals in terms of accounts of symbolism or hermeneutic dimensions. Goichon attempts to trace influences from Aristotle, Galen, the Stoics, Plato, and both Semite and Persian legends, the Qur'ān, al-Fārābī, and Islamic Neoplatonic emanation schemes. Her interpretation also covers images

[435] I have translated the following account that Goichon has written in French in: Avicenna, *Le Récit Visionnaire de Hayy Ibn Yaqzan*, trans. by A. M. Goichon (Paris: Desclée de Brouwer, 1959), pp. 14-15. "*À notre avis, il [Le Récit de Hayy Ibn Yaqzan] n'est pas un symbole, ni une allégorie, ni un ta'wil, ni un récit zahir, présentant une évidence littérale, ni un batin, ésotérique, récit au sens caché, ni un archétype, selon les diverses hypothèses que l'on pourrait envisager et qu'examine M. Corbin, ni le récit d'une initiation qui ne peut être donnée et racontée qu'en symboles, ni le propre roman spirituel de l'auteur, ni la rencontre des Archanges, ni le monde de l'imaginable.*"

from the recitals of Arab geographers, accounts of celestial bodies, faculties of the soul, as well as giving a consideration to the role of the *pneuma*. In this reading, Goichon attempts to demonstrate how the Recital of Ḥayy Ibn Yaqẓān does (indeed) summarize Avicenna's philosophical and scientific accounts in *Kitāb al-Shifā'*, *Kitāb al-Najāt*, the *Dānish Nāma*, and *Kitāb al-Ishārāt wal-Tanbīhāt*, while being at the same time tied to the above stated sources. From the onset, Goichon would take Avicenna's references to the narrator in the first person "I" to be a reference to the soul in its provenance from the Active Intellect (*al-ᶜaql al-faᶜāl*).[436]

While "whirling" with its companions,[437] the soul encounters a splendid majestic sage to whom the soul expresses its desire to be oriented towards the Intellect. The sage response is that of wishing the soul to have peace (*salām*) and long life, which is rather interpreted by Goichon as being an initiation of the soul and an expression of its immortality.[438] *Vivens* (*vivant*), the Living, is thus the name of *Ḥayy* the sage, the son of the vigilant and awakened and insomniac *Vigilantis* (*Yaqẓan*); Ḥayy Ibn Yaqẓān whose home is the dwelling of the sanctified, *bayt al-maqdis* (*al-quds*, Jerusalem). This sage points out to the soul that it has bad companions. And those are taken by Goichon to be bad sensible and carnal faculties that the rational self ought to direct and control.[439] In the context of interpreting the image of the "source of running water," Goichon takes it to be the expression of the movement of thought that prepares the soul to receive the intelligibles, while the immobility of the source reflects the immobility that characterizes contemplation.[440] On Goi-

---

436 *Ibid*, p. 22.

437 Like the whirling dervishes performing their *ṣūfī* dance.

438 Avicenna, *Le Récit Visionnaire de Hayy Ibn Yaqzan*, trans. by A. M. Goichon (Paris: Desclée de Brouwer, 1959), p. 34.

439 *Ibid*, pp. 56-59.

440 *Ibid*, p. 75.

chon's view, Avicenna would thus take thinking to be in motion while contemplation to be in the state of rest (*rākida*). This entails that movement characterizes research while rest is an aspect of acquisition or possession. This interpretation, of the running (*jāriya*) water and the source, in terms of being expressions of thought and contemplation, goes in accordance with the interpretation that Goichon offers of physiognomy in terms of an account of logic and syllogism. If the traveller is able to cross the desert, then according to Goichon, this is the gift of logic. On Goichon's view, logic (*al-manṭiq*) leads the self across deserts, i.e. what is called *majāhil*. And *majāhil* has the same Arabic root of *majhūl* (unknown) and *jahl* (ignorance). Therefore, *majāhil* may etymologically be taken to be the [deserted] places of ignorance. Therefore on Goichon's analysis, the deserts crossed by the traveller (*le voyageur, al-musāfir*) are sites of ignorance that the traveller crosses by virtue of logic which leads the self from the unknown (*majhūl*) to the known (*maʿrūf*). Syllogistic logic moves from premises to conclusions, transferring the self from the known to the unknown to be known.[441] On Goichon's reading of the recital, one finds an account that rejects H. Corbin's interpretation of the recital as being a mystic journey. On Goichon's view the recital expresses the development of the self due to the thrust of natural knowledge as opposed to an "*initium*" of a mystic knowledge as H. Corbin would hold. On this account, Goichon would hold that the barrier (*barzakh*), between the known and the unknown, cannot be transgressed but with the aid of the logic of concepts and reasoning by virtue of which the unknown is made known due to the known.[442] Goichon holds that "in this world, the soul remains immersed in matter, likened to the three inseparable companions."[443] This state of affairs shows that the soul, in its link to its inseparable

[441] *Ibid*, pp. 78-79.

[442] *Ibid*, pp. 89-90.

[443] *Ibid*, p. 175.

faculties, is thus disoriented since it is linked to the material sensible entities, and it is thus tempted to focus on the sensible realm by the temptation of clandestine inner senses. The inclination of the soul to benefit from material goods, its tendency to be violent and angry, and the fantasies that the soul draws to itself by virtue of imagination, all reflect that the soul is held captive within this world of sensible entities. The faculties of the soul, that keep the soul captive within the sensible realm, are faculties of a world in which forms are in matter. This region, where form is in matter, is the realm in which one desires, owns, and benefits from material goods. And it is also the region of violence, war, and anger in which the truth is mixed with falsity and facts mingled with fictions. The region that lies above the material region, is the region of forms and celestial souls. The occident is as such the realm of matter, the "desert of salt," the "sea of mud," the place of "privation and non-being."[444] Accordingly, matter is depicted as a *topos* that does not produce anything in and by itself. Accordingly, it needs forms in order to be inhabited and cultivated.

To contemplate the face of the Almighty is to contemplate that aspect due to which the Lord is known. Humans contemplate the face (*wajh*) of the Lord by contemplating the creation of the Lord. In quoting al-Fārābī's *Fuṣūṣ al-Ḥikma*, Goichon writes how in addressing us, al-Fārābī depicts a scene in which we are requested to contemplate the world of creation and to deduce from it the proof that it has been created. Al-Fārābī then adds that in order to put such contemplation into effect, one has to rise above the world of creation in ascension towards the Exalted who exists due to Itself.· That one has to know the true and to distinguish it from the false. And the ultimate ascension towards certitude is manifested in

---

[444] *Ibid*, pp. 95, 97, 101. All of these designations are meant to be expressions of what the realm of matter is, these are reflected in different parts of Goichon's analysis and in the French translations that she incorporates in her book from the Arabic version of Ḥayy Ibn Yaqẓān.

the contemplation of the face.[445] Al-Fārābī then says, "consider then the true. Then you will never love those who disappear, but on the contrary you will turn your face towards the only face [*wajh*] that remains." The allusion to those who disappear is taken by Goichon to be an allusion to Abraham's (The Prophet Ibrāhīm's) sighting of a star at night when he says: "This is my master," yet when the star disappeared, he said: "I do not like those who disappear."[446]

In another context, Aḥmad Amīn presents an interpretation of the Ḥayy Ibn Yaqẓān recital in a way that diverts from the Henry Corbin interpretation. Aḥmad Amīn holds that the three bad companions are none other than the human faculties, and that these faculties bring forth both anger and lust and therefore ought to yield to the authority of Reason which is represented by the figure of Ḥayy Ibn Yaqẓān (Amin, 1952, pp. 17-19). On Amīn's reading, the Recital of Ḥayy Ibn Yaqẓān is meant to be an expression of Avicenna's glorification of Reason and the demonstration of the extent of its powers and supremacy over the other human faculties. Consequently, Amīn holds that Avicenna expresses the need for Reason to take charge and to assume its authority and responsibility as a guide.[447] While in the *Encyclopaedia of Islam*, T.J. De Boer holds that the metaphysical doctrine of the Soul finds its profound expression in the mystic and poetic meditations of Avicenna which "crown" his system rather than "support" it.[448] In another context, and according to Dimitri Gutas, the interpretation that H. Corbin offers of Avicenna's recitals is due to an "obsession" with what is

---

445 *Ibid*, p. 220.

446 *Ibid*, p. 220.

447 Avicenna, *Hayy Ibn Yaqzān*, ed. by Aḥmad Amīn (Cairo: Dar al-Ma^{c}ārif, 1952), p. 21

448 *The Encyclopaedia of Islam*, ed. M. Th. Houtsma, A. J. Wensinck, T. W. Arnold, W. Heffening, E. Levi-Provencal (Leiden: E. J. Brill, 1927), p. 420.

perceived to be "an allegedly ineffable Iranian spirituality."[449] According to Gutas' reading, the use of symbolic and allegorical methods of communication was intended to be a way by virtue of which Avicenna aimed at transmitting the truths of demonstrative and expository language in a simplified manner that appeals to the understanding of the common people. On Gutas' interpretation, Avicenna's use of symbolic and allegorical language was directed to the common people who would not be able to understand the truths as they are expressed to the elect my means of demonstrative and expository modes of expression.[450] On this view, Gutas opposes those interpretations that attempt to show that Avicenna had an esoteric, oriental, mystic, or secretive doctrines that differ from his exoteric philosophical writings. The Aristotelian sort of knowledge, as expressed in Avicenna's writings, is for the elect (*al-khāṣa*), while the (esoteric) allegorical and symbolic recitals are for the common people (*al-ᶜāmma*). Gutas argues that the Aristotelian knowledge (meaning the demonstrative philosophical knowledge) must be withheld from the masses because they are "unable" to understand its "syllogistic structure." And Gutas also holds that the masses will be "corrupted" by the Aristotelian knowledge, since they will eventually adopt ideas that are "harmful" to society. Therefore, Gutas holds that something is to be withheld from them in the form of symbols.[451] He then claims that his arguments are advanced in support of Goichon's accounts. And he holds that every symbol, that one finds in Avicenna's Visionary Recitals, has its corresponding concept in the philosophical writings. Gutas even asserts that Goichon demonstrated that there is a "strict one-to-one correspondence between philosophical concepts and symbols," while still asserting that symbolic and allegorical presentations are "inferior" to demonstrative

---

449 Dimitri Gutas, *Avicenna and the Aristotelian Tradition: Introduction to reading Avicenna's Philosophical Works* (Leiden: E. J. Brill, 1988), p. 299 n.2.

450 *Ibid*, pp. 301-302.

451 *Ibid*, pp. 302, 303.

presentations. On this view, the truth that lies behind the symbol is higher than what is apparent. Yet that truth is also none other than the demonstrative philosophical truth that remains hidden from the masses. Gutas' thesis is supported by his reference to Goichon's meticulous and rigorous search for "phrase for phrase" and "word for word" correspondence between concepts and symbols.[452] Gutas' interpretation in support of Goichon's reading of the Avicennian Visionary Recitals might be more elucidated in a consideration of Ibn Rushd's *Faṣl al-Maqāl*.[453]

Ibn Rushd (Averroes) sets out to show that the Scriptural Law (*shar*^{C}) of Islam does not prohibit the study of philosophy (*falsafa* or *ḥikma*). According to Ibn Rushd, if the religious Law encourages and urges the reflection on beings, then the activity of philosophy is made obligatory by the Law. Ibn Rushd then adds that the study of philosophy must be conducted by demonstrative reasoning while being aware of the respects in which demonstrative reasoning differs from the dialectical, rhetorical, or fallacious reasoning. One has to study logic prior to philosophy that requires a mastery of the art of demonstrative syllogism.[454] The way to truth has been provided to believers each according to his/her own capacities. Some come to assent through demonstration, some through dialectics, while others come as firmly to assent through rhetoric.[455] Ibn Rushd

---

452 *Ibid*, pp. 304-306.

453 The title: *Faṣl al-Maqāl* is the abbreviation of the treatise of Ibn Rushd (Averroes) which is called: *Kitāb Fasl al-Maqāl wa Taqrir ma bayn ash-Sharī*^{C}*a wal-Hikma min al-Ittiṣāl*, which literally may be rendered into English as: "The Book of the decision (or distinction) of the discourse, and a determination of what there is of connection between religion and philosophy." This book is more known in English as the book: *On the Harmony of Religion and Philosophy*, Trans. by George F. Hourani (London: E. J. W. Gibb Memorial Trust and Luzac & Co., 1976).

454 *Ibid*, pp. 44, 45, 47.

455 *Ibid*, p. 49.

does not in any way reject the allegorical interpretation of *ta'wīl*. He believes that all Muslims accept *ta'wīl* (as allegorical interpretation). However this also means that *ta'wīl* should in no way violate Islamic consensus (*ijmāʿ*).[456] Having said that, Ibn Rushd cautions by saying that the "unlearned masses" must take religious texts in their apparent (*ẓāhir*) meaning. And he asserts that it is "unbelief" that the learned set down "allegorical interpretations" (*ta'wīl*) in popular writings. He therefore sees the threat that such *ta'wīl* poses on the understanding of the masses and the possibility of corrupting that understanding that is not appropriately prepared to receive allegorical interpretations. Ibn Rushd says that "allegorical interpretations ought to be set down only in demonstrative books," and that such books must be "banned from the unlearned, but not from the learned." Since on his view, if these allegorical interpretations were included in non-demonstrative books, they would corrupt rather than increase learning. On this reading, philosophical (and allegorical) interpretations of scripture should not be taught to the masses, since the Law provides other methods of instructing them. With the case of symbolization (*tamthīl*), each class of learning, according to its capacities, ought to attempt to decrypt the symbols in demonstrative, dialectical, or rhetorical methods. In case a class is unable to do so, those believers ought to rest content with the apparent meaning (*al-ẓāhir*). Therefore, the duty of the elect learned is to undertake demonstrative methods in conducting allegorical interpretations, while the unlearned ought to rest content with the apparent meaning. And, allegorical interpretations ought not to be included in dialectical or rhetorical books or else they would "injure" the masses, especially if such interpretations might be open to falsity.[457] Given this interpretation one realizes that demonstrative methods, which are higher than dialectical or rhetorical methods, ought to be used in relation to alle-

---

456 *Ibid*, pp. 51-52.

457 *Ibid*, pp. 65, 66.

gorical interpretations which on Ibn Rushd's view are given a high and prominent status that is accepted (on his view) by all Muslims. *Ta'wīl* as allegorical interpretation is then praised, and allegories or symbols are not classified as being inferior to demonstrative and expository methods as Gutas might have wanted to assert. The allegorical and symbolic method is turned into a textual and semiotic field that ought to be hermeneutically interpreted using demonstrative methods, and in a less effective way, using dialectical and rhetorical methods. So when one is endowed with demonstrative reasoning and expository analysis, one is then well prepared to tackle allegorical interpretations. Based on this view, demonstrative and expository methods are not higher than allegorical or symbolic expressions. This is the case given that the former is used to decipher the latter. Therefore demonstrative and allegorical methods are not subject to a comparative interpretation as Gutas attempts to advance. They are rather complementary of one another, especially in the works of the philosophers and the learned.

CHAPTER 8
LANGUAGE AND BEING

I- Being and Beings

The history of classical ontology, and mainly that of the Middle Ages, attests to long-standing traditions that attempt to link being to God. The question of being was a question of ontology that stood open to the question of the divine. This did not readily entail the assimilation of ontology to theology rather it implied that there existed an interplay between the concerns of the two disciplines.[458] To say that something is an entity is to say that it is "this something." The Ancients once wondered about why "something is" and "is not something else." The Scholars of the Middle Ages asked why "something is" and "is not nothing at all." With them, the wonder shifted from merely thinking identity and difference to theologically asking the ontological question: "why is there being rather than non-being?" God as being itself (*esse ipsum*) was the flight from non-being, since being was taken to be that which allows the entity to be. Given that God grants being, God is not entity at all. God is no-thing in terms of being the One who grants being. The question of being is connected to the question of non-being, and the study of being qua being entails a study of non-being. The being/non-being speculative state of affairs is also attested in Avicenna's ontology where the question of being (*al-wūjūd*) is also connected to the question of non-being (*al-ʿadam*). This being/non-being speculation was undertaken while having in view an attempt to avoid misconstruing God as

458 Jeff Owen Prudhomme is one of those contemporary philosophers who are interested in the connection between God and being. His attempts to interpret the relation of Heidegger's ontology to theology are part of his interest in the connection between God and being which leads to what he calls a "correlative" relation between theology and ontology. This thesis is advanced in Prudhomme's book: Jeff Owen Prudhomme, *God and Being, Heidegger's Relation to Theology* (New Jersey: Humanities Press International, Inc., 1997).

entity. This corrective request is later to be found in Heidegger's attempted thinking of the unthought ontological difference between being and beings, which is also attested in Avicenna's consideration of being. Even if God is taken to be the ultimate and most supreme and perfect being (*ens perfectissimum*), on such account God is still taken to be an entity though unlike any other entity.[459] God as an Idea of Reason, is for Critical Idealism the Idea of a necessary connection between subjectivity and objectivity, between the self and the world. And this is also the case with Cartesianism where God is the warrant for there being a world, and there being others.[460] With these traditions, God figures as the supreme entity, though still an entity. Faced with such instances, one might still run the risks of compromising the ultimacy of the divine. The difference of the *causa sui* (self-caused) from all that is, is not a difference between two species of being that are within an overarching one genus. At least this is what Heidegger might have wanted to avoid and what Avicenna attempted to show. This is marked as a corrective request to think the unthought ontological difference between being and beings in terms of fundamental ontology. However, if according to fundamental ontology, what is unthought in classical ontology is the ontological difference between being and beings, then one might have an intricate and solid case-study in investigations that attempt to find in Avicenna's ontology what could re-valuate the position of fundamental ontology. Since, Avicenna attempted to avoid the talk of a common denominator genus and species while he addressed the question of being from the standpoint of studying being as being. Avicenna's ontology might have avoided what Kockelmans pinpoints viz. Heidegger's project, that being ought not to be taken to be a common denominator to all that is, and thus not to take being (*das*

---

459 *Ibid*, pp. 22-24.

460 *Ibid*, p. 24.

Sein) as being the beingness (*das Seiendheit*) of beings.[461] Holderlin once asserted "the radical insufficiency of the measure established" by human beings, he asked: "Is there a measure on Earth?," and his answer was: "There is none."[462] The divine (θεῖον, *theion*) breaks into the non-divine by establishing the measure that is insufficiently drawn in the world of humans. Θεός (*theos*, God) breaks into the world in religious experiences, in scripture, and in the text where revelation takes place as the site of the divine annunciation of the measure in language. It is in the rule and the measure that the *sensorium* of divine providence is annunciated. It is in language, in the implications of scripture, of the text, and the hermeneutics of the text and its grammar, that this annunciation takes place.[463] The radical other is even beyond symbolic realities, beyond the Trinitarian incarnate deity. In language, the being of being is disclosed, and the place where the divine breaks into the non-divine is in language; in the divine as well as human language. Thus the issue is to think the being of beings in language. The study of being is thus to be opened up to a faithful existence, and revelation to be opened up to reflection. What would remain an issue is how not to compromise the ultimacy of the One God of monotheism in philosophical reflection, and how to relate in language to the ineffable? Such questions orient reflection toward language as a path of thinking that leads to onto-theology. The place of the disclosure of being, and the place where the divine breaks into the non-divine, find a site in speech and writing, a locus in a human language that "stands open to the divine and to being."

---

461 *Ibid*, p. 108. Also see: Josef Kockelmans, *"On the Truth of Being," Reflections on Heidegger's Later Philosophy* (Bloomington: Indiana University Press, 1984), p. 74.

462 See: Reiner Schurmann, "Symbolic Praxis." *Graduate Faculty Philosophy Journal*, vol.19 n.2-vol.20 n.1, 1997, p. 58.

463 This brings about almost the radicality that one might receive from Jacques Derrida's saying: "*il n'y a pas d'hors-texte*" (There is no outside-text).

II- Remarks on the "Language of Being"

In speculating about the topology of being, and the place where the divine breaks into the non-divine, the question that emerges is whether the site where the divine breaks into the non-divine is to be found in a human language that "stands open to the divine and to being." In this regard, the language that is the *topos* of disclosure is itself the language of being and that of the divine. And, this language requires linguistic devices by virtue of which the question of the divine and of being ought to be addressed and received. Avoiding misconstruing being as entity entails an avoidance of what might be taken to be a linguistic contribution to such misconstruing. Replacing the copula "is" or "are" with a colon (:) was one way of avoiding the self-predication of being which was taken to be some sort of "misconstruing" being as entity that stems from saying "being is...."[464] This self-predication might have been avoided by saying "it gives being" (*es gibt Sein*). In Theodore Kisiel's discussion of Heidegger's use of the colon (:), the attempt to avoid the verbal "to be" is connected to etymological variations in terms of "verbally iterative sentences" that are used in such a way that the "is" is avoided. In this sense, one would say that "language speaks" instead of saying "language is language," or one would say that "it gives being" (*es gibt Sein*) instead of saying "being is."[465] In this regard, the use of a colon (:) highlights the ontological difference between being and beings. This takes place in such a way that what precedes the colon opens itself to what proceeds from it. This linguistic practice is claimed to be a way by virtue of which a self-annunciation and disclosure of be-

---

[464] Jeff Owen Prudhomme, *God and Being, Heidegger's Relation to Theology* (New Jersey: Humanities Press International, Inc., 1997), p. 152.

[465] *Ibid*, pp. 150-152. Also see: Theodore Kisiel, *The Language of the Event: The Event of Language,' Heidegger and the Path of Thinking* (Pittsburg: Duquesne University Press, 1970), p. 98.

ing occurs in language.[466] The value behind such an exercise is gained in relation to the hermeneutics of language that would be conducted in a way that attends to the question of being through a language of being. This exercise is supposedly also applicable *vis à vis* the question of the divine; since the ultimacy of God ought not be compromised by misconstruing God as entity. This same misconstruing risk, which was marked with regard to the self-predication of being in connection with the verbal "to be," also holds with respect to the question of the divine. Thus avoiding misconstruing God and being as entity entails avoiding the verbal "to be." In all of this, what might be at stake is thinking the question concerning the verbal "to be" in general and its present tense in particular. This is the case given that the present tense is connected to the "metaphysics of presence." In order to avoid misconstruing being and God as entity, it was mentioned earlier how certain linguistic practices and exercises were devised. The use of tautologies, with what they hold as risks in terms of emptiness in meaning, constitutes an additional linguistic practice that avoids misconstruing God and being as entity. This practice may be illustrated in such utterances as: "being is being" or God is God."[467] When we say that "being is being" or "God is God," there is an exchange of place between the subject and the predicate. And when we say that a being is that which has being, or a being is existent, the existing (*exister*) or being (*être*) is conferred in terms of being some sort of predicate that does not add the same knowledge as external real predicates offer. Saying that: "this car is red," adds to our knowledge, identification, and definition of what that thing is, as opposed to what it is not. *Being* itself when predicated about something does indeed add to our knowledge of the thing that has being. That something is given being, that it exists,

---

466 Jeff Owen Prudhomme, *God and Being, Heidegger's Relation to Theology* (New Jersey: Humanities Press International, Inc., 1997), p. 152.

467 *Ibid*, p. 156.

adds to our knowledge of that subject despite what a Kantian might have argued in this regard, that being is not a real predicate.[468]

Thinking about the verbal "to be" in its present tense, and the "is" in particular, might itself be enriched with new linguistic as well as ontological possibilities when it is addressed from the standpoint of examining a Semitic language like Arabic. In Arabic (like all Semitic languages), the present tense of the verbal "to be" silently withdraws to underlie the said or the written. Arabic, in its syntax, grammar, style, and rhetoric grants the non-occurrence of the present tense of the verbal "to be" in neither speech nor writing. In this regard, Arabic might not have the same problem that French, English, and German have with regard to the use of the "is-form" and the thinking of this "is." The verbal, *Sein*, *être*, or "to be," appears as a copula, a bond between a subject and a predicate complement. In Arabic the verbal "to be" is not present in the present tense, rather it is absent, it is silent. Yet, this does not entail that the Arabic language (as a Semitic language) completely lacks copulative functions or existential predications. The verbal "to be" is not completely absent as some scholars, like Soheil Afnan or Angus Graham, might assert. This is the case given that other scholars dispute the claim that Arabic lacks copulative and existential functions (scholars of the caliber of Fadlou Shehadi and L. E. Goodman rightfully dispute the claims of Afnan and Graham).[469] However, it might be the case that in

---

468 This issue has been addressed in chapter 1, *The Metaphysical Tradition.*

469 Regarding the elaboration of the views of these scholars, one could refer to the following references: i- Soheil Afnan, *Avicenna: His Life and Works* (London: Allen & Unwin, 1958), p. 125; ii- Soheil Afnan, *Philosophical Terminology in Arabic and Persian* (Leiden: E. J. Brill, 1964), pp. 29-30; iii- L. E. Goodman, *Avicenna* (London: Routledge, 1992), pp. 101-109; iv- Angus Graham, "'Being' in Linguistics and Philosophy." *Foundations of Language 1* (Dordrecht: D. Reidel Publishing Company, 1965), pp. 223-231; v- Fadlou Shehadi, "Arabic and the Concept of Being," in Essays in *Islamic Philosophy and Science*, ed. G. Hourani (Albany: State University of New York Press, 1975), pp. 147-157.

Arabic, no apparent copula or bond occurs between subject and predicate. However, in the Arabic language, the verbal "to be" is partially un-hidden. Being, or the verbal "to be" is not present as it is the case with the use of "is." Nevertheless, in its very absence, being still underlies the said and the written. The partial un-hiddenness of being is unveiled when the question of being is asked. To say "the house is blue" you say "*al-bayt azraq,*" where *bayt* is house and *azraq* is blue. In "the house is blue," "is" acts as a copula that brings with it the verbal "to be." In "*al-bayt azraq*" there is no indication of being, yet when the question is addressed with respect to whether *al-bayt* "has being," the answer is that "*al-bayt mawjūd.*" This answer "*al-bayt mawjūd*" means that the house has being (*wūjūd*),[470] that the house "is an existent." The existence or being of the house is already presupposed without being written or uttered. There is no indicator of the verb "to be" yet in its absence, it silently underlies the said and the written, and it is thus not super-added neither in speech nor in writing as is the case with the occurrences of the verbal "to be" in French, English, or German. It is by the fact that we utter or write something about "*al-bayt,*" that this "*bayt*" is presupposed to be what is "*mawjūd*" (that it is given *wūjūd* [being]). For something *to be* is for that thing to be *mawjūd*, only when the question concerns the being of that which is *mawjūd* does the speculation about being start. *Mawjūd* itself is not like any other predicate. It is the predicate that appears only when the question of being is asked.

---

470 *Wūjūd* is rendered in English (French) "being" (*être*) or as "existing" (*exister*). The *mawjūd* is thus that which has being, that which exists. In this, the couple *être/étant* and *exister/existant* are exchanged as being valid French renderings of *wūjūd/mawjūd.* Thus *wūjūd* as being *(être)* and *mawjūd* as [the] being *(l'étant)* are also rendered as existing/existent (*exister/existant*). This linguistic exchange is reminiscent of Emmanuel Levinas' speculations, in *Le Temps et L'autre*, about being with regard to Heidegger's *Being in Time.* There, *être/étant* were suggested by Levinas to be exchanged with *exister/existant*, thus being/being(s) is replaced by existing/existent to stand for *Sein/Seiendes* which apparently is the dual French rendering of the Arabic *wūjūd* and *mawjūd.*

It is only from the standpoint of the question of being that the present tense utterance or writing about being appears. Before that, it subsists in silence, it is there yet withdrawing, until one has to address its question, the question that seeks being as being. When we say "A is *mawjūd*," we mean that "A is existent." Yet, the question regarding what A is, is not the same as the question whether A is existent or not. The essence of A or its quiddity (*māhīya*), as they figure in the question of A's whatness (*mā huwa*), are not the same questions as the question concerning A's existing (*wūjūd*). If "A is *mawjūd*" is equivalent to saying that it is the essence of A that "A is *mawjūd*," then "A is *mawjūd*" amounts to tautologically saying "A is A." Regarding the fact that A is an existent entity, A's existing is rather super-added to A's essence, while it is not the case with the divine where being or existing (*wūjūd*) is not added to essence. Given God's simplicity, Avicenna held that *dhāt* and existing (*wūjūd*) are one in the Necessary Existent due to Itself. This view was later held by Mūssa Ibn Maymūn (Moshe Bin Maymun, who was known through his Latin name as Maimonides), and it also found its echoes in Spinoza's philosophy.[471]

Given what has been stated above, with regard to *wūjūd* in the critical present tense, it might be also needed to briefly address what the past Arabic tense holds with respect to being. Instead of saying *"al-bayt azraq"* (the house is blue) one would say in the Arabic past tense: *"kāna al-bayt azraq"* (the house was blue). In this regard, we notice that in the past tense, "*kāna*" was added to "*al-bayt azraq*." Both *kana* and *kānat* (for the masculine and the feminine uses of "was") refer to the being/existing of something in the past tense. *Kāna* and *kānat* are derivatives of the root *kawn* (generation), the command *kun!* (be!), or *al-kawn* (universe or world). *Kāna* and *kānat* both imply generation in the past tense,

---

[471] Regarding this last point, see: Harry Austryn Wolfson, *The Philosophy of Spinoza* (New York: Meridian Books, The World Publishing Company, 1934), pp. 123-125.

Kāna and *kānat* both imply generation in the past tense, they entail being-in-the-past. *Kāna* (for the masculine use of "was") and *kānat* (for the feminine use of "was"). Both *wūjūd* and *kawn* are used as renderings of being, yet *kawn* accentuates generation while *wūjūd* accentuates existing. Some contemporary scholars use *kaynūna* (also from the root *kawn*) to designate being while others still use *wūjūd*. In the case of Avicenna, the use of *wūjūd* is the one that accounts for being, while *kawn* and its derivatives are more so assigned to generation. However this does not imply that *kawn* does not entail being. Faced with the linguistic intricacies of accounting for being, one could refer to what Rūmī utters in a mystic mood that shuns away philosophical drives to excessive speech: "keep silence, keep silence, for by virtue of the command 'Be!' (*kun*)[472] that silence of bewilderment has augmented beyond all speech." Jalāl al-dīn Rūmī (1207-1273).[473]

III- Hermeneutics and *Ta'wīl*

Our relationship to language has been of primary concern for the various schools of contemporary philosophy. Language is revealed as being the place that unveils our human finitude. It is the site in which the limits of subjectivity are unconcealed. Contemporary German Hermeneutics, as mainly exemplified by the works of Hans-Georg Gadamer, approaches language from the standpoint of dialogical conversation. On this account, language allows meaning to emerge as an event that reflects mutual understanding. This view is contended by a major contemporary French school of thought that is represented by Jacques Derrida's philosophic inclinations. Based on

---

472 Said in allusion to the following Qur'ānic verse: "The Sublime Originator of the heavens and the earth, who *when He decreeth a thing He simply telleth it Be, and it is.*" Qur'ān 2:117; 3:47; 16:40; 19:35; 36:82; 40:68

473 Jalāl al-dīn Rūmī, *Mystical Poems of Rūmī I, first selection, Poems 1-200,* trans. by A. J. Arberry (Chicago: The University of Chicago Press, 1968), poem 79.

a Derridean Deconstructivist account, one might say that the meanings that emerge in language exceed our intentions and are pervaded by absence and *otherness*. Instead of being based on a dialogical model of mutual understanding and commonality of meaning, language is rather revealed in a Deconstructivist thrust as being the site of the equivocation of meaning. Having said that, the two major contemporary schools of European thought do still adopt a Heideggerian account of the priority of language. Yet, these European schools of thought divert in their course of development. Hermeneutics recognizes a unity in meaning while Deconstruction reveals meaning as being multiple and disseminated. However, both schools hold that meaning and language are not at our disposal, and that the limits of our control over language are also the limits of our human finitude. The later works of Heidegger reflect deep interests in poetic language which some contemporary critics take to be a failed or weak attempt by virtue of which Heidegger tried to overcome the language of metaphysics and classical ontology (*ousiology* in particular). If this critique is advanced in relation to the later works of Heidegger, a similar claim may be raised *vis à vis* contemporary Hermeneutics and its stress on the unity of meaning. In a Derridean move, the Gadamerian line in Hermeneutics may itself get stamped by metaphysics and classical ontological dimensions due to the stress on the unity of meaning, and more so, due to the attempts to find a truth in texts. This critique reflects a double fold concern, it addresses the univocity of meaning that approximates the Hegelian totality, and at the same time, it deals with hermeneutic interpretations that seek to disclose hidden truths in texts. Both Hermeneutics and Deconstruction reflect the contemporary European philosophical interest in language, meaning, and interpretation. Hermeneutics privileges the word over the sign, it privileges speech over writing, while Deconstruction gives priority to the written. Hermeneutics engages in philosophical dialogues, in questions and answers. Like what was the case with Plato and Heidegger, Gadamer takes questioning to be (so to speak) the "piety of thought," where questioning is itself the path of thought that leads to the matter to be thought. Questioning is raised *vis à vis* the interpretation of interpretation, the interpretation of meaning, of intentionality, and of language itself. What constitutes the matter to be thought has to be brought into language. Such Hermeneutic attempt is rendered questionable by Deconstructivist strains in interpretation. On Derrida's view, philosophical thinking is taken to be the "other" that could not be fully assimilated into language nor could it be fully decrypted in words. With Hermeneutics, or with Deconstruction, the philosophical concerns echo Heidegger's concern with the overcoming of metaphysics. Hermeneutics attempts to draw the metaphysical meaning away from its determinacy by engaging it in speech and philosophical conversations. Deconstruction attempts to disengage itself from the metaphysical meaning by dismantling this meaning and ceding it to dissemination, rupture, and dispersal. Both schools attempt to overcome the metaphysical tradition from within, by moving on the limits between philosophy and non-philosophy. The attempt to undo the metaphysical tradition from within is still inscribed within the limits of the philosophy that one is trying to dismantle, dislocate, and displace. The attempts to undo what has been oppressive in thought is undertaken in the name of opening up a path for what has been philosophically obliterated or occluded by that thought. The unsaid, the unspoken, and the unthought, obsess this double fold European philosophical concern with *otherness*. This state of affairs reflects attempts to overcome the confines of the philosophical language that captivated Western thinking. Dialogues, conversations, negotiations, and speech, all cannot be assumed unless one is able to speak more than one language. Yet, speaking more than one language does presuppose translation, understanding, and a trustful intentionality. Unlike the Enlightenment conception of understanding, Gadamer expounds Heidegger's conception of "fore-understanding" by taking prejudice to be a positive feature of understanding that presumably reflects goodwill and an openness to *otherness*. Yet, language as that which allows us to bridge gaps may turn into that which places barriers between us.

This risk is always in sight within the Hermeneutic project where meaning is constantly open to interpretations without being taken to be determinate yet at the same time without giving its unity away. A Deconstruction counter-position attempts to dislodge this Hermeneutic confidence and hope by enacting a tension between the spoken and the written in a line that stresses absence and radical *otherness*. This incommensurability line in thought unsettles the hope of being satisfied with the determinacy in translation, synonymy, meaning, and interpretation. Hermeneutics faces this semantic, linguistic, and interpretive seriousness, with a play that shifts its grounds and never settles on determinate rigid positions. Hermeneutic strategies introduce conversational and dialogical interlocutors that debate a position and question it. However, Hermeneutics still reflects a deep longing for hidden truths and profound meanings that may eventually be excavated in texts. This interpretive seeking of "eternal" truths may be still in tune with classical philosophical inclinations (Plato, Hegel, German Romantics, even Heidegger). The same may also be the case with the Heideggerian question of the meaning, place, and truth of being which itself turned towards poetic language by way of overcoming metaphysics. This play on the limits between philosophy and non-philosophy might not appeal to some hard headed philosophers of the Anglo-American Analytic school in thought. Since such a play gives an important philosophical weight to literature which itself is the scene of a ceaseless interpretational play that Hermeneutics enacts on literary texts. If Heidegger was concerned with the question of the meaning, place, and truth of being, this did not entail that being has been fully unfolded by him. Rather, on Heidegger's own view, being is also a self-withdrawing that is as primordial as the sending and self-manifesting. Being is thus as mysterious as language that is never fully understood or fully uncovered in the intentionality of its incessantly modified meanings. The presence of *otherness* in language, as the trace of absence, confronts us with our self-narrowness and prejudices that pervade our "fore-understanding." Interpretations allow for some sort of dialogue to be enacted without assuming that a commonality of intentions and of meanings has been completely accomplished. Interpretations may mediate between different languages and horizons without necessarily turning into arbitrariness. Comprehension is essential to the Hermeneutic undertaking without assuming that what is being interpreted is exhaustible, since so much is left unsaid in the written, and what is said is always less than what has been intended. With writing, the said is not given the opportunity to be defended, and therefore, writing anticipates the readings and with them it anticipates the possibilities of mis-reading. Intentions and meanings are open to disputes, especially with narratives and texts. The literary text gives itself its own grounds from which the interpretation seeks its supports. The literary or philosophic text is unlike the legal contractual document and is also unlike speech. With the literary text, or recital narrative, words ground themselves and do not fall back but onto themselves. These words face the risks of being alienated from their ground by interpretations that mis-read them. These words must be left to speak for themselves without alienation, wherein the unity of meaning is countered by displacements that give hints of suggestive other meanings. The text has to be addressed with the voice of interlocutors, the hermeneutic task is to enact a conversation with the text rather than merely address it with a determinate over analytic reading. Let-the words-be what they, in their self-manifestation, want or wanted to be. But how would that task be achieved without facing our own limits and narrow perspectives? And how would we be able to admit the voices of others in the hope of reaching some form of agreement rather than exacting consensus or assent? Interpretation is then advanced as a hope that trans-subjective communication is still really possible. Interpretation and Hermeneutics may still reflect a hope in universality and Humanism without readily being stamped with Logocentrism or the assimilation of the other by the same. Interpretive readings are thus opened up to undecidability and hesitance while being at the same time in a play that shifts grounds and positions without leading to discontinuity, pure immediacy, and rupture.

Having briefly addressed some dimensions that underlie contemporary continental European philosophical concerns with interpretation, meaning, and language, what would the above entail in relation to the philosophical reception of Avicenna's Phenomenology? But to assume that Avicenna's philosophy is phenomenological, or pervaded by phenomenological dimensions, is itself a hermeneutic interpretive move that assumes a particular standpoint from which Avicenna's philosophy is taken to be phenomenological in character. Interpretation is assumed from the onset by this "prejudice" or inclination in reading Avicenna's work in conjunction with Contemporary European Continental schools of thought. To call Avicenna's philosophy a phenomenology is already a move towards a particular way of reading Avicenna. And this way reflects certain interpretational perspectives or horizons that address Avicenna's work from within the confines of contemporary European philosophic concerns. Much has been written about Avicenna and his role within the course of development of Islamic Philosophy, and much more has been written among western scholars about Avicenna's work in relation to Greek thought and to Neoplatonism. Yet, some contemporary scholars are starting to reflect on Avicenna's work from the standpoint of contemporary developments in Western thought. This sort of interest has been mostly inscribed within the confines of comparative philosophy, while others are attempting to go beyond these scholarly confines towards different philosophical concerns that reflect an interest in philosophy proper and in the future of philosophy. This interest in the destiny of philosophy is an interest in what is left unsaid in the history of philosophy. And when one is saying philosophy what is mainly meant by the term is metaphysics (as First philosophy) and the long-standing metaphysical Western tradition. The concern with issues of Logocentrism, oppressiveness of metaphysics, and *otherness*, all reflect a deep interest in seeking to awaken and recover what has been hidden, occluded, or obliterated. The contemporary preoccupations with discourse, textuality, writing, intentionality, understanding, meaning, and language, all constitute grounds that allow us to apply Hermeneutic and other interpretational strategies to our reading of Avicenna. However, this application is double fold in the sense that it serves Hermeneutics and Continental thought as much as it serves the purposes of scholars that are interested in Avicenna and in Islamic or Near Eastern philosophy. In this spirit, one may enact a conversation with the Avicennian textual heritage, be it the primary texts or the interpretations of these texts. Our contemporary attempts to save the textual heritage from the consequences of our own philosophical reflections must not turn the interpretation of the text into that which is ambiguous. Held between an incommensurability line of thought and hopeful Hermeneutic accounts, the textual heritage is itself brought into the fore within the contemporary debates about textuality, discourse, meaning, and language. To save the textual heritage from the unfolding philosophical interpretations of interpretation, one has to be engaged with these debates while engaging the text with strategies of interpretations that play between skeptically forbidding interpretation or allowing it to be open to further readings. If equivocity, complexity, and multiplicity of meaning all point towards incommensurability, one may still have to account for these radical claims with a readiness to shift in positions or in readings without losing continuity and ceding to ruptures. To save the textual heritage, and to keep it as a heritage, is to save the significance of the text in the course of development of philosophy. To save the Avicennian text as heritage is to safeguard the significance of the text for our contemporary debates. This involves a readiness to engage this text in the interpretational debates or disputes that address issues of interpretation, intentionality, meaning, and language. An incommensurability line in thought takes understanding to be none other than an assimilation of the *otherness* of the *other*. Yet, in the face of such claim, one may still contend that extreme caution by engaging in interpretations that keep a vigilant eye on such distortions while still hoping that an engagement in interpretation would furnish an understanding that does not occlude the other. Contemporary philosophical concerns do reflect a deep interest in undoing what keeps the Western Mind entrapped within a metaphysical horizon that destines that Western Mind to be an *Understanding Mind* that is always engaged with concepts and shunning away the sentimentality of metaphors. This contemporary philosophic scene provides significant themes that allow us to uncover dimensions and issues that were left unthought in relation to the other occluded traditions that were obliterated by an over-dominant metaphysical language. And the contemporary interest in interpretation is itself the site from which new readings and approaches to texts is unfolding. It is in this sense that an exegesis of Avicenna's work may be undertaken given that Hermeneutics itself has had long standing working features within the Islamic tradition, where classical Hermeneutics took the forms of *al-ta'wīl* and *al-tafsīr*. This itself provides another ground for engaging ourselves in conversations about the philosophical conditions, dimensions, and features of *al-ta'wīl* and *al-tafsīr* while being aware of the developments of contemporary thought. And even being engaged in philosophical negotiations with that thought whenever it places significant challenges or possibilities for our understanding of *al-ta'wīl* and *al-tafsīr* and of the texts that we seek to interpret.

The interpretation of Avicenna's Visionary Recitals is one arena of disputes that reflect a variety of hermeneutic methods. The above addressed Corbin, Goichon, Amīn, and Gutas arguments offer an adequate setting in which differences in interpretation are well manifested.[474] However, those commentators and interpreters have brought with them a variety of philosophical influences (be it Orientalist inclinations or scholarly approaches to Avicenna's work) that are mediated through interests in Ancient and Neoplatonic thought. By addressing philosophical issues of interpretation, meaning, and language, *al-ta'wīl* and Hermeneutics offer an interesting setting for the assessment of the work of Avicenna. This may rigorously be conducted in terms of exploring contemporary developments in

[474] Refer to the previous chapter 7 "The Authenticity of Being."

European Hermeneutics while also giving attention to inner and profound developments in *ʿulūm al-ta'wīl* (Sciences of hermeneutic interpretation) and their links to *ʿulūm tafsīr al-Qur'ān al-Karīm* (Sciences of the exegesis of the Holy *Qur'ān*).

IV- *Al-Ta'wīl*

Being thrown into the world is being thrown into a world of "metaphor" (*al-majāz*). This is what may be deduced from Ṭūsī's commentary on Avicenna's Recital of Ḥayy Ibn Yaqẓān, and this is what Henry Corbin reads in his interpretation of Avicenna's recital and Ṭūsī's commentary. If the world of "thrownness" is the world of "metaphors," then which world would be that of reality (*ḥaqīqa*)? Corbin's interpretation and Ṭūsī's commentary both tell us that to come into this world [of thrownness, of the fall] is to pass from the world of reality (*ḥaqīqa*) to the world of metaphor (*majāz*). Such a passage is then a fall from the world of the real to the world of metaphor that presents itself as the world of the real. And it does so in terms of construing the real as being that which is of the order of the collective common sense and common consciousness; i.e. as the reality of the "they-self" (*das Man*). To be called to one's own reality is to be awakened to the estrangement of being in the un-homelike world of everydayness. To be called to recollect one's own self is to be awakened to one's own reality as being a stranger in a world of metaphor that the neuter "they" (*das Man*) take to be the true world of reality.[475] To pass from *majāz* (metaphor) to *ḥaqīqa* (reality or truth) is to pass from alienation to a state of self-awareness that requires in its own right an alienation of the self from what alienates it. It requires an estrangement from those who keep the self entrapped in a world of estrangement. The path of *ḥaqīqa*, as the path of truth and reality, is the path to the Orient; it is the path that alienates

---

[475] Henry Corbin, *Avicenne et le Récit Visionnaire (Tome II): Étude sur le Cycle des Récits Avicenniens* (Tehran: Société des Monuments Nationaux de l'Iran, 1954), p. 31.

the self from what keeps it alien. The way to the Orient is an *exodus* from the world of the exiling "they-self." It is by way of a hermeneutic interpretive spiritual exegesis that the self is led back to a recollection of its primordial originary self. This hermeneutic and interpretive spiritual self-exegesis is a form of *ta'wīl*. And *al-ta'wīl* is originally understood as being a way by virtue of which Divine Revelation (*al-tanzīl*) is brought back to its origin. In this context, *ta'wīl* is taken to be a hermeneutic textual exegesis that brings back in ascension what *al-tanzīl* by way of revelation brings down to this world. *Ta'wīl* is then an ascending proceeding that brings back what has fallen in *tanzīl* as a divine revelation that broke into the non-divine world. *Ta'wīl* brings back what is the case to its origin. It is a hermeneutic move that uncovers the hidden esoteric reality or truth that underlies the exoteric apparent meaning. *Ta'wīl* is a hermeneutic move that unveils the true and hidden esoteric (*bāṭin*) meaning that underlies the apparent exoteric (*ẓāhir*) meaning.[476] *Ta'wīl* complements *tanzīl* in the same way that the *bāṭin* complements the *ẓāhir* and *ḥaqīqa* complements *majāz*. If *tanzīl* is the fall of revelation into the world of *majāz* (metaphor) and the world of the *ẓāhir* (exoteric/apparent) meaning, then *ta'wīl* is an ascending bringing back of the *bāṭin* (esoteric) hidden meaning into the world of *ḥaqīqa* from where it originated. *Ta'wīl* is not solely a hermeneutic move that is concerned with textual and scriptural exegesis; rather *ta'wīl* is also a spiritual interpretive exegesis of the self. In this sense, *ta'wīl* is a personal story, a personal recital, a personal experience, since the self cannot bring back language to its truth unless it brings itself back to its truth. *Al-ta'wīl* of the *bāṭin* that underlies the *ẓāhir*, or of the *ḥaqīqa* that underlies the *majāz*, all cannot be realized unless they are accompanied by *al-ta'wīl* of the self (*dhāt*), since in this context the text becomes "a trace" of the *ta'wīl* of the self. The text as the "trace" of the exegesis of the self

---

[476] *Ibid*, pp. 33-36.

is then itself symbolizing the exegesis of the soul in its *exodus* from the world of *majāz* to the world of *ḥaqīqa*. The *tanzīl* is then followed by a *miʿrāj* (ascension) of the soul along the path of its hermeneutic exegesis of the revealed text. The interpretation of the world, its *ta'wīl* is also itself a *ta'wīl* of an awakened self that puts the exegesis of its own modes of being-in-the-world into effect.[477] Like it is the case with Heidegger's account in *Being and Time*, that philosophy (as phenomenological ontology) is a hermeneutic of *Dasein*;[478] Avicenna's consideration of *al-nafs* is also by way of *ta'wīl* (hermeneutic) as an analysis of the existentiality of the existence of *al-nafs* (*anima*/*Dasein*). The Avicennian analytic of *al-nafs* was undertaken in terms of epistemological views ("Suspended Person Argument," and the account of *al-wahm*), and it has been developed in terms of mystical accounts (Orientation, journeying, self-realization, death, and the quest of Union).

In *ta'wīl*, the self, the world, and beings, all are encountered as being in relation to their originary source. Therefore, everything is considered as being in a relation with the Orient. In this sense, Avicenna's Visionary Recitals turn his philosophy into a philosophical inclination towards the Orient. Avicenna's philosophy then tends to be an oriental philosophy that seeks the Orient as the place of origin, of being, and return. A place that orients by way of calling thought to think by way of being oriented towards that orient that orients, whereby, an oriented thinking pays heed and thanks to that towards which it is oriented. Thinking is therefore a thanking of what grants being while at the same time being that which is the origin, source, and place of return.

---

477 *Ibid*, pp. 36-40.

478 Martin Heidegger, *Being and Time*, trans. by Joan Stambaugh (Albany: State University of New York Press, 1996), pp. 33-34.

V- Doctrinal Accounts of *al-Ta'wīl*

The focus on the hermeneutic *ta'wīl* reflects an inclination to adopt a line of interpretation that places Avicenna within a long standing tradition of Shīᶜīsm in general, with a bent on Ismāᶜīlī doctrines in particular. Even if scholars of Ismāᶜīlī studies do not assert that Avicenna was influenced by Ismāᶜīlī doctrines, yet one cannot avoid mentioning that Avicenna's father and brother were influenced by the Ismāᶜīlī *daᶜwa* (call). And that the Epistles of the Bretheren of Purity (*Rasā'il Ikhwān al-Ṣafā'*) were made available to the young Avicenna. However, if Henry Corbin insists on bringing a focus on the notion of *ta'wīl* in his interpretation of the Avicennian Visionary Recitals, this does not readily entail that he wants to track Shīᶜī or Ismāᶜīlī doctrinal traces in Avicenna's works. Yet, this does not rule out the fact that by focusing on *ta'wīl* one is also focusing on a notion, or a process, that was of prime importance in Shīᶜī circles, and particularly in Ismāᶜīlī practices and teachings. In reflecting some aspects of *ta'wīl*, Farhad Daftary writes the following:

> The notion of *ta'wīl* affirms the Shīᶜī belief in the existence of the separate exoteric and esoteric dimensions in all religious scriptures and teachings, necessitating the spiritual comprehension of, and initiation into, their hidden and true meaning. Herein lies the essence of the imam's role, and the justification for the importance assigned to esotericism and gnosis (*ᶜirfān*) by some Shīᶜī groups. Shīᶜī esotericism found its fullest development in Ismāᶜīlism, by far the most representative Shīᶜī sect designated with the term *Bāṭinīyya*; referring to those who give primacy to the inner, esoteric, or *bāṭinī* meaning behind the literal wording of all religious texts and formulations.[479]

---

479 Farhad Daftary, *The Ismāᶜīlīs their History and Doctrines* (Cambridge: Cambridge University Press, 1990), p. 87.

In another context, Daftary also mentions that *ta'wīl* was a method of allegorical interpretation of the *Qur'ān* that was associated with the Ismāᶜīlīs who refined it to its fullest extent.[480] The notion of *ta'wīl* implies that one could educe an inner meaning (*bāṭin*) from a literal wording of a text or a ritual, especially those texts which draw religious prescriptions. According to Daftary, the Ismāᶜīlīs extensively used *ta'wīl* (hermeneutic exegesis) in their allegorical, symbolic, and esoteric interpretation of the *Qur'ān* and the *Sharīᶜa* (religious law).[481] *Ta'wīl* suggests that every appearance implies that there is a hidden inner true reality that lies behind it. The apparent exoteric *ẓāhir* undergoes changes while the *bāṭin,* as the hidden and esoteric, holds an immutable and eternal reality or truth (*ḥaqīqa*). It is by virtue of *ta'wīl,* as a hermeneutic, allegorical, symbolic, and esoteric interpretation, that the *bāṭin* truth is educed from behind the *ẓāhir*. *Ta'wīl* is a leading back to the first and primordial origin *al-awal* that educes the *bāṭin* from the *ẓāhir,* while *tafsīr* is an explicative commentary and philological exegesis of the external apparent meaning of the religious texts and of the revelation of the sacred scripture by *tanzīl* (revelation).[482] Those who exalted the *bāṭin* and their contained *ḥaqā'iq* (truths) were regarded as being Shīᶜī extremists (*ghulāt*) who adopted esotericism and gnosticism and herein became known as *Bāṭinīyya*. The passage from *ẓāhir* to *bāṭin* is also a passage from *tanzīl* (as a descending revelation) to *ta'wīl* (as a hermeneutic interpretational ascending return). This is also a passage from appearance to truth and reality (*ḥaqīqa*), which on a certain interpretation could also be seen as be-

---

480 *Ibid*, pp. 73, 89. Also refer to the "Ismāᶜīlīyya" section in: *Encyclopaedia of Islam*, ed. by M. Th. Houtsma, A. J. Wensinck, T. W. Arnold, W. Heffening, E. Levi-Provencal (Leiden: E. J. Brill, 1927), p. 203.

481 Farhad Daftary, *The Ismāᶜīlīs their History and Doctrines* (Cambridge: Cambridge University Press, 1990), p. 566.

482 *Ibid*, pp. 138, 566.

ing a passage from the *phenomenon* to the *noumenon*.[483] If the early Ismāᶜīlīs stressed on the *bāṭin* over the *ẓāhir*, the Fāṭimī Ismāᶜīlīs insisted on giving a balanced and equal importance to the *bāṭin* and the *ẓāhir* while attempting to show that the one could not "meaningfully exist" without the other. They therefore focused on *ᶜilm al-ẓāhir* (the science of appearance) in relation to jurisprudence (*fiqh*) and exoteric aspects of the *Sharīᶜa* (Religious Law) while *ᶜilm al-bāṭin* (the science of the esoteric) contemplated treatises on *ta'wīl* and truths (*ḥaqā'iq*).[484] However, the focus on the prime importance of the *bāṭin* was further carried to extreme limits by some Nizārī Ismāᶜīlīs who believed in the existence of a *bāṭin* side to the *bāṭin*.[485] On the view of those *Bāṭinīyya* exponents, the world of the *bāṭin* behind the *bāṭin*, as the third level of being, is the world of ultimate reality and truth. On this view, one finds the first level of being in the level of the exoteric *ẓāhir*, while the second level is that of the *bāṭin* of the *ẓāhir* as the truth-of-appearance, and the third level is that of the *bāṭin* of the *bāṭin* as the truth of the truth-of-appearance. *Ta'wīl* might also be interpreted in terms of the Sufi path (*ṭarīqa*) or journey that is a passage from the world of the physical *ẓāhir* to the realms of *ḥaqīqa* (truth).[486] It is held that some *ṣūfīs* might have relied on the *bāṭinī* Ismāᶜīlī *ta'wīl* in their gnostic accounts of the spiritual *ṭarīqa* (mystic path). Yet, whether with the *Bāṭinīyya* or those who followed their path of the *ṣūfīs*, the accusations of having undermined the *ẓāhir* (as the *Sharīᶜa* or religious law) in favor of the *bāṭin*, have led some heresiographers to consider the *bāṭinī* doc-

---

483 *Ibid*, p. 138. This is the case with Daftary's own interpretation of *ta'wīl*.

484 *Ibid*, pp. 232-233.

485 *Ibid*, pp. 393-395, 412.

486 *Ibid*, pp. 453, 455, 469, 477.

trines as being heresies.[487] *Al-ta'wīl* itself describes a field of tension that lies between the risks of anthropomorphism from one side and *Bāṭinīyya* extremism from the other side. In stressing on the literal interpretation of the exoteric *ẓāhir*, the interpreter might fall into anthropomorphist accounts that compromise transcendence (*tanzīh*). The stress on the esoteric *bāṭin* might lead to extreme positions similar to those advocated by the *Bāṭinīyya* adherents. In this sense, *al-ta'wīl* is a field of hermeneutic interpretations that lies between the two poles of literal anthropomorphism and the overcoming of anthropomorphism in an emphasis on the transcendence of the divine. Extreme focus on the *ẓāhir* from one side or the *bāṭin* from the other side, leads in both instances to heresies with regard to the *ta'wīl* of the divine revelation (*al-tanzīl*). This hermeneutic tension reflects the focus on the textuality of what is to be interpreted. On this account, speech is subordinate to writing, and the text as language is revealed as being not at our disposal. The openness in interpretation and the equivocal character of meaning are to be carefully measured in *ta'wīl* in order to avoid extreme interpretive positions. *Ta'wīl* stresses on the priority of writing in language where the spoken is in service of the written. *Ta'wīl* entails that the said is always less than the saying. This in itself grounds the need for the hermeneutics of *ta'wīl* that reveals the equivocal char-

---

[487] *Ibid*, pp. 453, 454, 455, 705. On the affinity between some Sufis and Ismāᶜīlī *Bāṭinīyya* exponents, the *Ḥurūfīyya* is a gnostic group that focused on the *bāṭinī* (hidden) meaning of letters and adopts *ta'wīl* as a main interpretation method rather than *tafsīr*. By the 15th century, the *Ḥurūfīyya* started spreading in Anatolia and as a doctrine, it has been eagerly adopted by Sufi orders like the *Bektāshī* Dervishes of Turkey. The *Jafr* (loosely: Arabic Cabalistic-Gnosticism) is another form of the *Shīᶜī Ḥurūfīyya* tendency which represents a systematization of the symbolic and mysterious value of the alphabetic letters. Also see: Henry Corbin, *Avicenne et le Récit Visionnaire (Tome II): Étude sur le Cycle des Récits Avicenniens* (Tehran: Société des Monuments Nationaux de l'Iran, 1954), p. 321; M. Louis Massignon, *La Philosophie Orientale d'Avicenna et son Alphabet Philosophique* (Cairo: Institut Français d'Archéologie Orientale, 1952), vol. IV, p. 16.

acter of intentionality, meaning, and textuality. And it does so while at the same time revealing interpretation as being a serious responsibility that requires careful measure and deliberation that avoids what leads to heretic accounts viz. Scripture or misreadings viz. any textual heritage. *Ta'wīl* is measure taking, canonization, and regulation. In this sense, *ta'wīl* reveals a long standing Semitic and Near-Eastern tradition that focuses on the convergence between textuality (Scripture, *al-naṣ*), legislation (Law, *al-Sharīᶜa*), and ethos. *Ta'wīl* is itself pragmatic, legislative, doctrinal, and reflects a stress on truth in terms of its ethical and legal value. *Ta'wīl* reveals the priority of writing over speech. The said is in the service of the saying, the spoken and recited in the service of what is read in the written. And writing thus presents the field of what is to be read, recited, heard, and listened to. *Ta'wīl* as such calls for a textuality that affects the self in its own attempts to unveil the written by way of undertaking an ethical self-exegesis.

VI- *Ta'wīl* and the Unveiling of Truth

If the search for a profound truth, as that which is deeply hidden and awaiting disclosure is metaphysical, then what would be the case with the unveiling of truth that one practices in *ta'wīl*? A correctness conception of truth does not qualify to be the truth of unveiling by *ta'wīl*. The unveiling of truth by way of the hermeneutic movement of *ta'wīl* is called *kashf al-maḥjūb* which may be rendered as an unconcealing or unveiling of that which is veiled or concealed. *Kashf al-maḥjūb* by *ta'wīl* already points in the direction of the self-withdrawal of that which is unveiled. *Kashf al-maḥjūb* therefore differs from the revealing by way of disclosure. The unveiling of truth is a mode of revealing that is irreducible and cannot be assimilated. It always points to the otherness and alterity of a self-withdrawing truth. *Kashf* is itself a journeying on the path of truth, it is a *taḥqīq* as a realization of truth (*ḥaqīqa*). *Kashf al-maḥjūb*, as an unveiling of truth by *ta'wīl*, is a happening of truth.

It is therefore part of a process that is temporal and that describes a journeying towards truth as exemplified in the mystic voyage or ascension. Truth as *al-ḥaqīqa* is not discovered and afterwards assimilated. Truth as *ḥaqīqa* is not reducible to what the *Ge-stell* (Enframing) turns into a *Bestand* or "standing reserve." The unveiled truth is not assimilated in its otherness and externality. It is self-withdrawing and it is therefore not brought into an assimilative totality. In *ta'wīl*, the unveiling of truth is also an unveiling of selfhood. The *ta'wīl* as *taḥqīq* of truth, is also a path of self-exegesis. *Kashf al-maḥjūb* is an unveiling of truth by way of self-exegesis. The unveiling of truth is a happening of truth as a granting. Yet, this happening is not abstract, it is an existential experience that happens to the self. As it was the case with the encounter of being as *anā* (I), where the self stands in being. The happening of truth is an unveiling of truth at the same site where the self stands. Rather than being assimilated, truth is an otherness that is unveiled in its mystery and alterity while withdrawing from assimilation or reduction. Truth by *kashf* is revealed as that which is self-withdrawing. Truth is as such a self-granting that is irreducible and inexhaustible. Unveiling, *taḥqīq* (as "truthing"), and *ta'wīl*, all express the happening of a veiled truth. Truth thus remains *maḥjūba*, i.e. truth remains veiled in its very unveiling. In its happening as truth, truth is self-withdrawing. Its unveiling of itself is mysteriously veiling. In this sense, truth is not reduced to what is other than itself as correctness. The unveiled truth as *ḥaqīqa* is mysterious, since it is pervaded by alterity.

VII- Mystery and Poetizing

If the coming into the light points as well to darkness, then for every un-concealing there is a prevailing of concealing. Every "appropriative event" like *Ereignis* is coupled with an "expropriative event" like *Enteignis*. Light is pervaded by what is of the realm of darkness, it is not merely luminous, it is also mysterious. What is most mysterious is that which unveils mystery and brings it into the light. On Heidegger's view, *Dasein*'s mode of being is that of "disclosure," as being the "clearing" as *Lichtung*. In *Being and Time*, he holds that the existential-ontological structure of the human being is "illuminated" as being-in-the-world, yet, it is itself the "clearing." However, even with disclosure, the coming into the light implies darkness. In the sense that the interplay of light and darkness figures in the occurrence of being and ultimately of truth, which in its turn is determined in relation to un-truth. If *Dasein*'s mode of being is that of disclosure, then truth and untruth both belong to that constitution of *Dasein*. The authenticity of untruth lies in mystery and not in a correctness conception of truth that takes untruth to be error. Untruth as mystery is distinct from untruth as error. The mysterious (as the untrue) is the self-concealment of clearing (*Lichtung*); since what is unconcealed will still be pervaded by mystery as concealing. Concealing and un-concealing, veiling and unveiling, light and darkness, mystery and truth, all are in an interplay of strife (like that strife between World and Earth, as illustrated in Heidegger's *The Origin of the Work of Art*). On this reading, mystery as un-truth must not be understated based on successes in disclosure. After all, disclosure itself is pervaded by mystery and its truth is therefore open to [becoming] un-truth. The veiling mystery might preserve that which is harmful in the unveiling of truth. Mystery is a veil that keeps behind it what is harmful in truth.

In Chapter 22 of "*Reading Heidegger*," under the title: "*Overcoming Metaphysics in the Holderlin Lectures*," Dominique Janicaud quotes a passage from Heidegger's works where he says: "Holderlin is one of our most promising thinkers, because he is our greatest poet. The poetical turning toward his poetry is only possible as *meditative* debate with the *revelation* of being which has been achieved in his poetry."[488] One evidently sees the eminent status that

---

[488] Dominique Janicaud, "Overcoming Metaphysics in the Holderlin Lectures," in *Reading Heidegger "Commemorations"*, ed. by John Sallis (Bloomington Indianapolis: Indiana University Press, 1993), p. 386.

Heidegger accords to Holderlin in relation to the revelation of being. And this reflects an appreciation and taste for a particular sort of poetic language that becomes the site of the unfolding of being. Heidegger's appreciation of Holderlin's poetry is mediated through a transmutation of the poetic words into words of being. The poetic language calls for an interpretation that turns its poetic words into becoming words of being. Avicenna's Visionary Recitals are also addressed in terms of how they put into effect a transmutation of the sensible world into a world of symbols which becomes open to profound hermeneutic readings. Such Visionary Recitals are themselves subject to attempts that try to transmute their allegorical, mystic, and poetic icons, into icons of being. After all, the Avicennian Visionary Recitals are either turned into profound allegorical texts that veil an ineffable reality and truth, or these Visionary Recitals are seen as being a summary of a complex ontological cosmology. In both readings, the Visionary Recitals might constitute some sort of a transmutation of the cosmos into a language of being. If the Recitals were open to a hermeneutic reading that attempts to unveil hidden and ineffable truths, then already these Recitals are speaking the language of truth and being that bears inexhaustible interpretations. If the Visionary Recitals just crown Avicenna's system and, in an allegorical and poetic way, i.e. give expression to what his ontology and cosmology is about, then these Recitals are also transmutable into a language of being. In all cases, thinking and poetizing are intertwined in the sense that poetizing bears fruit for thinking, and thinking occurs in poetizing. At least this was the case in Heidegger's overpraising of Holderlin's poetic verses that awaken us to the "granting." And (supposedly) these verses bring about the "turn" through which the "saving power" of deliverance emerges in the face of the perils that the terminal configuration of metaphysics (as essence of technology) brings about. In wondering about the lack of measure on Earth (as Holderlin wonders), poetry (Holderlin's) is itself revealed by Heidegger as being that which takes "measures." Since on Heidegger's account, poetizing is "measure-taking."[489] Poetizing brings the "measures of divinity" to language, and by being a *work*, poetizing is also a generator of significant meanings. Yet, this generation of significant meanings may not count philosophically. After all, Heidegger's turn towards poetizing is seen by some critics (including Derrida and Gadamer) as being a weak attempt to overcome metaphysics. This poetizing turn in Heidegger's thought might not count as being a philosophical discursive attempt to overcome metaphysics. On this reading, the very place of being is itself still metaphysical even if it is not being expressed through a conceptual and metaphysical language. In this sense, the nostalgia of poetizing or the evasion of the metaphysical parlance through poetry, do not overcome metaphysics, yet they display attempts to dismantle, disrupt, and displace metaphysical inclinations in thinking from within. Therefore, like Gadamer, and Derrida, Heidegger is attempting to undo the metaphysical tradition from within. Like his European Continental philosophic successors, Heidegger attempted to explore the limits that separate philosophy from non-philosophy. Yet poetizing might not be philosophizing based on what the metaphysical tradition describes as being philosophy or non-philosophy. In this sense, the boundary of philosophy is itself delimited by philosophy itself. And this is done in terms of occluding, marginalizing, and subordinating what lies on the limits as being external to philosophy. By addressing what is poetic, Heidegger already is addressing that which is non-philosophic. At least this is the case based on what the metaphysical tradition qualifies as being philosophic. By addressing poetry philosophically, Heidegger gives expression to what is taken to be the limits of philosophy. To account for poetizing philosophically, is to address the limits that separate philosophy from non-philosophy. And this is done in such a way as to trace these limits by virtue of carefully delimiting what is

---

[489] Marx Werner, *Heidegger and the Tradition* (Evanston: Northwestern University Press, 1971), pp. 236-237.

other. Philosophically accounting for poetizing is already a stretching of the limits of philosophy from within. Heidegger did not overcome the metaphysical tradition as much as he was delimiting its extreme limits. Poetry and mystic features in his thinking might have been the risky dimensions that tinted his philosophical attempts to undo philosophy from within, while still realizing that such undoing is not yet a realized overcoming. It is in this sense that one may attempt to seriously read Heidegger's consideration of poetizing while at the same time taking into consideration that the value of the attempt lies in its being undertaken rather than in its being a successful step. In Heidegger's stress on Holderlin's verse: "poetically dwells Man," one notices how poetizing grounds human existence on "dwelling." At least this is the immediate "thought" that the verse brings about. However, the verse already presupposes and supports its own truth by grounding itself within its own saying. After all, grounding human existence in dwelling is not the full message that the poetic verse brings about. Human existence is grounded in poetic dwelling, not any dwelling, but poetic dwelling which itself requires the acceptance of the very poetic verse that calls for poetic dwelling. This poetizing thought calls for a poetizing dwelling as "thinking about dwelling" that gathers what Heidegger calls the "fourfold." Dwelling is therefore a dwelling on Earth, under the Heavens, with mortals, and among things. Poetic dwelling gathers the fourfold as a bringing together of the neighborhoods (*Gegenden*) of the world. To dwell poetically is to dwell in the gathering of the fourfold.

Heidegger has received much criticism for his turn towards poetic language. This has been seen by some as being a failed or weak attempt to overcome the language of metaphysics. Derrida and Gadamer, each in his own way criticized this poetic turn in Heidegger's later works. Yet, the turn towards poetry is also a turn towards a practice of listening that avoids debate and argumentation. In this sense, poetizing is also a recital, a call for hearing that requires listening and thinking. Poetry speaks to those who are willing or able to listen. And listening is itself poetizing, and what is heard is heard as such by an inner ear that calls for a certain knowledge that lies within us, and that calls us to strife for the sake of our own selves. Derrida himself offers an eloquent account of hearing that he expresses in relation to Heidegger's work. Derrida recites, "the ear is not for Heidegger an organ of the auditory sense *with* which we hear. Hearing (*das Horen*), in the authentic sense, is a gathering, a self-recollection (*Sichsammeln*) toward the word [*parole*] that is addressed to us."[490]

VIII- World, Things, and the Fourfold

Being-in-the-world constitutes *Dasein*'s basic structure. The Earth, the Heavens, the Divine, and the Mortals are revealed as being the four neighborhoods (*Gegenden*) of the world. The world in its "worlding" grants significant meanings and gathers its four neighborhoods while *Dasein* stands within this worlding/gathering; since *Dasein*'s basic structure is that of being-in-the-world, i.e. of belonging to a world that worlds and gathers the fourfold. In this state of affairs, being is revealed as being the place of this "worlding" of the world, i.e. as the place of the gathering of the fourfold. Being-in-the-world is also being amidst things, since the world is a with-world. However, things are revealed as being ready at hand (*Zuhandene*) or present at hand (*Vorhandene*), which does not unveil the state of affairs of things that "thing." If the world "worlds," then some wordly things "thing," i.e. they are "thinging" things. And a thing that "things," is a thing that grants a place for the gathering of the four neighborhoods of the world; so a thing is more complex than being merely ready at hand or present at hand. A "thinging" thing, in its own style and way, gathers the fourfold. The "thinging" of new things brings new possibilities of gathering the fourfold by granting a spot for the fourfold. The thing of technological import and character is thus opposed to the thing that turns into the place where truth

---

490 Jacques Derrida, "Heidegger's Ear *Philopolemology* [*Geshlech IV*]," in *Reading Heidegger "Commemorations,"* ed. by John Sallis (Bloomington Indianapolis: Indiana University Press, 1993), pp. 187-188.

happens; this is what Heidegger advocates in *Building Dwelling Thinking*. The Van Gogh's painting of the "peasant's shoes" is taken as an example of analyzing the "equipmentality" of equipment, the "thingly" character of a thing, and the "workly" character of a work. And, this is what Heidegger attempted to do in *The Origin of the Work of Art* and is then debated by Meyer Schapiro and problematized by Derrida's intervention in "*Restitutions*" in his book: *La Vérité en Peinture*. What Heidegger does with the painting of the "peasant's shoes," or the "temple-work," is to set examples that show how a work of art acts as the place where the setting-into-work of truth takes place. In this regard, poetry is taken to be a founding art that sets truth into work. And it does so by setting up a world and setting itself (as work) back in order that Earth comes forth and shelters. However, this setting-into-work of truth, and this setting up of a world and setting forth of Earth is what the work of Art grants as a spot for the world/Earth strife. Things (some things) do grant or allow for a spot where the fourfold is gathered, and in *Building Dwelling Thinking*, Heidegger offers an elaborate account of a "bridge" as that which grants a spot for the gathering of the fourfold. The "bridge" gathers to itself, in its own way, Earth and sky, divinities and mortals. In *The Origin of the Work of Art*, Heidegger holds that to think about what is "thingly" in the thing brings us closer to thinking about the being of beings. So, newness in creativity and innovation is something to be praised, given that new things bring about new possibilities of gathering the fourfold, granting that these things are "thinging" things. However, things that "thing" appeal to creative human beings; they are things that appeal to thinkers, poets, and artists. Things that "thing" are encountered in a "worlding" world that *Dasein* poetically dwells. Dwelling poetically is itself dwelling in the gathering and therefore dwelling in a "worlding" world, amidst "thinging" things, where the gathering of the fourfold is granted numerous spots, and where poetizing turns into a thinking about being. In such a "worlding" world, poetizing tends to be thinking, to be a commemorating, and to be a thanking that pays heed to granting. And in this sense it approximates the *ṣūfī* ethics that cosmologically transmute the world into a world of icons, signs, and symbols, and pay heed to the gift of being while being oriented in a quest of the origin and of Union (*itiḥād*, *itiṣāl*, *ḥulūl*). To be worldly, in both cases would mean to poetically dwell on Earth, under the Heavens, with the Divine and the Mortals. After all this is an instance of what Heidegger is trying to sketch as being a new essence of a human being that overcomes substance and subject. And this is done with the hope of marking the "turn" that in Heidegger's eyes does indeed usher an overcoming of metaphysics (as an overcoming of the ontology of substance and subject). This Heideggerian cosmological utopia might be brought to a closer relation to reality through an account that understands the essence of human beings in terms of worldliness without claiming that substance and subject are (finally and fully) dispensable. And I take it that Avicenna was closer to this position than Heidegger. After all, Heidegger attempts to establish the beginnings of a new cosmology grounded by an ontology that is claimed to be prior to all the sciences. This cosmology will be based on the revelation of the existential mode of *Dasein*'s being-in-the-world, where *Dasein* is taken to be the locus of existential meaning or meaninglessness, whereby meaning (mainly that of being) is the sphere to which *Dasein* belongs.

CHAPTER 9
CONCLUDING REMARKS

The ontological account of being that has been addressed in chapter four (The Ontology of Being) reflected an encounter with being that is conceptual and analytic in character. Being *qua* being has been analyzed in terms of its modalities of necessity, contingency, and impossibility. This analysis oscillated between the *ousiological* metaphysics and an analytic approach that overcomes some aspects of this *ousiological* Aristotelian tradition. Based on Avicenna's accounts, one holds that the Necessary Existent due to Itself (*wājib al-wūjūd bi-dhātihi*) is not a substance (*ousia, jawhar*), nor is it a genus (*jins*), nor species. On this view, a classical *ousiological* account of being cannot help in accounting for the Necessary Existent due to Itself which is without definition or description (*lā ḥad lahu wa lā rasm*). In this sense, being (as Necessary Existent due to Itself) is irreducible, in the sense that it is not reducible to something other than itself. Being is being and nothing other than being. It is not *ousia*, and in this sense it surpasses the realms of Aristotelian *ousiological* accounts of being. Furthermore, the Necessary Existent due to Itself cannot be accounted for in terms of a language that relies on genus or species. This in itself shows that the ontological difference between being and beings cannot be resolved in terms of an account of species under an overarching genus. On this view, Avicenna's account of being does not fall under the rubric of what Heidegger takes to be a history of a metaphysical oblivion of being. What may be deduced from this account is that Avicenna's consideration of the modalities of being has paved the way for a double fold account of being, one account is still metaphysical in the classical sense of metaphysics, while the other account overcomes this classical metaphysical tradition. The Necessary Existent due to Itself reflects an account of being *qua* being that is not *ousia* based, thus being is not reduced to what is other than itself. And at the same time, this account reveals that the ontological difference between being (as Necessary Being) and beings (as contingent beings) is not simply accounted for in terms of a metaphysical reliance on genus and species. Given this state of affairs, Avicenna's ontology of being is not stamped by the oblivion of being nor does it leave the ontological difference between being and beings unthought. This is the case given that on Heidegger's view, or the thrust of his view, the ontological difference between being and beings remains unthought even if one finds an account of this difference in terms of genus and species. Yet, such an account of the ontological difference in terms of genus and species is not sufficient and it is still metaphysical in character. Given that Avicenna's ontological account of being does not rely on genus and species, this account is not considered a metaphysics that is oblivious of being. Having addressed the above issues in terms of the ontological analysis of being and its modalities, it appears that Avicenna's ontology of being already overcomes some features of the *ousiological* tradition. Instead of being a substance based ontology, Avicenna's ontology is a process-ontology, and this in itself already transgresses the confines of *ousiology*. Whether in terms of his ontological account of the modalities of being, or in his reliance on an Islamic Neoplatonic account of Emanation and participation in being (by way of *al-tashkīk*), Avicenna already is overcoming some dimensions of the classical ontological tradition while working his way out from within. In analyzing the essence/existence distinction, the claim that Avicenna's philosophy is a metaphysics of essence is revealed as being a disputable and somehow un-founded claim. It is in the light of the analysis of the essence/existence distinction that Avicenna's metaphysics is revealed as being a metaphysics of being rather than being a metaphysics of essence. Existence is qualified as being a perfection, and pure existence is the highest and purest perfection. The Necessary Existent due to Itself is held as being that which has no quiddity and that whose essence is none other than existence. Existence is then taken to be the purest qualification of something. An entity is higher in the hierarchy of being the more it participates in being and existence. The more intense its existence is, the closer it is to perfection. An existential line is therefore a line of perfection. The highest essential qualification is that of finding the last determination of essence in existence. And this differs from what one finds in the culmination of the essentialist line that reaches its highest manifestations in Hegel's Science of Logic. Based on the ontological analysis of the modalities and on the essence/existence distinction, Avicenna construes the encounter with being in terms of a happening that is temporal and processional. In both instances one is not reducing being into *ousia* nor into essence.

In Avicenna's epistemological accounts of the "Suspended Person Argument," and the consideration of *al-wahm*, the encounter with being is not merely conceptual or solely analytic. In the "Suspended Person Argument," being is convergent with thinking, and the processional unfolding of the affirmation of the existence of the *nafs* by itself, and the self-reflexive recognition that the affirmed *nafs* is one's own *nafs*, all point to a self-presence based knowledge (*ʿilm ḥuḍūrī*). Yet, presence itself points towards absence and otherness. The convergence between being and thinking is revealed as an encounter with being in terms of *al-anā* (I). By pointing towards otherness, the encounter with being in terms of *al-anā* reveals being as the site in which one's own being stands. Being is revealed as being a granting or a happening to *al-nafs*. Therefore, being is analyzed in an existential analysis of the self (like it is the case with the existential analytic of *Dasein*). The analysis of *al-wahm* reveals some pragmatic dimensions in Avicenna's epistemological account of knowledge that emphasizes intentionality and contextuality as being what grounds the cognitive emergent significant meanings that the pragmatics of knowledge entail.

The *nafs* is affirmed in its existence in terms of what the analysis of the "Suspended Person Argument" leads to. And this affirmation is not inscribed within the horizon of metaphysics and subjectivity. In this sense, the overcoming of the metaphysical subject reflects the merits and value of the account of being in terms of a self-unfolding and processional self-generating of a soul-field that gathers experiences around a center of being. All that this shows is that selfhood is not a "static metaphysical subject" or a substance (*jawhar*, *ousia*). It is "it" (*al-nafs*) that self-unfolds and what is a primary encounter is that of being which converges with thinking. And based on an interpretation of the mystic voyage (*safar*), *al-nafs* journeys in ascension on the path of truth and being. The mystic journey starts by an orientation towards being. The emanation cosmological account is interiorized in the *nafs* that journeys in love (*ʿishq*) towards what allows the self to overcome itself. This overcoming of subjectivity is also an overcoming of alienation and a breaking away from the realm of the fall and separation. The mystic journey is intertwined with a self-exegesis that is put into effect in terms of a hermeneutic *ta'wīl* of the self that seeks truth and being. *Ta'wīl* (as hermeneutics) is turned into a *taḥqīq*, as a realization of *ḥaqīqa*, (truth) which takes place in terms of the mystic *kashf al-maḥjūb* (unveiling of truth). In this sense, truth is irreducible and cannot be assimilated or brought into an accumulative totality. The otherness and alterity of truth is revealed in the very self-withdrawal that characterizes its unveiling. This state of affairs also reflects an overcoming of the metaphysical and enframing (*Ge-stell*) based account of truth.

In the above ontological, epistemological, and mystic accounts about being, Avicenna's philosophy evades the over generalized Heideggerian claims about the history of metaphysics. Avicenna's philosophy cannot be read as being a metaphysics that is characterized with the oblivion of being. Moreover, Avicenna's philosophy or thought of being does not culminate in the modern pervasion of all spheres by enframing (*Ge-stell*). The accounts of truth and being, that one finds in Avicenna's thought, do not fall under the rubric of the essence of technology, nor do they metaphysically remain entrapped within the confines of a classical ontological reliance on the notions of substance and subject. However, Avicenna's thought of being, and the existential encounter with being, do not lead to a nostalgic and utopian philosophical position that enacts the drama of crisis and salvation. Avicenna's philosophical accounts do overcome some features of a particular metaphysics without claiming that indispensable metaphysical notions of substance, essence, and subjectivity can be fully overcomed. Avicenna is able to use the language of classical metaphysics while at the same time being able to overcome some dimensions of a particular metaphysics that is oblivious of being. In overcoming a particular sort of metaphysics, or some features of a particular classical ontology, Avicenna's thought already addresses us in terms of some of the contemporary philosophic concerns or demands to overcome metaphysics (This is at least the case with the post-Heideggerian schools of European Continental thought). Avicenna's accounts of being pave the way for a consideration of a philosophic heritage that offers ways of overcoming some features of metaphysics while standing within the tradition that is being undone. The overcoming of metaphysics is undertaken from within while moving along the limits between philosophy and non-philosophy which reveal ways of overcoming metaphysics without a use of a nostalgic, reactionary, dramatic, or utopian philosophic language. Avicenna's accounts of being address our contemporary philosophic sensitivity without addressing us through a dramatic language of crisis and saving powers. The shift across the lines between philosophy and non-philosophy is smoothly undertaken while keeping the analysis of being clear and multi-perspectival. After all, Avicenna's consideration of being is ontological, epistemological, mystic, and linguistic. Each of these encounters with the question of being expresses some ways of overcoming "classical ontology," i.e. the metaphysics of *Vorhandenheit* and substance.

The interpretation of the Avicennian corpus admits rich hermeneutic possibilities. And these possibilities cannot be addressed through a rigid categorization of the intellectual history of Islamic philosophy that captivates the work of scholars who cannot address Islamic thought or Avicennism but through a consideration of this tradition in terms of being a Medieval tradition. What this book reveals is that Avicennism may be hermeneutically read in terms of being confronted with contemporary philosophic concerns. The philosophical Avicennian heritage is also a living tradition that is still practiced in contemporary Persian seminaries and other schools that are influenced by the *ashᶜarī* line of development of *kalām*. The place of Avicennism in the history of Western philosophy and Latin scholasticism is supported by many scholarly approaches to the intellectual history of philosophy. Apart from merely addressing Avicennism through historical doctrinal concerns, the consideration of the Avicennian living heritage presents a way by virtue of which one could address the Logocentric and ethnocentric side of Western metaphysics. After all, some deeply rooted and profound developments in the Latin and Eurocentric intellectual history have led to the rise of some strains in Western metaphysics that are occlusive of other traditions. To address Avicennism in terms of contemporary philosophic concerns is itself a hermeneutic move that contributes to the undoing of the occlusion and obliteration of the other tradition that underlies Western thought. And it does so without being itself responsible for the oppressive course of development which that thought has undertaken. Avicennism vibrantly lived within the history of Western metaphysics despite the attempts to occlude it within that history. It is from the site of marginalization, and in times when the Western metaphysical tradition is under intense critique, that Avicennism has to be given back the voice by virtue of which it could address our contemporary concerns with the history, destiny, and renewal of philosophy. It is in this sense that Avicenna's account of being has been addressed in this book in terms of calling for the undoing of the tradition of the oblivion of being and undoing the tradition that occludes. A tradition that veils the otherness of the other, by assimilating that otherness in terms of doctrinal biases, is a tradition that developed while being characterized by a particular interpretation/mis-interpretation of a metaphysical inclination in thought. By these concluding remarks I hope that this book would have humbly contributed to a possible bringing together of research interests that attract contemporary philosophers as well as Medievalist scholars.

Addressing the subsequent ontological tradition that develops with the successors of Avicenna (like Suhrawardī, Ṭūsī and Mullā Ṣadrā) reveals the course of development of a philosophical tradition that departs from the confines of medieval and ancient philosophy and attests to the emergence of phenomenological and hermeneutic dimensions. In this sense the post-Avicennian ontological developments offer alternative hermeneutic and phenomenological perspectives on the question of being that reaffirm what figures in Heidegger's thought while being precedent to that thought. This is the case, given that the subsequent developments of Avicenna's philosophy has led to the emergence of a tradition that overcomes the Peripatetic tradition and the Aristotelian categories by accounting for "temporality/time" and "processes/motions" (Mullā Ṣadrā's "substantial motion" *al-ḥaraka al-jawharīya* is one example). And this tradition gives prominence to the immediate knowledge and experience (*al-ʿilm al-ḥuḍūī*), and shifts from creation *ex nihilo* due to various accounts of emanation and illumination that address the question of being in terms of a fourfold process of the unfolding (or unveiling) of being. This starts with a primary encounter with being, then the *anā* (the "I") is shown as that which reveals this primary encounter with being while moving in quest for the origin that grounds self-being. And this leads to the fourth movement in the unfolding of being that integrates (re-folds) the above stages of the unfolding of being within a conception of the unity of being as *wiḥdat al-wūjūd*. The post-Avicennian ontological developments offer alternative approaches to the question of being that answer to some aspects of what Heidegger's thought might have sought. And this state of affairs reveals that the phenomenological method in ontology has a cross-cultural universal character. Investigating post-Avicennian philosophical developments would present a contribution to the contemporary philosophical concerns with the renewal of philosophy and metaphysics.

This becomes more of a pressing issue in an epoch that is considered by some to be the epoch of "the closure of metaphysics;" or more so the closure of a "particular" sort of metaphysics.

BIBLIOGRAPHY

I- Texts by Avicenna (Ibn Sīnā)

Kitāb al-Shifā', al-Nafs (De Anima), ed. G. C. Anawati, Ibrahim Madkour, Sa^c^id Zayed. Cairo: al-hay'a al-miṣrīya al-^c^āmma lil-kitāb, 1975.

Nafs (al-Shifā'), Avicenna's De Anima, ed. F. Rahman. London: Oxford University Press, 1960.

Kitāb al-Shifā', al-Ilāhīyāt (La Métaphysique), ed. G. C. Anawati, Ibrahim Madkour, Sa^c^id Zayed, 2 vols. Cairo: al-hay'a al-miṣrīya al-^c^āmma lil-kitāb, 1975.

Kitāb al-Najāt, ed. Majid Fakhry. Beirut: dār al-'āfāq al-jadīda, 1985.

Kitāb al-Ishārāt wal-Tanbīhāt, ed. Sulayman Dunia. Cairo: dār al-ma^c^ārif, 1960.

Livre des Directives et Remarques (Kitāb al-Ishārāt wal-Tanbīhāt), ed. and trans. by Goichon A. M. Paris: Librairie Philosophique J. Vrin, 1951.

Dānish Nāma (The Metaphysica of Avicenna), English Translation and Commentaries by Parviz Morewedge. New York: Columbia University Press, 1973. French Translation: *Le Livre de Science*, ed. Mohammad Achena & Henri Masse. Paris: Les Belles Lettres, 1958.

Ḥayy Ibn Yaqẓān, Risālat al-Ṭayr, Salmān wa Absal, ed. and French trans. Henry Corbin in: Corbin, Henri. *Avicenne et Le Récit Visionnaire (Tome II): étude sur le cycle des récits Avicenniens*. Tehran: Société des Monuments Nationaux de l'Iran, 1954. Also, ed. Arabic texts by August F. Mehren in: Mehren, August F. *Traités Mystiques d'Avicenne*. Amsterdam: Philo Press, 1979.

Ḥayy Ibn Yaqẓān, ed. Arabic text by Aḥmad Amīn. Cairo: dār al-ma^c^ārif, 1952.

Le Récit Visionnaire de Ḥayy Ibn Yaqẓān, trans. by A. M. Goichon. Paris: Desclée de Brouwer, 1959.

Salmān wa Absal, ed. and French trans. by Henry Corbin in: Corbin, Henri. *Avicenne et Le Récit Visionnaire*. Tehran: Société des Monuments Nationaux de l'Iran, 1954.

Kitāb al-Hidāya, ed. Mohammad 'Abdo. Cairo: maktabat al-qāhira al-ḥadītha, 1974.

Al-Taᶜlīqāt, ed. A. R. Badawi. Cairo: al-hay'a al-miṣrīya al-ᶜāmma lil-kitāb, 1973.

Kitāb al-Ḥudūd, Arabic text with French trans. in: Goichon, A. M. *Avicenne Livre des Définitions*. Cairo: Institut Français d'Archéologie Orientale du Caire, 1963.

Avicenna Latinus (*De Anima, I-V*), ed. and French translation by Van Riet Simone. Leiden: E. J. Brill, 1972.

Avicenna Latinus (*Scientia Divina*, I-IV), ed. and French translation by Van Riet Simone. Leiden: E. J. Brill, 1977.

II- Texts by Martin Heidegger (English Translations)

Being and Time, trans. by Joan Stambaugh. Albany: State University of New York Press, 1996.

Basic Writings, ed. David Farell Krell. New York: Harper & Row, 1977.

What is Called Thinking? (*Was Heisst Denken*?), trans. by J. Glenn Gray. New York: Harper & Row, 1968.

The Concept of Time, (German & English text), trans. by William McNeill. Oxford: Blackwell, 1996.

The Question Concerning Technology and Other Essays, trans. by William Lovitt. New York: Harper & Row, 1977. Text: Vorträge und Aufsätze. Pfullingen: Günther Neske Verlag, 1954.

What is Metaphysics? trans. in Werner Brock, Existence and Being. London: Vision Press, 1949. Text: *Was ist Metaphysik*? Frankfurt: Klostermann,

1949. French translation in: Corbin, Henri. Questions I. Paris: Gallimard, 1968.

Aristotle's Metaphysics Θ 1-3: on the essence and actuality of force, trans. by Walter Brogan & Peter Warneck. Bloomington & Indianapolis: Indiana University Press, 1990.

"Hegel and the Greeks," trans. by Robert Metcalf in *Pathmarks* (*Wegmarken*), ed. William McNeill. Cambridge: Cambridge University Press, 1998.

"Kant's Thesis about Being," trans. by Ted E. Klein and William E. Pohl in *Patmarks* (*Wegmarken*), ed. William McNeill. Cambridge: Cambridge University Press, 1998.

III- References & Sources

The Encyclopaedia of Islam, ed. M. Th. Houtsma, A. J. Wensinck, T. W. Arnold, W. Heffening, E. Levi-Provencal. Leiden: E. J. Brill, 1927.

Encyclopaedia Iranica, Vol.III, ed. Ehsan Yarshater. London: Routledge & Kegan Paul, 1989.

Al-Muʿjam al-Falsafī, ed. Jamil Saliba (Vol. II). Beirut: dār al-kitāb al-lubnānī, 1971.

Al-Muqadima, Kitāb al-ʿIbar (*Ibn Khaldūn's Introduction to History*), trans. by Franz Rosenthal, ed. N. J. Dawood. Princeton: Princeton University Press, 1989.

Aristotle. *Metaphysics*, trans. by W. D. Ross, rev. J. Barnes. Oxford: Revised Oxford Aristotle, 1984. Greek text: ed. W. D. Ross. Oxford: Oxford University Press, 1924.

______. *Categories*, trans. by A. J. Ackrill. Oxford: Clarendon Aristotle Series, 1963. Greek text: ed. L. Minio-Paluello. Oxford: Oxford Classical Texts, 1956.

______. *A New Aristotle Reader*, ed. J. L. Ackrill. Princeton: Princeton University Press, 1987.

Al-Ghazālī, Abū Ḥāmid. *Tahāfut al-Falāsifa*, ed. Fakhry Majid. Beirut: dār al-mashreq, 1990.

Averroes (Ibn Rushd). *Faṣl al-Maqāl* (On the Harmony of Religion and Philosophy), trans. by Georges F. Hourani. London: Gibb Memorial trust, 1976.

Aquinas, Thomas. *S. Thomas Aquinatis opusculum De ente et essentia*, ed. C. Boyer. Rome: Gregorian University, 1933.

______. *On Being and Essence*, trans. by A. Maurer. Toronto: The Pontifical Institute of Medieval Studies, 1949.

Descartes, René. *Meditations On first Philosophy*, trans. by John Cottingham. Cambridge: Cambridge University Press, 1994.

Hegel, Georg Wilhelm Friedrich. *Science of Logic*, trans. by A. V. Miller, ed. H. D. Lewis. New Jersey: Humanities Press International Inc., 1996.

Kant, Immanuel. *Critique of Pure Reason*, trans. by Norman Kemp Smith. New York: St. Martin's Press, 1965; text *Kritik der reinen Vernunft* (1787).

Khūsraw, Naṣīr. *Knowledge and Liberation* (*Kashāyish wa Rahāyīsh*), trans. by Faquir M. Hunzai, intro. Parviz. Morewedge. London: I. B. Tauris, 1998.

Rūmī, Jalāl al-dīn. *Mystical Poems of Rūmī*, trans. by A. J. Arberry. Chicago: The University of Chicago Press, 1968.

Ṣadr al-dīn Shīrāzī [Mullā Ṣadrā]. *Book of Prehensions* (*Kitāb al-mashāᶜir*), trans. by Parviz Morewedge. Binghamton: SSIPS, 1992.

Ṭūsī, Naṣīr al-dīn. *Metaphysics*, trans. by Parviz Morewedge. Binghamton: Society for the Study of Islamic Philosophy and Science, 1992.

Wittgenstein, Ludwig. *Tractatus Logico Philosophicus*, trans. by C. K. Ogden. London: Routledge & Kegan Paul, 1988.

______. *Philosophical Investigations*, trans. by G. E. M. Anscombe. New York: Macmillan Publishing co., Inc., 1968.

IV- General Works by Others

Acikgenc, Alparslan. *Being and Existence in Ṣadrā and Heidegger*. Kuala Lumpur: International Institute of Islamic Thought and Civilization (ISTAC), 1993.

Afnan, Soheil. *Avicenna: His Life and his Works*. London: Allen & Unwin, 1958.

______. *Philosophical Terminology in Arabic and Persian*. Leiden: E. J. Brill, 1964.

Brisart, Robert. *La Phénoménologie de Marbourg, ou la résurgence de la métaphysique chez Heidegger a l'époque de Sein und Zeit*. Paris: Grasset, 1993.

Caputo, John. *Heidegger and Aquinas: An Essay on Overcoming Metaphysics*. New York: Fordham University Press, 1982.

______. *The Mystical Element in Heidegger's Thought*. New York: Fordham University Press, 1986.

Carra de Vaux, Bernard. *Avicenna*. Amsterdam: Philo Press, 1974.

Cavell, Stanley. *Conditions Handsome and Unhandsome: The Constitution of Emersonian Perfectionism*. Chicago: The University of Chicago Press, 1988.

Daftary, Farhad. *The Ismāᶜīlīs, their History and Doctrines*. Cambridge: Cambridge University Press, 1990.

Derrida, Jacques. *La Vérité en Peinture*. Paris: Flammarion, 1978

______. *Positions*, trans. by Alan Bass. Chicago: The University of Chicago Press, 1981.

Gardet, Louis. *La Connaissance Mystique chez Ibn Sina et ses Présupposés Philosophiques*. Cairo: Publications de l'Institut Français d'Archéologie Orientale du Caire, 1952.

Goichon, A. M. *Léxique de la Langue Philosophique d'Ibn Sina (Avicenne)*. Paris: Desclée de Brouwer, 1938.

______. *Vocabulaires Comparés d'Aristote et d'Ibn Sina (Avicenne)*. Paris: Desclée de Brouwer, 1939.

Goodman, Lenn E. *Avicenna*. London: Routledge, 1992.

Graham, Angus. "Being in Linguistics and Philosophy," in *Foundations of Language*, I. Dordrecht: D. Reidel Publishing Company, 1965, pp. 223-231.

Gutas, Dimitri. *Avicenna and the Aristotelian Tradition*. Leiden: E. J. Brill, 1988.

Hamburger, Michael. *Patmos: Friedrich Holderlin Poems and Fragments*. Ann Arbor: The University of Michigan Press, 1966.

Heath, Peter. *Allegory and Philosophy in Avicenna (Ibn Sīnā), with a translation of the Prophet Muhammad's Ascent to Heaven (Miʿrāj Nāma)*. Philadelphia: University of Pennsylvania, 1992.

Houben, Jean Joseph. *Avicenna and Mysticism*. Calcutta: Commemoration Publication, 1956.

Hyman, Arthur & Walsh, James. *Philosophy in the Middle Ages*. Indianapolis: Hackett Publishing Company, 1986.

Kisiel, Theodore. *"The Language of the Event: The Event of Language," Heidegger and the Path of Thinking*. Pittsburg: Duquesne University Press, 1970.

Kisiel, Theodore J. & Kockelmans, Joseph. *Phenomenology and the Natural Sciences*. Evanston: Northwestern University Press, 1970.

Kockelmans, Joseph. *'On the Truth of Being,' Reflections on Heidegger's Later Philosophy*. Bloomington Indianapolis: Indiana University Press, 1984.

Levinas, Emmanuel. *Le Temps et l'Autre*. Paris: Quadrige, Presses Universitaires de France, 1979.

______. *Dieu, la Mort, et le Temps.* Paris: Grasset, 1993.

Marmura, Michael. "Avicenna's 'Flying Man' in Context." *The Monist* 69, 3, 1970, pp. 383-395.

Mashran, Salam. *Al-Jānib al-Ilāhī ᶜinda Ibn Sīnā.* Damascus: dār quṭayba, 1992.

Massignon, M. Louis. *La Philosophie Orientale d'Ibn Sina et son Alphabet Philosophique.* Cairo: Institut Français d'Archéologie Orientale, 1952.

Megill, Allan. *Prophets of Extremity.* Berkeley: University of California Press, 1987.

Merleau-Ponty, Maurice. *Phénoménologie de la Perception.* Paris: Éditions Gallimard, 1945.

Morewedge, Parviz. *Essays in Islamic Philosophy, Theology, and Mysticism.* Oneanta: State University of New York, 1995.

________. *Islamic Philosophical Theology.* Albany: State University of New York, 1979.

Michelfelder, Diane P. & Palmer, Richard E. *Dialogue and Deconstruction.* Albany: State University of New York Press, 1989.

Owens, J. *The Relevance of Avecinnian Neoplatonism and Islamic Thought.* Albany: State University of New York, 1992.

Peters, F. E. *Aristotle and the Arabs.* New York: New York University Press, 1968.

Prudhomme, Jeff Owen. *God and Being, Heidegger's Relation to Theology.* New Jersey: Humanities Press International Inc., 1984.

Sallis, John. *Reading Heidegger, Commemorations.* Bloomington Indianapolis: Indiana University Press, 1993.

Schimmel, Annemarie. *Deciphering the Signs of God: A Phenomenological Approach to Islam.* Albany: State University of New York Press, 1994.

Schürmann, Reiner. "Symbolic Praxis." *Graduate Faculty Philosophy Journal*, Vol. 19, No. 2 - Vol. 20, No. 1, 1997.

Shehadi, Fadlou. "Arabic and the Concept of Being," in *Essays in Islamic Philosophy and Science*, ed. G. Hourani. Albany: State University of New York Press, 1975.

Sikka, Sonya. *Forms of Transcendence: Heidegger and Medieval Mystical Thought*. Albany: State University of New York Press, 1997.

Werner, Marx. *Heidegger and the Tradition*. Evanston: Northwestern University Press, 1971.

Witt, Charlotte. *Substance and Essence in Aristotle: An Interpretation of Metaphysics VII-IX*. Ithaca & London: Cornell University Press, 1989.

Wolfson, Harry Austryn. *The Philosophy of Spinoza*. New York: Meridian Books, 1961.

Yazdi, Mahdi. *Haram al-Wūjūd*. Beirut: dār al-rawḍa, 1990.

GLOSSARY OF ARABIC KEY TERMS

ᶜadam: Non-being, nothingness.

anā: I (As myself, "I").

anīyya: Thatness.

ᶜaql: Reason.

ᶜaraḍ: Accident.

ᶜārif: Mystic or gnostic (endowed with mystic knowledge or gnosis).

ᶜārifīn: Plural of *ᶜārif*.

ashkhāṣ: Individuals.

aṣl: Origin, source, *archē*.

awal: The primordial One, the One.

āya: Divine sign, and also Divine verse of the Qur'an.

āyāt: Plural of *āya*.

badāha: Familiarity, or immediate evidence.

baqā': Subsistence, also linked to the mystic annihilation and overcoming of the self.

basīṭ: Simple (as opposed to *murakab*: composite).

bāṭin: Esoteric, hidden (as opposed to *ẓāhir*: the exoteric and apparent).

burhān: Demonstration, or proof.

dahr: Perpetuity, or perpetual time.

dhāt: Essential self, or nature.

ḍarūra: Necessity.

falsafa: Philosophy.

fasād: Corruption (As in generation and corruption).

faṣl: Differentia.

fayḍ: Emanation.

firāq: Separation, alienation.

fiʿl: Actuality, or act.

gharb: Occident.

gharība: Stranger.

ḥad: Definition, or limit.

ḥadīth: Caused, or made.

ḥāl: A mystic state that allows the gnostic to move from one mystic stage to another.

ḥaq: True, real.

ḥaqīqa: Truth, reality.

ḥaraka: Movement, motion.

hawīya: Identity.

ḥay: Alive or living.

ḥayāt: Life.

ḥayyīz: Space, or occupied space.

hayūlī: Material.

ḥiss: Sense (As in the inner or outer senses).

ḥikma: Philosophy.

ḥudūd: Definitions, or limits.

ḥulūl: Mystic Union with the Origin of being.

idrāk: Perception.

ightirāb: Alienation (it is linked to *gharīb*: i.e. stranger, and has the root shared with *gharb*: i.e. occident, as if alienation is thus linked to a migration to the occident).

ʿila: Cause.

ilāhīyāt: Metaphysics, or Divine sciences.

ʿilal: Causes.

ʿilm: Knowledge, science, or discipline.

imkān: Contingency, or possibility.

imtināʿ: Impossibility.

insān: Human being.

ishrāq: Illumination.

ʿirfān: Gnostic or mystic knowledge, mysticism or gnosticism.

ishtidād: Intensification (As in the intensification in the participation in being).

istiḥāla: Impossibility.

itiḥād: A form of Union by way of obeying the Divine Law (less intense Union than *itiṣāl*).

itiṣāl: A form of Union by way of sharing (More intense form of Union than *itiḥād* and lesser in degree than *ḥulūl*).

jahl: Ignorance.

jawhar: Substance.

jins: Genus.

jism: Body.

juz': Part, or Atom.

kalām: Speech, or Dialectical Theology.

kamāl: Perfection.

kashf: Unveiling, unconcealment.

kawn: Universe, world, or sometimes used as 'being'.

kaynūna: Being (not a being, but 'Being').

khāṣṣa: Elect learned.

khayāl: Imagination.

khayr: Good

khayrīa: Goodness.

kulī: Universal.

kun: The command "Be !", to be.

ma^{c}ād: Return (As in the processional return to the primordial One).

mādda: Matter.

māhīya: Quiddity, essence.

maḥjūb: Veiled, hidden.

majāz: Metaphor.

majāhil: Deserts, places or sites that are unknown.

majhūl: Unknown.

makān: Place.

maʿlūl: Caused.

mantiq: Logic.

maqām: Mystic stage.

maqāmāt: Mystic stages.

maqūlāt: Categories.

maʿrifa: Knowledge and sometimes it refers to gnosis.

mashriq: Orient.

mawjūd: Existent.

mawt: Death.

miʿrāj: Ascension.

muḥāl: Impossible.

mumkin: Contingent, possible.

murakab: Composite.

murīd: Seeker (as a seeker in quest for mystic Union with the One)

musabab: Caused.

mustaḥīl: Impossible.

nafs: Soul, self, or mind (Yet not used in the sense of designating a substance, a subject, or a static state).

naṣ: Scripture.

nawʿ: Species.

nutq: Speech.

quwa: Potentiality.

rasm: Description.

rūḥ: Soul, *pneuma*, *spiritus*.

sabab: Cause.

safar: Mystic journey.

sharīʿa: Divine Law.

sharq: Orient.

ṣūra: Form.

ṭabīʿa: Nature (The nature of something).

taḍāʿuf: De-intensification and weakening in the participation in being.

tafsīr: Explication.

taḥqīq: Realization of truth, or going towards truth.

takhayul: Imagining, to imagine.

takwīn: Generation.

tanzīh: Transcendence.

tanzīl: Descent, or Revelation.

ṭarīqa: Mystical path of self-realization (in General it designates a path, or a way).

taṣawūr: Conception.

taṣdīq: Assertion, assent.

tashkīk: Analogical gradation in being.

tawḥīd: Unification.

ta'wīl: Hermeneutic interpretation or exegesis

wahm: A pragmatic inner sense of prehension.

wajh: Face.

wājib: Necessary.

waqt: Time.

wūjūb: Necessity.

wūjūd: Being, Existence.

zāhid: Pious.

ẓāhir: Exoteric, or apparent.

zaman: Time.

INDEX